T0178537

# Communications
# in Computer and Information Science     1828

## Rationale

The CCIS series is devoted to the publication of proceedings of computer science conferences. Its aim is to efficiently disseminate original research results in informatics in printed and electronic form. While the focus is on publication of peer-reviewed full papers presenting mature work, inclusion of reviewed short papers reporting on work in progress is welcome, too. Besides globally relevant meetings with internationally representative program committees guaranteeing a strict peer-reviewing and paper selection process, conferences run by societies or of high regional or national relevance are also considered for publication.

## Topics

The topical scope of CCIS spans the entire spectrum of informatics ranging from foundational topics in the theory of computing to information and communications science and technology and a broad variety of interdisciplinary application fields.

## Information for Volume Editors and Authors

Publication in CCIS is free of charge. No royalties are paid, however, we offer registered conference participants temporary free access to the online version of the conference proceedings on SpringerLink (http://link.springer.com) by means of an http referrer from the conference website and/or a number of complimentary printed copies, as specified in the official acceptance email of the event.

CCIS proceedings can be published in time for distribution at conferences or as post-proceedings, and delivered in the form of printed books and/or electronically as USBs and/or e-content licenses for accessing proceedings at SpringerLink. Furthermore, CCIS proceedings are included in the CCIS electronic book series hosted in the SpringerLink digital library at http://link.springer.com/bookseries/7899. Conferences publishing in CCIS are allowed to use Online Conference Service (OCS) for managing the whole proceedings lifecycle (from submission and reviewing to preparing for publication) free of charge.

## Publication process

The language of publication is exclusively English. Authors publishing in CCIS have to sign the Springer CCIS copyright transfer form, however, they are free to use their material published in CCIS for substantially changed, more elaborate subsequent publications elsewhere. For the preparation of the camera-ready papers/files, authors have to strictly adhere to the Springer CCIS Authors' Instructions and are strongly encouraged to use the CCIS LaTeX style files or templates.

## Abstracting/Indexing

CCIS is abstracted/indexed in DBLP, Google Scholar, EI-Compendex, Mathematical Reviews, SCImago, Scopus. CCIS volumes are also submitted for the inclusion in ISI Proceedings.

## How to start

To start the evaluation of your proposal for inclusion in the CCIS series, please send an e-mail to ccis@springer.com.

Marcelo Naiouf · Enzo Rucci ·
Franco Chichizola · Laura De Giusti
Editors

# Cloud Computing, Big Data & Emerging Topics

11th Conference, JCC-BD&ET 2023
La Plata, Argentina, June 27–29, 2023
Proceedings

 Springer

*Editors*
Marcelo Naiouf 🆔
Universidad Nacional de La Plata
La Plata, Argentina

Enzo Rucci 🆔
Universidad Nacional de La Plata-CIC
La Plata, Argentina

Franco Chichizola 🆔
Universidad Nacional de La Plata
La Plata, Argentina

Laura De Giusti 🆔
Universidad Nacional de La Plata-CIC
La Plata, Argentina

ISSN 1865-0929         ISSN 1865-0937 (electronic)
Communications in Computer and Information Science
ISBN 978-3-031-40941-7         ISBN 978-3-031-40942-4 (eBook)
https://doi.org/10.1007/978-3-031-40942-4

This Springer imprint is published by the registered company Springer Nature Switzerland AG
The registered company address is: Gewerbestrasse 11, 6330 Cham, Switzerland

# Preface

Welcome to the full paper proceedings of the 11th Conference on Cloud Computing, Big Data & Emerging Topics (JCC-BD&ET 2023), held in a hybrid setting (both on-site and live online participation modes were allowed). JCC-BD&ET 2023 was organized by the III-LIDI and the Postgraduate Office, both from the School of Computer Science of the National University of La Plata, Argentina.

Since 2013, this event has been an annual meeting where ideas, projects, scientific results and applications in cloud computing, big data and other related areas are exchanged and disseminated. The conference focuses on the topics that allow interaction between academia, industry and other interested parties.

JCC-BD&ET 2023 covered the following topics: high-performance, edge and fog computing; internet of things; modelling and simulation; big and open data; machine and deep learning; smart cities; e-government; human-computer interaction; visualization; and special topics related to emerging technologies. In addition, special activities were also carried out, including 1 plenary lecture and 1 discussion panel.

In this edition, the conference received 38 submissions. The authors of these submissions came from the following 10 countries: Argentina, Bulgaria, Chile, Colombia, Ecuador, India, Mexico, Spain, Uruguay and Vietnam. All the accepted papers were peer-reviewed by at least three referees (single-blind review) and evaluated on the basis of technical quality, relevance, significance and clarity. To achieve this, JCC-BD&ET 2023 was supported by 52 Program Committee (PC) members and 56 additional external reviewers. According to the recommendations of the referees, 14 of them were selected for this book (37% acceptance rate). We hope readers will find these contributions useful and inspiring for their future research.

Special thanks to all the people who contributed to the conference's success: program and organizing committees, authors, reviewers, speakers and all conference attendees. Finally, we want to thank Springer for its support in publishing this book.

June 2023

Marcelo Naiouf
Enzo Rucci
Franco Chichizola
Laura De Giusti

# Organization

## General Chair

Marcelo Naiouf                                   Universidad Nacional de La Plata, Argentina

## Program Committee Chairs

Armando De Giusti                                Universidad Nacional de La Plata-CONICET,
                                                 Argentina
Franco Chichizola                                Universidad Nacional de La Plata, Argentina
Laura De Giusti                                  Universidad Nacional de La Plata and CIC,
                                                 Argentina
Enzo Rucci                                       Universidad Nacional de La Plata and CIC,
                                                 Argentina

## Program Committee

María José Abásolo                               Universidad Nacional de La Plata and CIC,
                                                 Argentina
José Aguilar                                     Universidad de Los Andes, Venezuela
Jorge Ardenghi                                   Universidad Nacional del Sur, Argentina
Javier Balladini                                 Universidad Nacional del Comahue, Argentina
Oscar Bria                                       Universidad Nacional de La Plata and INVAP,
                                                 Argentina
Silvia Castro                                    Universidad Nacional del Sur, Argentina
Mónica Denham                                    Universidad Nacional de Río Negro and
                                                 CONICET, Argentina
Javier Diaz                                      Universidad Nacional de La Plata, Argentina
Ramón Doallo                                     Universidade da Coruña, Spain
Marcelo Errecalde                                Universidad Nacional de San Luis, Argentina
Elsa Estevez                                     Universidad Nacional del Sur and CONICET,
                                                 Argentina
Pablo Ezzatti                                    Universidad de la República, Uruguay
Aurelio Fernandez Bariviera                      Universitat Rovira i Virgili, Spain
Fernando Emmanuel Frati                          Universidad Nacional de Chilecito, Argentina
Carlos Garcia Garino                             Universidad Nacional de Cuyo, Argentina

# Additional Reviewers

Laura Aballay
Silvana Aciar
Hugo Alfonso
Analía Amandi
Javier Apolloni
Agustina Buccella
Alejandra Cechich
Karina Cenci
César Collazos
Leonardo Corbalan
Pedro Dal Bianco
Sebastián Dapoto
Marisa De Giusti
Javier Diaz
César Estrebou
Marcelo Falappa
Guillermo Feierherd
Alejandro Fernández
Pablo Fillotrani
María Luján Ganuza
Mario Alejandro Garcia
Christian Garcia Bauza
Alejandra Garrido
Sergio Alejandro Gomez
Julián Grigera
Wenny Hojas Mazo
Jorge Ierache
Horacio Kuna

Martín Larrea
Xaviera Lopez Cortez
Antonio Lorenzo
Ana Maguitman
Diego Martinez
Lía Molinari
Diego Montezanti
Antonio Navarro Martin
Carolina Olivera
Ariel Pasini
David Petrocelli
Joaquín Pina
María Florencia Pollo-Cattaneo
Claudia Pons
Facundo Quiroga
Hugo Ramón
Andrés Rodriguez
Franco Ronchetti
Gustavo Salazar
Carolina Salto
Cecilia Sanz
Matías Selzer
Pablo Thomas
Diego Torres
Dana Urribarri
Pablo Vidal
Augusto Villa Monte
Gonzalo Villarreal

## Sponsors

CONICET

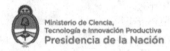

Sistema Nacional de
Computación de Alto
Desempeño

Agencia Nacional de Promoción
Científica y Tecnológica

RedUNCI

Red de Universidades Nacionales con
Carreras de Informática

# Contents

**Parallel and Distributed Computing**

Exploring Heterogeneous Computing Environments: A Preliminary
Analysis of Python and SYCL Performance ............................. 3
 *Youssef Faqir-Rhazoui and Carlos García*

Towards Reducing Communications in Sparse Matrix Kernels ............... 17
 *Manuel Freire, Raul Marichal, Ernesto Dufrechou, and Pablo Ezzatti*

Distributed Architectures Based on Edge Computing, Fog Computing
and End Devices: A Conceptual Review Incorporating Resilience Aspects ..... 31
 *Santiago Medina, Diego Montezanti, Lucas Gómez D'Orazio,*
 *Francisco Garay, Armando De Giusti, and Marcelo Naiouf*

Resilience Analysis of an Emergency Department in Stressful Situations ...... 45
 *Mariela Rodriguez, Francesc Boixader, Francisco Epelde,*
 *Eva Bruballa, Armando De Giusti, Alvaro Wong, Dolores Rexachs,*
 *and Emilio Luque*

**Big Data**

CoVaMaT: Functionality for Variety Reuse Through a Supporting Tool ........ 57
 *Líam Osycka, Alejandra Cechich, Agustina Buccella,*
 *Ayelén Montenegro, and Angel Muñoz*

Local Pluralistic Homophily in Networks: A New Measure Based
on Overlapping Communities ......................................... 75
 *Fernando Barraza, Carlos Ramirez, and Alejandro Fernández*

**Machine and Deep Learning**

The Implementation of the RISE Algorithm for the Captum Framework ....... 91
 *Oscar Stanchi, Franco Ronchetti, and Facundo Quiroga*

Drug Repurposing Using Knowledge Graph Embeddings with a Focus
on Vector-Borne Diseases: A Model Comparison .......................... 105
 *Diego López Yse and Diego Torres*

An Analysis of Satellite-Based Machine Learning Models to Estimate
Global Solar Irradiance at a Horizontal Plane ............................ 118
   Paula Iturbide, Rodrigo Alonso-Suarez, and Franco Ronchetti

An Architecture and a New Deep Learning Method for Head and Neck
Cancer Prognosis by Analyzing Serial Positron Emission Tomography
Images ...................................................................... 129
   Remigio Hurtado, Stefanía Guzmán, and Arantxa Muñoz

## Smart Cities and E-Government

Designing a Data Strategy for Organizations ............................. 143
   Fabiola del Toro Osorio, Victoria Eugenia Ospina Becerra,
   and Elsa Estévez

A Maturity Model for Data Governance, Data Quality Management,
and Data Management ..................................................... 157
   Ismael Caballero, Fernando Gualo, Moisés Rodríguez, and Mario Piattini

Examining Factors of Acceptance and Use of Technology in Digital
Services in the Context of Ecuador ...................................... 171
   Pablo Pintado, Sebastián Wiesner, Daniela Prado, and Elsa Estevez

## Visualization

UVAM: The Unified Visual Analytics Model. The Unified Visualization
Model Revisited .......................................................... 189
   María Luján Ganuza, Dana K. Urribarri, Martín L. Larrea,
   and Silvia M. Castro

**Author Index** ......................................................... 205

# Parallel and Distributed Computing

# Exploring Heterogeneous Computing Environments: A Preliminary Analysis of Python and SYCL Performance

Youssef Faqir-Rhazoui[ID] and Carlos García[✉][ID]

Department of Computer Architecture and Automatics,
Universidad Complutense de Madrid, Madrid, Spain
{yelfaqir,garsanca}@ucm.es

**Abstract.** Python's popularity has grown rapidly over the past decade due to its high productivity factor. While Python is popular in scientific computing, its interpreted nature and limitations on parallelization result in slower performance compared to compiled languages. Despite this, Python is still a valuable tool for high-performance computing (HPC) due to its ease of programming and optimization capabilities. This paper discusses the performance gap between Python and compiled languages like SYCL when working with heterogeneous computing environments and the challenges in developing portable and high-performance native extensions. It highlights the development of the dpctl Python library, which provides a portable and architecture-agnostic API for writing extensions and supports asynchronous SYCL kernel execution. We developed four benchmarks across CPU, integrated GPU, and discrete Intel Arc GPU, finding that SYCL outperformed Python in all cases, but optimizations could be made to improve Python performance. This research also highlights issues encountered when porting Python code, limitations in using Numpy, and current Intel Arc performance issues.

**Keywords:** Python · SYCL · oneAPI · HPC

## 1 Introduction

Python has become increasingly popular since the past decade due to its high productivity factor [16], which has also led to its inclusion in academic curriculums [19]. Python is currently ranked number one on the TIOBE Programming Community index with a 14.8% rating [7], which measures the popularity of programming languages. Further evidence that confirms this trend is the number of pull requests for Python projects on Github [3] which has also been consistently high and at the top spot since the previous year.

This paper has been supported by the EU (FEDER), the Spanish MINECO and CM under grants S2018/TCS-4423, PID2021-126576NB-I00 funded by MCIN/AEI/10.13039/501100011033 and by "ERDF A way of making Europe".

© The Author(s), under exclusive license to Springer Nature Switzerland AG 2023
M. Naiouf et al. (Eds.): JCC-BD&ET 2023, CCIS 1828, pp. 3–16, 2023.
https://doi.org/10.1007/978-3-031-40942-4_1

Although Python has gained popularity in scientific computing due to its vast collection of scientific libraries such as SciPy [21], NumPy [15], Matplotlib [20], and scikit-learn [18], its performance is still slower in comparison with the compiled languages due to its interpreted nature and limitations on parallelization [13]. In order to overcome this limitation, the Python community has developed various solutions such as NumPy's specialized data structures and SciPy's utilization of C and FORTRAN. Besides, PyPy [12] is a Python implementation written in RPython that compiles and optimizes RPython code to generate the PyPy interpreter in C. Focusing on the exploitation of hardware accelerators we can find PyCUDA [9] and PyOpenCL [10] which are Python wrappers for the CUDA and OpenCL libraries, respectively. Both wrappers provide a high-level interface for utilizing GPU acceleration within Python programs, allowing for significant performance gains on suitable hardware.

Nevertheless, developing portable and high-performance native extensions is still challenging due to the complexity of the hardware. This often results in a fragmented software ecosystem and duplicated development efforts. The CuPy library [14] is an example of this issue, as it is a reimplementation of a significant portion of NumPy for Nvidia GPUs using CUDA [6], requiring extensive programmer effort. Attempting to replicate this approach for other large native extensions and various architectures is impractical. Therefore, there is a need for a portable and architecture-agnostic API for writing extensions. Recently a new framework for building and using SYCL-based Python native extensions supports asynchronous SYCL kernel execution known as dpctl Python library [17]. Dpctl implements a subset of SYCL's API providing wrappers for the SYCL runtime classes.

This paper evaluates the API to execute SYCL kernels asynchronously via Python available in the oneAPI Python distribution promoted by Intel known as Data Parallel Extension for Python [17]. This extension offers various levels of abstraction when programming for heterogeneous architectures with Python. Specifically, at top abstraction level, it expands the functionality of the NumPy library to XPUs (Intel denotes XPUs as processing units that are designed to accelerate specific workloads such as CPUs, GPUs or FPGAs) utilizing SYCL's API through Dpctl. Additionally, it permits the expression of kernel code at a lower level in the SYCL format by means of numba-dpex[1].

The rest of the paper is organized as follows. Section 2 presents concepts of SYCL and Data Parallel Extension for Python. Sections 3 and 4 describe the benchmarks chosen and the methodology applied. In Sect. 5, we describe the experimental conditions and Sect. 6 discusses the main results observed. Finally, Sect. 7 summarizes the conclusions reached.

## 2   Background

This section presents a brief introduction to some of the key concepts of SYCL and Python that are referred to in the rest of this paper.

---

[1] Data-Parallel Extension for Numba: https://github.com/IntelPython/numba-dpex

## 2.1   SYCL

The SYCL language is a domain-specific language based on C++17 that provides a single-source programming environment for heterogeneous architectures, similar to other accelerator programming languages such as OpenCL and CUDA. One of the benefits of SYCL over OpenCL and CUDA is its unified single-source programming model that combines host and device code in a single source file. This feature simplifies the task of coding, comprehension, and maintenance.

SYCL consists of a set of runtime classes that abstract offload kernel programming concepts and an API for kernel development that includes indexing functions, synchronization functions, memory operations, and mathematical functions. There are numerous implementations of SYCL available nowadays, such as ComputeCpp from Codeplay,[2] triSYCL from Xilinx,[3] OpenSYCL from Universitat Heidelberg,[4] and DPC++ from Intel.[5] DPC++ is included in the oneAPI toolkit,[6] an initiative that aims to bring together a single API to program multiple devices. Moreover, it includes optimized libraries on multi-devices such as oneMKL for linear algebra, oneDAL for machine learning, or oneDPL, which adds additional functionalities to the language.

Code snippets 1.1 shows an example of vector addition using SYCL. The first step is selecting the device to execute the kernel using the *gpu_selector* class. Memory allocation is performed using the USM mechanism which allows using the same pointer in both the host and device ambit. Then the kernel is enqueued asynchronously using the *submit* class. And finally, the host waits for the completion of the kernel's execution before displaying the sum result.

**Listing 1.1.** Vector adding wrote in SYCL

```
#define N 16
using namespace sycl;

int main() {
    sycl::queue q(sycl::gpu_selector{});

    auto a = sycl::malloc_shared<float>(N, q);
    auto b = sycl::malloc_shared<float>(N, q);
    auto c = sycl::malloc_shared<float>(N, q);

    // Init a and b in host
    for(int i=0; i<N; i++){
        a[i]=1.0f;
        b[i]=i;
    }
```

---

[2] https://developer.codeplay.com/products/computecpp/ce/home.

[3] https://github.com/triSYCL/triSYCL.

[4] https://github.com/OpenSYCL/OpenSYCL.

[5] https://www.intel.com/content/www/us/en/developer/tools/oneapi/dpc-compiler.html.

[6] https://www.intel.com/content/www/us/en/developer/tools/oneapi/toolkits.html.

```
q.submit([&](handler& h) {
    h.parallel_for(N, [=](item<1> idx) {
        c[idx] = a[idx]+b[idx];
    });
}).wait();

for (int i=0; i<N; ++i)
    std::cout << c[i] << "\n";
}
```

## 2.2  Data Parallel Extensions for Python

The Data-Parallel Extensions for Python aim to facilitate the integration of Python with oneAPI and enable Python programmers to use the oneAPI programming model. The extensions consist of several Python packages, which are:

- **dpctl**: a package for accessing data-parallel computing resources targeted by oneAPI, allowing for device selection, queue construction, USM allocation, and creation of USM-based ND-array objects.
- **dpnp**: a library similar to NumPy but built using oneAPI DPC++ compiler and optimized libraries as oneMKL for matrix and vector operations.
- **numba-dpex**: a standalone extension to the Numba JIT compiler that offers an OpenCL-style compute API for writing oneAPI kernels directly in Python, and extends Numba's parallelizer to generate kernels from data parallel code regions.

**dpctl.** The Python interface for SYCL only binds to a subset of SYCL's API, specifically device selection, queue creation, and kernel execution. There are various implementations of the SYCL specification, and the dpctl library supports them. The dpctl library has two main components: the dpctl module, which provides Python bindings for the SYCL platform, context, device, queue, and event classes, and the dpctl.memory module, which manages MemoryUSM operations and supports Python classes for memory allocation, such as *array.array* and *numpy.ndarray*. The dpctl library also offers a C-API to integrate with other Python native extensions using either Cython [5] or pybind11 [8]. The dpctl library only supports the DPC++/SYCL implementation and relies on the filter-selector and other features of the SYCL standard.

**dpnp.** The dpnp library [2] is designed to be compatible with NumPy and can be used on SYCL-based devices. Its purpose is to speed up the processing of arrays and matrices on Intel devices. It offers Python interfaces for many NumPy functions and a subset of methods from the dpnp.ndarray class. The library is built on native C++ and uses oneMKL-based kernels to perform its operations. It supports *ufuncs* which are grouped on math, trigonometric and comparison element-wise operations.

**numba-Dpex.** Numba [11] is an extension that enables parallelism in heterogeneous architectures via low-level programming in kernels. The Data-Parallel Extension for Numba, or *numba-dpex* [1], is an autonomous extension for the Numba Python JIT compiler that interacts with the data-parallel compiler. It offers a universal kernel programming API and an offload functionality that expands Numba's auto-parallelizer for parallel-for loops. The kernel API is structured similarly to Numba's *cuda.jit* module, but employs the SYCL language instead. It supports SPIR-V-based OpenCL and oneAPI Level Zero devices that the Intel DPC++ SYCL compiler runtime supports. The numba-dpex API includes features such as replacing NumPy expressions with the dpnp library, low-level kernel programming, and exploiting ad-hoc parallelism through NDRange parallelism expression, hierarchical parallelism, memory hierarchy exploitation and lower-level operations as barriers.

The code Listing 1.2 is an example of vector addition implemented in Python with support for dpctl. The code begins by selecting the device and assigning an execution queue, then allocating memory using the USM mechanism. The vector initialization is performed using the Numpy library. The kernel function is decorated with *@dpex.kernel* in which each *idx* instance performs the addition of the vector component. Finally, the results are displayed.

**Listing 1.2.** Vector adding wrote in DPCTL

```python
import dpctl
import numpy as np
import numba_dpex as dpex


@dpex.kernel
def vector_add_dpex(a, b, c):
    idx = dpex.get_global_id(0)
    c[idx] = a[idx]+b[idx]


# Set main values
N = 16
Nsize = N*np.dtype(np.float32).itemsize
fp32=np.float32
localsize = dpex.DEFAULT_LOCAL_SIZE


def main():
    device = dpctl.SyclDevice("gpu")
    q = dpctl.SyclQueue(device)
    device.print_device_info()

    a_buf = dpctl.memory.MemoryUSMShared(Nsize, queue=q)
    b_buf = dpctl.memory.MemoryUSMShared(Nsize, queue=q)
    c_buf = dpctl.memory.MemoryUSMShared(Nsize, queue=q)
```

```
a_usm = np.ndarray(N, buffer=a_buf, dtype=fp32)
np.copyto(a_usm, np.ones(N, dtype=fp32))
b_usm = np.ndarray(N, buffer=b_buf, dtype=fp32)
np.copyto(b_usm, np.arange(N, dtype=fp32))
c_usm = np.ndarray(N, buffer=c_buf, dtype=fp32)

with dpctl.device_context(device):
    vector_add_dpex[N, localsize](a_usm, b_usm, c_usm)
    q.wait()

print(c_usm)

if __name__ == "__main__":
    main()
```

# 3   Target Applications

This section outlines the algorithms that have been selected to assess the heterogeneous computing capabilities of the Intel Distribution for Python tool, which is accessible through the oneAPI suite.

## 3.1   Matrix Multiplication

General Matrix Multiply (GEMM) is a commonly used algorithm for matrix multiplication that plays a crucial role in many scientific and engineering applications. Due to its extensive usage, GEMM has been widely adopted as a standard performance indicator within the scientific and computer architecture communities. GEMM is an ideal candidate for benchmarking, which enables researchers to evaluate not only performance but also new features of Data Parallel for Numpy. Furthermore, the optimized Intel Math Kernel Library (MKL) provides speedy implementations of this operation through the SGEMM/DGEMM routines. The election of this benchmark is to analyze the additional expenses incurred while executing a Python-interpreted code, given that the most significant computational burden lies on the multiplication operation optimized by MKL.

## 3.2   Monte Carlo

The Monte Carlo method is a well-known numerical technique that involves generating random numbers to estimate the value of an integral or simulate a physical process for problem-solving. One of the exemplary instances of this method is the estimation of pi value by generating random numbers. The Monte Carlo algorithm for pi estimation is inherently parallel, as each point calculation is independent of others. However, it also involves a reduction operation that poses challenges to the scalability of parallel computation systems. The selection of this benchmark is influenced by the simplicity of presenting this method using vector operations that can be effortlessly represented with NumPy. This approach facilitates the assessment of the performance of dpnp.

## 3.3   Nbody

The n-body benchmark involves simulating the interactions between a large number of particles, such as stars or planets, in a gravitational field. The simulation requires performing pairwise interactions between each particle, resulting in a computationally intensive task that is suitable for parallelization. Additionally, this highly parallel benchmark poses a challenge in terms of effectively utilizing the memory hierarchy by implementing memory access schemes that rely on array structures and prioritize vectorized exploitation. The Nbody benchmark facilitates the evaluation of the performance of the Data-Parallel Extensions for Python API in a practical code scenario that necessitates exploiting parallelism and memory hierarchy at a finer level to achieve optimal performance.

## 3.4   VCA

Vertex Component Analysis (VCA) is a signal processing technique used for hyperspectral unmixing, which refers to the process of decomposing a mixed spectrum into its constituent spectral signatures. The VCA algorithm is based on the concept that the vertices of a convex polytope, enclosing the observed data, correspond to the pure spectral signatures present in the mixture. Parallelizing the VCA algorithm is possible despite its iterative nature and the need for a large amount of data communication between parallel processing units. Each iteration of the algorithm requires the computation of a correlation matrix, which involves a significant amount of matrix multiplication and vector addition operations. Additionally, the selection of the vertex with the highest correlation requires global communication among all processing units to ensure that the correct vertex is selected.

# 4   Methods

This section briefly describes the configuration and methodology used for the experimentation.

It is worth mentioning that all the code used is freely available in the following GitHub repository.[7]

## 4.1   Benchmark Methodology

Since the benchmarks will run over different languages (Python and SYCL), the underlying code was designed to keep the same structure whenever it was possible. These benchmarks were run ten times to reduce variability, using single precision and the following parameters:

- Gemm: $M = 8192, N = 8192, K = 8192$
- Pi-calculus: $N = 327680000$

---

[7] https://github.com/artecs-group/ipython-bench.

- Nbody: $N = 15000, Iters = 100$
- VCA: $Image = SubsetWTC, Endmembers = 30, SNR = 0$

Moreover, we developed three implementations to run all the benchmarks with the target of evaluating the performance gain of Data Parallel Extension available on the oneAPI suite:

1. `Python` version which corresponds to a baseline code written in Python whose computations are based on vector operations expressed with the universal function of the Numpy library.
2. `IPython` version which code is based on vector operation expressed with Numpy but runs using Intel's Python distribution. Heterogeneous computing is performed by means of Data Parallel Extension for Python with dpctl. Low-level coding is also carried on with numba-dpex features (titled as `ipython-dpex`).
3. `SYCL` version resembles the parallel coding using the SYCL programming paradigm.

Table 1 provides a summary of the software and hardware features of the versions being studied.

**Table 1.** Versions and supported devices of the benchmark implementations.

| Implementation | Software version | Device |
|---|---|---|
| Python | - Python 3.10.6<br>- Numpy 1.24.2 | CPU |
| iPython | - oneAPI 2023.1<br>- AI Analytics Toolkit 2023.1 | CPU and GPU |
| SYCL | - oneAPI 2023.1 | CPU and GPU |

### 4.2   Environment Configuration

In Table 2, the main characteristics of the devices used in the experimentation are summarized. The *Intel UHD 11th Gen* and the *Intel Arc A770* are the GPUs used. The *UHD 11th Gen* is an integrated GPU that complements certain tasks of the CPU, while the Arc A770 is a discrete GPU. Although the Arc A770 lacks double precision and performance issues due to unpolished drivers, we chose to use the Arc GPU because of it enables the potential accelerations to be extrapolated in the future.

As it is noticed in Table 2, we have specified two drivers. Both iPython and SYCL implementations use another language as a backend to run on the devices. When running on the CPU only, we use the OpenCL driver. However, for Intel GPUs, we can also use the Level0 backend, which is essentially Intel's low-level implementation. For the sake of comparison, we also introduced both backends to the results.

**Table 2.** Technical specifications of the devices used.

|  | i9-9900K | UHD 11th Gen | Arc A770 |
|---|---|---|---|
| Frequency | 3.6 GHz(base) 5.0 GHz(boost) | 0.35 GHz(base) 1.45 GHz(boost) | 2.1 GHz(base) 2.4 GHz(boost) |
| Cores | 2 × 8 | 32 | 512 |
| Performance (FP32) | 0.46 TFLOPS | 0.74 TFLOPS | 16.66 TFLOPS |
| OpenCL driver | 2023.15.3.0.20 | 22.35.24055 | 23.05.25593.11 |
| Level0 driver | - | 1.3.24055 | 1.3.25593 |

## 5   Experimental Results

The following section presents the execution times obtained from the tests, which have been grouped into subsections referring to the devices for the sake of clarity.

### 5.1   CPU Results

Figure 1 shows the execution time achieved for each benchmark and implementation developed: regular Python (Python), Intel's Python distribution based on dpnp and numba-dpex (iPython, iPython-dpex), and SYCL.

Since most of the Nbody (Python) implementation uses plain Python (without Numpy), the code is greatly inefficient. Because the benchmark took 101 s to complete, we shortened the chart to enhance its readability.

Regarding the results, the SYCL versions achieve the best execution times. Comparing SYCL to iPython implementation, SYCL implementation is on average 3.6 times faster than the iPython counterparts.

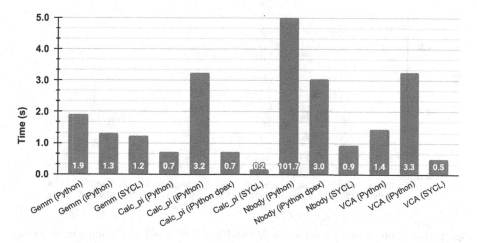

**Fig. 1.** Benchmark times for i9-9900K with Python, iPython and SYCL implementations.

When comparing the performance of Python and iPython implementations, iPython came out ahead in 2 out of 4 benchmarks and tied in the *Calc_Pi* benchmark. This translates to a significant speed advantage of 9.2 times in favour of the iPython version. However, upon removing the Nbody test, which is responsible for the speed difference, the speedup falls to just 0.96. In this case, it can be concluded that both implementations performed similarly.

## 5.2   GPU Results

Figures 2 and 3 depict times obtained in the Intel Arc A770 and Intel UHD 11th Gen GPUs respectively. In both cases, we included the execution times for both drivers *Level0* and *OpenCL*.

In relation to the Intel Arc A770, we observed time differences when changing the driver used to run the tests. The OpenCL backend outperformed in six out of nine tests and achieved the same time as the Level0 backend in one (Calc_pi SYCL). Therefore, by using the OpenCL backend, the speedup increased to 1.4.

When comparing the SYCL and iPython versions, it is clear that the SYCL implementation outperforms iPython in all benchmarks, resulting in a speedup of 3.5 times.

In Fig. 3, we examine the performance of the Intel UHD 11th Gen iGPU. Upon analysis, we observed that both drivers produced similar results. Specifically, the Level0 backend outperformed OpenCL in three out of nine tests, fell behind in one, and drew in the remaining five. However, the performance difference was only around 3%, excluding the *Calc_pi SYCL* test.

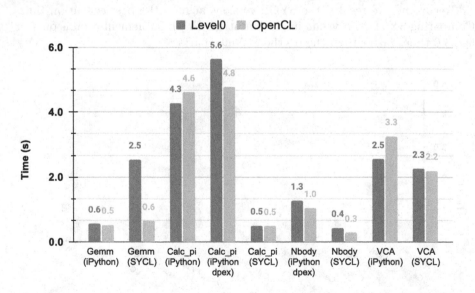

**Fig. 2.** Benchmark times for Intel Arc A770 with iPython and SYCL implementations.

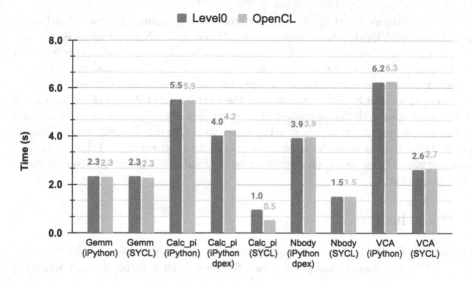

**Fig. 3.** Benchmark times for Intel UHD 11th Gen with iPython and SYCL implementations.

Facing the SYCL and iPython implementations, again, SYCL implementation outperforms iPython in all the benchmarks, this results in a speedup of 4.3 times.

## 6 Discussion

Based on the results got in the previous Sect. 5, we can assert that the SYCL implementation, as was expected, gives the best performance. Hence, we will centre the discussion on the performance difference between Python and iPython, and the gap between SYCL and iPython.

Some issues we found in porting iPython code were related to numba-dpex and the early stage it is. *Calc_pi* is an example of it. An issue[8] related to defining local variables in kernels makes it impossible to resize work batches to work-groups[9].

The same issue mentioned earlier also affects the *Nbody* test, as this benchmark employs local variables to obtain partial results. Due to this problem, it becomes impossible to define these variables, and therefore, we had to create local dynamic arrays to simulate them.

Other issues which increase the gap between iPython and SYCL include: the lack of implementation of the *numba.guvectorize* decorator to vectorize the *Calc_pi dpex* in the same way as SYCL does [4]; besides optimization issues already reported[10].

---

[8] https://github.com/IntelPython/numba-dpex/issues/829.
[9] A work-group is how SYCL defines the work batch sent to each thread.
[10] https://github.com/IntelPython/numba-dpex/issues/974.

We encountered certain limitations when using Numpy in the *VCA* benchmark. While SYCL treats all arrays as unidimensional, Numpy requires the definition of array dimensions. This makes it challenging to perform matrix-vector operations (+,-,*,/) efficiently. In order to overcome this limitation, matrix transposition operations are necessary at expenses of performance degradation.

Finally, we would like to remark on the current Intel Arc performance some issues also observed. As discussed in the previous section, there is a significant performance degradation when using different backends (about 40%). Despite being Level0 the native Intel backend we should expect to get better performance rates. Other users also reported issues related on performance and memory corruption[11].

## 7   Conclusion

Developing for HPC systems typically requires significant efforts in development and code maintenance, especially when working with heterogeneous computing environments. In such scenarios, Python is often considered as an attractive alternative due to its ease of programming and optimization capabilities using Numba or CPython.

To assess the performance gap between Python and a compiled option such as SYCL, we ran four benchmarks across CPU, integrated GPU, and discrete Intel Arc GPU. As expected, the results showed that the SYCL version outperformed Python in all cases. However, we found that we could improve the performance of the Python base code significantly by running certain tasks on a GPU or parallelizing Python functions. Moreover, these optimizations can be implemented with minimal changes to the original Python code.

Although the experiment revealed several limitations resulting from the immaturity of the Data Parallel extension in Python, upcoming enhancements could enable the community to embrace the utilization of XPUs in Python-based development, which is currently prevalent. Furthermore, Intel Python aims to deliver on the promise of code and runtime portability across different targets, including Nvidia, AMD, and Intel GPUs. This will enable the code to run seamlessly across various platforms that support SYCL.

Finally, it is important to acknowledge that the obtained results should be regarded as preliminary findings from experiments conducted on the Intel Python platform. These findings are subject to future improvements, as anticipated resolutions of code-related and performance-related issues are expected to be implemented in the near future. Consequently, these anticipated resolutions hold the promise of enhancing language expression and bridging the existing performance gap. Moving forward, potential future extensions of this research endeavor involve evaluating the performance of Intel Python on the latest generation of Intel processors. Specifically, the assessment would encompass servers equipped with the Xeon architecture, namely the Sapphire Rapids and in desktop based on the Core Raptor Lake architectures. Furthermore, an evaluation

---

[11] https://github.com/intel/compute-runtime/issues/627#issuecomment-1469079188.

within the Internet of Things (IoT) domain is contemplated, utilizing the latest X7000 Atom processors and Intel's GPU devices. These assessments aim to ascertain the compatibility and efficiency of Intel Python in diverse computing environments.

Moreover, it is of interest to conduct an evaluation of the well-known benchmark suite for Python, commonly referred to as NPBench. This comprehensive benchmark suite covers a wide range of domains, including linear algebra, physics simulations, and deep learning, while emphasizing the utilization of Python and SYCL for execution on heterogeneous devices. The assessment of Intel Python's performance within the context of the NPBench suite will provide valuable insights into its suitability and effectiveness across various computational domains.

# References

1. Data-parallel extension for numba. https://github.com/IntelPython/numba-dpex
2. Dpnp - data parallel extension for numpy. https://github.com/IntelPython/dpnp
3. Githut 2.0, a small place to discover languages in github (2023). https://madnight.github.io/githut/#/pull_requests/2022/undefined
4. Anaconda, I., et al.: Numba docs (2023). https://numba.pydata.org/numba-doc/latest/user/vectorize.html#the-guvectorize-decorator
5. Behnel, S., Bradshaw, R., Citro, C., Dalcin, L., Seljebotn, D.S., Smith, K.: Cython: the best of both worlds. Comput. Sci. Eng. **13**(2), 31–39 (2010)
6. Garland, M., et al.: Parallel computing experiences with Cuda. IEEE Micro **28**(4), 13–27 (2008)
7. TIOBE Index: Tiobe-the software quality company (2023)
8. Jakob, W., et al.: pybind11-seamless operability between C++ 11 and python. https://github.com/pybind/pybind11
9. Klöckner, A.: Pycuda: even simpler GPU programming with python. In: Proceedings of the GPU Technology Conference, Berkeley, CA, USA, pp. 20–23 (2010)
10. Klöckner, A., Pinto, N., Lee, Y., Catanzaro, B., Ivanov, P., Fasih, A.: Pycuda and pyopencl: a scripting-based approach to GPU run-time code generation. Parallel Comput. **38**(3), 157–174 (2012)
11. Lam, S.K., Pitrou, A., Seibert, S.: Numba: a LLVM-based python JIT compiler. In: Proceedings of the Second Workshop on the LLVM Compiler Infrastructure in HPC, pp. 1–6 (2015)
12. Lavrijsen, W.T., Dutta, A.: High-performance Python-C++ bindings with PyPy and cling. In: 2016 6th Workshop on Python for High-Performance and Scientific Computing (PyHPC), pp. 27–35. IEEE (2016)
13. Marowka, A.: On parallel software engineering education using python. Educ. Inf. Technol. **23**(1), 357–372 (2018)
14. Nishino, R., Loomis, S.H.C.: CuPy: a numpy-compatible library for nvidia GPU calculations. In: 31st Conference on Neural Information Processing Systems, vol. 151, no. 7 (2017)
15. Oliphant, T.E., et al.: A Guide to NumPy, vol. 1. Trelgol Publishing USA (2006)
16. Ozgur, C., Colliau, T., Rogers, G., Hughes, Z., et al.: Matlab vs. python vs. r. J. Data Sci. **15**(3), 355–371 (2017)

17. Pavlyk, O., Deb, D.: Interfacing SYCL and python for XPU programming. In: International Workshop on OpenCL, pp. 1–10 (2022)
18. Pedregosa, F., et al.: Scikit-learn: machine learning in python. J. Mach. Learn. Res. **12**, 2825–2830 (2011)
19. Simon, Mason, R., Crick, T., Davenport, J.H., Murphy, E.: Language choice in introductory programming courses at Australasian and UK universities. In: Proceedings of the 49th ACM Technical Symposium on Computer Science Education, SIGCSE 2018, pp. 852–857. Association for Computing Machinery, New York (2018). https://doi.org/10.1145/3159450.3159547
20. Tosi, S.: Matplotlib for Python developers. Packt Publishing Ltd. (2009)
21. Virtanen, P., et al.: Scipy 1.0: fundamental algorithms for scientific computing in python. Nat. Methods **17**(3), 261–272 (2020)

# Towards Reducing Communications in Sparse Matrix Kernels

Manuel Freire⬤, Raul Marichal⬤, Ernesto Dufrechou^(✉)⬤,
and Pablo Ezzatti⬤

Instituto de Computación, INCO Facultad de Ingeniería,
Universidad de la República, Montevideo, Uruguay
{mfreire,rmarichal,edufrechou,pezzatt}@fing.edu.uy

**Abstract.** The significant presence that many-core devices like GPUs
have these days, and their enormous computational power, motivates the
study of sparse matrix operations in this hardware. The essential sparse
kernels in scientific computing, such as the sparse matrix-vector multiplication (SpMV), usually have many different high-performance GPU
implementations. Sparse matrix problems typically imply memory-bound
operations, and this characteristic is particularly limiting in massively
parallel processors. This work revisits the main ideas about reducing
the volume of data required by sparse storage formats and advances
in understanding some compression techniques. In particular, we study
the use of index compression combined with sparse matrix reordering
techniques. The systematic experimental evaluation on a large set of
real-world matrices confirms that this approach is promising, achieving
meaningful data storage reductions.

**Keywords:** sparse matrices · memory access · reordering technique ·
matrix storage reduction

## 1 Introduction

The evolution of the sparse matrix research has evolved constantly since the
'50s when the pioneer works by Gustavson and others [12] made the first steps
in this field. Nowadays, sparse matrices are employed in different contexts in science and engineering, and the resolution of many scientific computing problems
implies an intensive use of sparse matrix operations. Maybe the most relevant
of these is the product of sparse matrices with dense vectors (SpMV) since it
is the heart of iterative methods to solve sparse linear systems. This has motivated several works to improve its performance on different hardware platforms
in the last 40 years. A related aspect that has a strong impact on sparse matrix
research, and scientific computations, is the evolution of hardware platforms in
the HPC field. The main design trend of modern computer architectures is to
integrate many lightweight cores and provide high memory bandwidths. These
are referred as throughput-oriented architectures. GPUs are key examples that,

M. Naiouf et al. (Eds.): JCC-BD&ET 2023, CCIS 1828, pp. 17–30, 2023.
https://doi.org/10.1007/978-3-031-40942-4_2

since the appearance of CUDA in 2007, dominated the HPC landscape of numerical linear algebra. Like other throughput-oriented hardware platforms, such as FPGAs or some multi-core CPUs, these devices offer impressive peak performance in floating-point operations (FPOs) as long as a high memory throughput can be maintained. However, the latency of memory accesses has not improved as much as the computing power for HPC platforms. This situation poses important challenges in the context of memory-bound problems, where few FPOs are performed for each memory access [7,8]. Besides being inherently memory-bound, sparse matrix problems generally present other performance restrictions such as load imbalance, indirect access to memory, and low data locality. However, despite being capable of reaching only a mild fraction of the peak performance in these devices, it is still possible to achieve important gains by exploiting their superior memory bandwidth. Therefore, it is mandatory to apply techniques that allow transferring less data between the memory and the cores for each FPO, increasing the achieved computational intensity.

In this work, we review the state-of-the-art techniques devoted to improving sparse matrix storage, such as efforts to improve the data locality and reduce the volume of data movements between levels of the memory hierarchy. Also, we identify some promising techniques and study them in detail, performing an extensive experimental evaluation. The main contribution of our work is an extensive evaluation performed on the SuiteSparse matrix collection[1] of the impact of index compression and reordering on the storage volume of sparse matrices. The obtained results show that important storage reductions can be reached in the sparse matrices evaluated. This reductions are highly relevant because they can lead to improvements in the relation between communications and FPOs, transferring less data from memory.

The rest of the article is structured as follows. In Sect. 2 we summarize some basic concepts about sparse matrices. Next, in Sect. 3, we revisit several works that are strongly related to our objectives. A systematic experimental evaluation of some highlighted strategies for these purposes follows in Sect. 4. At the end of our article, in Sect. 5, we offer some concluding remarks and identify promising future lines of work.

## 2   Basic Concepts

*Sparse Matrix Storage Formats.* They are strategies that avoid storing redundant matrix information by storing the nonzero values of a matrix together with a combination of data structures that allow determining the coordinates associated with each element. For example, the coordinate format (COO) stores the nonzero values and their coordinates as three arrays. Another standard format, Compressed Sparse Row (CSR), shares the array of values and columns of COO, but compresses the array of row coordinates, storing only the index where each row starts in the other two arrays. The main advantages of CSR are its compactness, and that it allows accesssing all the elements of a row directly. On

---

[1] https://sparse.tamu.edu/.

the other hand, it requires additional operations to access each value. Various formats similar to CSR have been proposed, such as the Compressed Sparse Column (CSC) format, which is analogous to CSR but compresses the column array. Another alternative is *Compressed Diagonal Storage* (CDS), which takes advantage of the band matrix structure to represent the matrix by eliminating the row and column arrays. *Block Compressed Row Format* (BSR) divides the original matrix into dense blocks of equal size and makes the array of columns represent block positions. The block compressed row array is analogous to the corresponding CSR array but considers rows of blocks instead of scalars. This format requires the elements of the same block to be contiguous in the array of values and uses *padding* in that array to fill the blocks with zeros since it assumes they are the same size. Other formats use variable-size blocks. Among them, two of the most prominent are 1D-VBL (*Variabable Block Length*) [19], which uses one-dimensional blocks, and VBR (*Variable Block Row*) [20], in which the blocks are two-dimensional.

There are multiple possible criteria to evaluate formats. In [15] the authors review the available literature on the subject and note that commonly used evaluation criteria depend on a variety of parameters, such as architecture dependencies, implementation quality, and representation used for the values.

*The Cuthill-McKee Algorithm.* [6] It is a reordering technique based on the application of a Breadth-First-Search (BFS) traversal strategy, in which the graph associated with the matrix is traversed by levels. Starting from a root node (level 0), the unvisited adjacent nodes of the nodes on each level are sorted and added to the list of nodes of the next level. Then the ones in the current level are numbered and the procedure repeats for the next level until all nodes are visited. The order in which each level is numbered gives rise to different orderings or permutations of rows and columns. In the Cuthill-McKee algorithm, the adjacent nodes to a visited node are always traversed from low to high degrees. A popular variant of the CM algorithm is the Reverse-CM, in which the order obtained for the rows/columns is "reversed". The RCM heuristic results in arrays with the same bandwidth as CM, but with a lower *profile*. In the original version of the RCM proposed by A. George, those nodes in the graph with minimum degree are also selected as initial vertices. The bandwidth and profile reductions of the resulting matrix, obtained by the CM and RCM heuristics strongly depend on the choice of the initial vertex. For this reason, several studies have been carried out on how to choose the initial vertex.

# 3    Related Work

Perhaps one of the simplest strategies to improve the memory access pattern in sparse methods is to save the diagonal of the matrix separately. In this line, Sun et al. presented the Compressed Row Segment with Diagonal-pattern (CRSD) format [21]. The format is focused mainly on matrices with diagonal patterns on groups or segments of adjacent rows. It consists of storing the components of each diagonal in a segment, in vectors whose index corresponds to the offset with respect to the main diagonal. Another example can be the HYB format that combines the ELL and COO formats, proposed by Bell and Garland [2]. The idea is to divide the matrix into a $A_{ELL}$ array of size $n \times k$ where the number of elements per row is close to $k$ and $A_{COO}$ for the rest of the elements. Choosing the column $k$ that determines the partition can be solved, as in the implementation of $CUSP$ [3] library, with a heuristic. Other hybrid format, that combines ELL and Vectored CSR is EVC-HYB [11], focused on improving the performance of the SpMV in GPUs. First, the authors sort the rows based on their lengths, from smallest to largest, and then they partition the rows into two groups, long and short. Centered in this partition, the matrix entries are stored in ELL or VCSR as appropriate, seeking to exploit the strenghts of both formats. While ELL works well with arrays whose number of nonzero elements per row is low and regular, VCSR works better with matrices whose rows are of sufficient length and, if possible, multiples of 32.

In recent years, various efforts in sparse ALN worked with reduced precisions or modifications of standard formats. An example is [1], where the authors evaluate the use of reduced precisions (half and single) to store some coefficients of preconditioners. This format aims to reduce the overhead produced by data transfers. Similar ideas are applied in [10], but decoupling the floating-point format used for arithmetic operations from the format used to store data in memory. A complementary approach is to reduce the precision of the indices associated with the coefficients. In this sense, in the work of Shiming Xu et al. [24] an optimization of the SpMV is proposed, based on the ELL format, whose objective is to reduce the number of bits needed to represent the indices. The authors explore the possibility of using the distance to the diagonal instead of the actual value of the coordinate as the column index. They target a set of square matrices where they also seek to reduce the distance of the nonzero elements to the diagonal through rearrangements or permutations such as the RCM method. Other authors also tried other heuristics instead of RCM [17]. Another idea is the CoAdELL format [16], focused on the division by warps of the computations with matrices stored in ELL-based formats. This is achieved using a compression technique to reduce the storage associated with column indexes. The idea is to use an encoding based on the difference between the indices of two consecutive nonzero elements in the same row, a technique that most authors call *delta encoding*. As these differences or deltas will have lower values than the indices, they can be represented with fewer bits. Tang et al. [22] propose using a family of efficient compression schemes, which they call *bit-representation optimized* (BRO), to reduce the number of bits required to represent indices. For the design of the BRO storage schemes, the authors considered essential aspects related to the target architectures. Without going into implementation details, the authors study the impact of the steps necessary to apply these techniques. For example, to be able to perform decompression on the GPU, it must be relatively light compared to the addition and multiplication operations of the SpMV so that most of the GPU cycles are allocated to useful work and not used only to decompress the index data. In this sense, two index compression techniques are presented, BRO-ELL and BRO-COO, based on the formats ELL and COO, compressing the column indices using delta encoding. For example, in BRO-ELL, once the column index vectors have been transformed into delta encoding, the authors suggest dividing each of these into segments (called slices) of height $h$. Subsequently, each slice is compressed by an independent thread according to the number of bits needed for each delta index. In addition to BRO-COO and BRO-ELL, the authors also present BRO-HYB, useful in cases when the number of nonzero elements per row varies substantially. This format is analogous to HYB, storing the regular component in BRO-ELL and the irregular component in BRO-COO.

Willcock and Lumsdaine proposed *Delta-Coded Sparse Row* (DCSR), a compression scheme based on the delta encoding of the indices is proposed, encoding the indices as the differences between the column positions of nonzero elements in a row, using the minimum number of bytes possible. For this, a set of six command codes is used to encode the index data. In another investigation, Monakov et al. [18] propose a new format that they called sliced ELLPACK, to improve the performance of SpMV in GPUs. This format has the main parameter $S$, which is the size or number of rows in each *slice*. Each of these slices is stored in ELL format. While the storage overhead in the sliced ELLPACK format is limited to slices with an imbalance in the number of nonzero elements per row, this can still cause noticeable performance degradation. The authors then propose a simple reordering heuristic that can substantially improve the performance of the SpMV implementation for that format, based on grouping rows with the same number of nonzero elements.

To take advantage of compression methods, the same authors of [22] extended their first proposals with the use of an ordering strategy that they called *BRO-aware reordering* (BAR). This strategy consists of bringing together those columns with similar patterns in terms of the number of bits necessary for their encoding to reduce the total space and, consequently, possibly reduce the number of transactions when operating with the matrix. The authors formulate the obtention of the permutation $P$ as a clustering problem. The increasing use of Machine Learning in multiple areas, and the computational capacity these methods need, motivated several studies that seek to optimize sparse operations that arise in these contexts, such as the SpMM (Sparse-dense Matrix Multiplication) and SDDMM (Sampled Dense Matrix Multiplication) [9,13,25]. For example, in Hong et al. [13], an ordering strategy based on adaptive *tiling* is designed, called Adaptive Sparse Tiling (ASpT). The technique is applied to improve the performance of the two primitives (SpMM and SDDMM). *Tiling* is a fundamental technique for data locality optimization. It consists of grouping elements of the matrix into blocks or tiles, usually 2D, with which certain operation is carried out, for example, multiplications and convolutions. This technique is widely used in high-performance implementations of dense matrix-matrix multiplications, both for CPU and GPU.

Other operation that has gained popularity in recent years is the SpGEMM (Sparse Matrix-Sparse Matrix multiplication) since it is an important part on many graph problems as well as in the field of data science. Since SpGeMM involves two sparse matrices the irregularity is one of the main problems, in the format presented in Berger et al. the authors use a blocked format with bitmaps to address irregularity [4, 5].

## 4    Systematic Experimental Evaluation

This section studies the effectiveness of techniques for sparse matrix compression, focusing on reducing index storage volume. The dataset used for our study is the group of matrices with symmetric non-zero patterns of the *SuiteSparse Matrix Collection*, which comprises 1407 matrices with different sizes and nonzero structures. Our purpose is to identify the most promising techniques to reduce index storage. In this context, we employ the sparse matrices represented with the CSR format as a baseline, which we call direct index compression. Then, we evaluate two different strategies: delta-to-diagonal encoding and delta encoding, assessing the effect of applying a previous reordering on each one.

### 4.1    Direct Index Compression

The first effort explores the original indices (i.e., in CSR), which will serve as the baseline to assess the rest of the strategies. Our evaluation classifies each index into three categories based on the minimum number of bits required to represent it. The categories comprise the indices requiring less than 8 bits, those requiring 9 to 16 bits, and those requiring 17 to 32 bits, respectively. In this case, all the indices are non-negative values. We also classify each matrix into the same three categories according to its largest index (or the largest index of each row or column). As we deal with square matrices and there are no empty rows or columns at the end, applying this procedure to the baseline matrix representation is equivalent to taking the matrix dimension, equal to the largest column index value. Therefore, we need to determine if the matrix dimension is less or equal to $2^8 - 1$, $2^{16} - 1$ or $2^{32} - 1$.

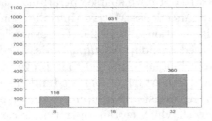 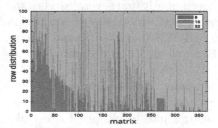

**Fig. 1.** Index size distribution of the studied matrices for direct-indexing.

The left image in Fig. 1 presents a bar chart with the results of the direct-index classification. We can see that from the 1407 studied matrices, 116 require 8 bits, 931 require 16 bits, and 360 require 32 bits. In other words, approximately 25% of the total matrices require 32 bits to store their indices.

In this and the following studies, we expand the evaluation over the matrices that require 32 bits. Specifically, we analyze the number of rows falling in each of the three categories for each of these matrices. The right image of Fig. 1 summarizes these results, showing the percentage of the total rows that imply 8, 16, and 32 bits for each matrix. It is easy to see that most rows lie in the 16 or 32-bit classes. In this figures each value in the x-axis represents one matrix. In other words, only a few matrices present a large number of rows storable with 8-bit indices, where a hybrid strategy that uses different integer sizes according to the row classification could be applied.

## 4.2    Delta-to-Diagonal Encoding

This encoding replaces the column index value in the CSR representation by the difference between the corresponding column and the diagonal. Therefore, the integer size required to represent each row is determined by the distance of the first nonzero value to the diagonal (a value equivalent to the bandwidth of each row, $\beta(A_i)$). As before, left part of Fig. 2 presents the number of matrices in each family (8, 16 or 32 bits). Notice that unlike the previous analysis, where we need to manipulate only positive indices, we need to employ integer numbers in this technique. Expressly, we assume symmetric ranges relative to zero (the column index of the diagonal values in the new encoding). Thus, we obtain the next ranges $[-2^7, 2^7]$, $[-2^{15}, 2^{15}]$ y $[-2^{31}, 2^{31}]$.

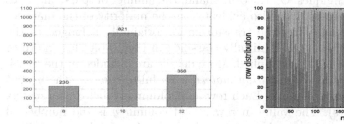

**Fig. 2.** Index size distribution of the studied matrices for delta-to-diagonal compression.

Expanding the analysis as in the previous case, we take the matrices of the 32-bit class and evaluate the percentage of rows that could be stored with fewer bits. The right-hand side of Fig. 2 shows a significant increase in the fraction of rows that require fewer bits compared to the previous representation. Furthermore, several large matrices with a high percentage of rows representable with 8-bits can be observed.

## 4.3    Delta-to-Diagonal Encoding with Reordering

This variant applies a reordering to the sparse matrix previous to the diagonal encoded. Specifically, and following the proposal of Xu et al. [24], we use the

RCM heuristic on each sparse matrix, and later we replace the column indices by the difference with the diagonal (the encoding presented in Sect. 4.2) in the reordered matrix.

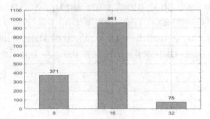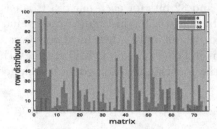

**Fig. 3.** Index size distribution of the studied matrices for delta-to-diagonal compression after applying RCM reordering.

The number of matrices that are representable using the delta-to-diagonal technique with 8, 16, and 32 bits, with and without the reordering, can be compared observing Figs. 2 and 3. From these charts, we can deduce that using the RCM heuristic offers substantial benefits, significantly diminishing the number of matrices that require 32 bits to store their indices from 353 to 63. In other words, 290 matrices (82%) that initially needed 32-bit indices can benefit from applying these two techniques. On the other hand, the number of sparse matrices in the 16-bit class increases. It is also evident that the majority of the matrices that form the 16-bit class after the transformation originally belonged to the 32-bit class. In fact, 154 matrices initially classified in the 16-bit class move to the 8-bit class when the RCM is applied. More details are included in the Fig. 4. This chart, which we name *composition matrix*, is useful to compare the benefit of applying a reordering technique. Each row and column is labeled as a matrix class (8, 16, or 32-bits). The value in row $x$ and column $y$ is the number of matrices of class $x$ that move to class $y$ after the reordering. In the composition matrix, it is easy to see that, although the numbers in the upper triangle are generally low, we have several nonzero values (only one is zero). This means that, in a few matrices, the reordering technique affects the number of bits needed for column index storage negatively. In particular, 15 sparse matrices move from 8 to 16 bits, and two matrices move from 16 to 32 bits. Although these numbers are significantly smaller than those of the matrices that benefit, this situation evidences that there are problems where applying these reordering techniques handicaps the compression.

Figure 5 shows the case of the matrix FIDAP/ex25, which moves from the 8-bit to the 16-bit category after the application of the RCM heuristic. In the original form, its 848 rows can be represented with 8 bits while, after the reordering, only 475 rows can be represented with 8 bits and 376 rows requiere 16 bits. This matrix shows a block-diagonal or periodic nonzero pattern, which is lost when RCM is applied. Similar to the previous example, in Fig. 6 we show the case

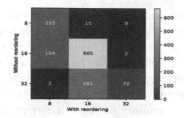

**Fig. 4.** The Composition Matrix shows the number of matrices that move form one category to the other after reordering with RCM, applying delta-to-diagonal encoding.

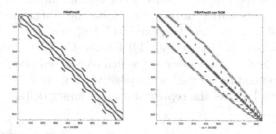

**Fig. 5.** An example of a matrix that moves from the 8-bit to the 16-bit category after applying RCM using delta-to-diagonal encoding.

of `Sinclair/3Dspectralwave2` matrix, where the application of the reordering technique does not improve the index representation. In this case, the matrix moves from the 16-bit to the 32-bit class. The causes of this situation are similar to the previous one.

At this point, it is difficult to establish a general rule that predicts the volume of storage saved using RCM reordering heuristic with delta-to-diagonal encoding. However, the nonzero structure of the matrix needs to be carefully considered before the transformation. In some cases, the reordering breaks a convenient pattern, even increasing the number of bits required to store the indices.

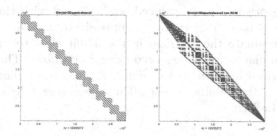

**Fig. 6.** Example of a matrix that moves from the 16-bit to the 32-bit category after applying RCM using delta-to-diagonal encoding.

As in the case without reordering, we expand our study focusing on the matrices of the 32-bit category and we evaluate which percentage of rows can be stored with less bits. These results can be observed in the right part of Fig. 3. In general, the figure shows that after the application of the RCM, the matrices in this category have relatively few rows storable with a smaller integer size. Additionally, it does not seem to be a strong correlation between the number of nonzero coefficients and the number of rows that require fewer bits.

## 4.4   Delta Encoding

This study modifies the rule to substitute the column index value by the difference between two consecutive indices, i.e., delta encoding. This idea is similar to those presented in works as Maggioni et al. [16], where the authors propose the CoAdELL format, Kourtis et al. [14] for the CSR-DU format, and other efforts [22,23]. Unlike the previous case, which considered positive and negative distances, in this encoding all values are positive. This provides an extra bit to store the indices and allows the representation of larger deltas.

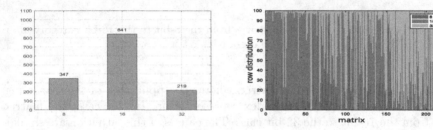

**Fig. 7.** Index size distribution of the studied matrices for delta encoding.

As before, the left part of Fig. 7 shows the categorization of sparse matrices according to the number of bits required to store the largest column index. Comparing delta encoding with the delta-to-diagonal variant (results in Fig. 2), the benefits achieved by the former are clear. Specifically, the number of matrices in the 32-bit category is heavily reduced, and, aligned with this, the number of matrices in the 8 bits category grows impressively. Similar to the previous experiments, we evaluate the matrices in the 32-bit class to understand how many rows of each matrix could be stored using 8 or 16 bits. The results of this study are summarized in rigth part of Fig. 7. As in delta-to-diagonal encoding without reordering, the results do not allow considering a hybrid strategy to store the column indices.

## 4.5   Delta Encoding with Reordering

Considering the benefits reached using the RCM reordering heuristic in the delta-to-diagonal encoding studied previously, in this work, we propose the application

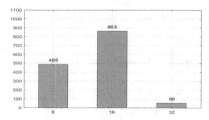 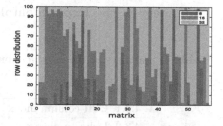

**Fig. 8.** Index size distribution of the studied matrices for delta encoding after applying RCM.

of the ideas of Maggioni et al. to the delta encoding strategy. Similar ideas were explored in [22]. Figure 8 summarizes the experimental results reached in this case. The figure shows that the effect of reordering produces similar results using delta encoding and delta-to-diagonal. The application of the RCM heuristic drastically improves the compression, actually achieving more significant improvements in the case of delta encoding. Comparing the use of delta encoding with and without the previous reordering, we can see that with reordering, the number of matrices that require 32 bits is reduced in the order of 75%.

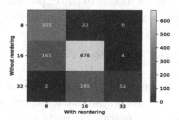

**Fig. 9.** Composition Matrix for the delta encoding strategy, showing the number of matrices that form each category with and without reordering

Observing the composition matrix that is presented in Fig. 9 it is possible to notice some matrices that increment the number of bits needed for its representation after the RCM. In this case, the upper triangle corresponds to 22 matrices that move from the 8 to the 16-bit class and four that move from the 16 to the 32-bit class. These numbers are a bit higher than the previous matrix.

Following the same procedure as the previous approaches, we analyze the matrices in the 32-bit category, which is the most interesting from the compression perspective. The right side of Fig. 8 shows the percentage of rows that require 8, 16, and 32 bits for the 56 matrices in this category, sorted by their number of nonzeros. The results are similar to those reached in previous experiments.

## 4.6   Summary of the Experimental Evaluation

**Table 1.** Summary of the classification results for the evaluated strategies

| Variant | 8 | 16 | 32 |
|---|---|---|---|
| 4.3.1. CSR column index | 116 | 931 | 360 |
| 4.3.2. Delta-to-diagonal | 230 | 821 | 356 |
| 4.3.3. Delta-to-diagonal with RCM | 371 | 961 | 75 |
| 4.3.4. Delta encoding | 347 | 841 | 219 |
| 4.3.5. Delta encoding with RCM | 488 | 863 | 56 |

To summarize and analyze the obtained results, we include Table 1 that lists the classification of the total matrices evaluated with each approach. From this table, we can highlight several results. First, the results show that the reduction of the number of matrices that require 32 bits is considerable for all the evaluated techniques. Although the gap is of only four matrices in the delta-to-diagonal encoding, the benefits are substantial in other cases. As second observation, the addressed reordering technique (RCM) improves the matrix classification. This affirmation can be corroborated, by the reduction of the number of matrices in the 32-bit category. These results motivate the exploration of methods for matrix index compression and storage formats that consider different integer sizes.

## 5   Final Remarks and Future Work

We evaluated the strategies proposed to reduce the storage volume of sparse matrix formats. Our effort includes a systematic experimental evaluation of some of the most promising ones. We thoroughly review the different techniques presented in previous efforts that align with our objective. Specifically, we identify two methods based on index compression techniques, i.e., the delta-to-diagonal encoding and delta encoding, and assess their use with sparse matrix reordering procedures such as the RCM heuristic. We perform our experimental evaluation on 1407 matrices from the Suite Sparse Matrix Collection. Our purpose is to avoid the potential bias in the analysis that can arise in small sets, caused by specific patterns. Considering the experimental results, we can affirm that these techniques strongly reduce the storage required by sparse matrices. In particular, the combination of delta encoding with reordering techniques allows storing the column indices of 96% of the evaluated matrices using at most 16-bit integers.

As part of future work, we plan to advance in four distinct directions. One interesting line of work is developing a computational method to address the sparse matrix-vector product using sparse formats that incorporate these index compression ideas. Although the RCM method is a heuristic specifically designed to optimize the sparse matrix profile, other heuristics could be explored with the specific focus of harnessing techniques such as delta encoding. Another interesting line is the creation of a new storage format that mixes 8, 16 and 32 bits representation for indices depending of the matrix. The general idea would be to divide the matrix into three blocks in which have the rows use each number of bits. Finally, developing a publicly available software library is essential to use and experimentally evaluate these techniques.

**Acknowledgments.** We acknowledge support of the ANII MPG Independent Research Group: Efficient Heterogeneous Computing at UdelaR, a partner group of the Max Planck Institute in Magdeburg. This work is partially funded by the UDELAR CSIC-INI project *CompactDisp: Formatos dispersos eficientes para arquitecturas de hardware modernas*. We also thank PEDECIBA Informática and the University of the Republic, Uruguay.

# References

1. Anzt, H., Dongarra, J., Flegar, G., Higham, N.J., Quintana-Ortí, E.S.: Adaptive precision in block-jacobi preconditioning for iterative sparse linear system solvers. Concurrency Comput. Pract. Experience **31**(6), e4460 (2018). https://doi.org/10.1002/cpe.4460
2. Bell, N., Garland, M.: Implementing sparse matrix-vector multiplication on throughput-oriented processors. In: Proceedings of the Conference on High Performance Computing Networking, Storage and Analysis, pp. 1–11 (2009)
3. Bell, N., Garland, M.: Cusp library (2012). https://github.com/cusplibrary/cusplibrary
4. Berger, G., Freire, M., Marini, R., Dufrechou, E., Ezzatti, P.: Unleashing the performance of bmsparse for the sparse matrix multiplication in GPUs. In: Proceedings of the 2021 12th Workshop on Latest Advances in Scalable Algorithms for Large-Scale Systems (ScalA), pp. 19–26, November 2021
5. Berger, G., Freire, M., Marini, R., Dufrechou, E., Ezzatti, P.: Advancing on an efficient sparse matrix multiplication kernel for modern gpus. Practice and Experience, Concurrency and Computation (2022)
6. Cuthill, E., McKee, J.: Reducing the bandwidth of sparse symmetric matrices. In: Proceedings of the 1969 24th National Conference, pp. 157–172. ACM Press (1969). https://doi.org/10.1145/800195.805928
7. Dufrechou, E., Ezzatti, P., Freire, M., Quintana-Ortí, E.S.: Machine learning for optimal selection of sparse triangular system solvers on GPUs. J. Parall. Distrib. Comput. **158**, 47–55 (2021). https://doi.org/10.1016/j.jpdc.2021.07.013
8. Dufrechou, E., Ezzatti, P., Quintana-Ortí, E.S.: Selecting optimal SpMV realizations for GPUs via machine learning. Int. J. High Perform. Comput. Appl. **35**(3) (2021). https://doi.org/10.1177/1094342021990738
9. Gale, T., Zaharia, M., Young, C., Elsen, E.: Sparse GPU kernels for deep learning. In: Proceedings of the International Conference for High Performance Computing, Networking, Storage and Analysis. SC 2020, IEEE Press (2020)
10. Grützmacher, T., Cojean, T., Flegar, G., Göbel, F., Anzt, H.: A customized precision format based on mantissa segmentation for accelerating sparse linear algebra. Concurrency Comput. Pract. Experience **32**(15) (2019). https://doi.org/10.1002/cpe.5418
11. Guo, D., Gropp, W., Olson, L.N.: A hybrid format for better performance of sparse matrix-vector multiplication on a GPU. Int. J. High Perform. Comput. Appl. **30**(1), 103–120 (2015). https://doi.org/10.1177/1094342015593156

12. Gustavson, F.G., Liniger, W., Willoughby, R.: Symbolic generation of an optimal crout algorithm for sparse systems of linear equations. J. ACM **17**(1), 87–109 (1970)
13. Hong, C., Sukumaran-Rajam, A., Nisa, I., Singh, K., Sadayappan, P.: Adaptive sparse tiling for sparse matrix multiplication. In: Proceedings of the 24th Symposium on Principles and Practice of Parallel Programming, ACM, February 2019. https://doi.org/10.1145/3293883.3295712
14. Kourtis, K., Goumas, G., Koziris, N.: Optimizing sparse matrix-vector multiplication using index and value compression. In: Proceedings of the 2008 Conference on Computing Frontiers, ACM Press (2008). https://doi.org/10.1145/1366230.1366244
15. Langr, D., Tvrdík, P.: Evaluation criteria for sparse matrix storage formats. IEEE Trans. Parall. Distrib. Syst. **27**(2), 428–440 (2016). https://doi.org/10.1109/TPDS.2015.2401575
16. Maggioni, M., Berger-Wolf, T.: CoAdELL: adaptivity and compression for improving sparse matrix-vector multiplication on GPUs. In: 2014 IEEE International Parallel & Distributed Processing Symposium Workshops, IEEE, May 2014. https://doi.org/10.1109/ipdpsw.2014.106
17. Marichal, R., Dufrechou, E., Ezzatti, P.: Optimizing sparse matrix storage for the big data era. In: Naiouf, M., Rucci, E., Chichizola, F., De Giusti, L. (eds.) JCC-BD&ET 2021. CCIS, vol. 1444, pp. 121–135. Springer, Cham (2021). https://doi.org/10.1007/978-3-030-84825-5_9
18. Monakov, A., Lokhmotov, A., Avetisyan, A.: Automatically tuning sparse matrix-vector multiplication for GPU architectures. In: High Performance Embedded Architectures and Compilers, pp. 111–125. Springer, Berlin Heidelberg (2010)
19. Pinar, A., Heath, M.T.: Improving performance of sparse matrix-vector multiplication. In: Proceedings of the 1999 ACM/IEEE Conference on Supercomputing, pp. 30-es. SC 1999, Association for Computing Machinery, New York, NY, USA (1999)
20. Saad, Y.: Sparskit: a basic tool kit for sparse matrix computations - version 2 (1994)
21. Sun, X., Zhang, Y., Wang, T., Zhang, X., Yuan, L., Rao, L.: Optimizing SpMV for diagonal sparse matrices on GPU. In: 2011 International Conference on Parallel Processing, IEEE, September 2011. https://doi.org/10.1109/icpp.2011.53
22. Tang, W.T., et al.: Accelerating sparse matrix-vector multiplication on GPUs using bit-representation-optimized schemes. In: Proceedings of the International Conference on High Performance Computing, Networking, Storage and Analysis, ACM (2013). https://doi.org/10.1145/2503210.2503234
23. Willcock, J., Lumsdaine, A.: Accelerating sparse matrix computations via data compression. In: Proceedings of the 20th Annual International Conference on Supercomputing - ICS 2006, ACM Press (2006). https://doi.org/10.1145/1183401.1183444
24. Xu, S., Lin, H.X., Xue, W.: Sparse matrix-vector multiplication optimizations based on matrix bandwidth reduction using NVIDIA CUDA. In: 2010 Ninth International Symposium on Distributed Computing and Applications to Business, Engineering and Science, IEEE, August 2010
25. Yang, C., Buluç, A., Owens, J.D.: Design principles for sparse matrix multiplication on the GPU. In: Aldinucci, M., Padovani, L., Torquati, M. (eds.) Euro-Par 2018. LNCS, vol. 11014, pp. 672–687. Springer, Cham (2018). https://doi.org/10.1007/978-3-319-96983-1_48

# Distributed Architectures Based on Edge Computing, Fog Computing and End Devices: A Conceptual Review Incorporating Resilience Aspects

Santiago Medina[1] ⓘ, Diego Montezanti[1(✉)] ⓘ, Lucas Gómez D'Orazio[1],
Francisco Garay[1], Armando De Giusti[1,2] ⓘ, and Marcelo Naiouf[1] ⓘ

[1] Instituto de Investigación en Informática LIDI (III-LIDI), Facultad de Informática,
Universidad Nacional de La Plata – Comisión de Investigaciones Científicas de la Provincia de
Buenos Aires, La Plata, Argentina
{smedina,dmontezanti,lgomez,fgaray,degiusti,
mnaiouf}@lidi.info.unlp.edu.ar
[2] CONICET – Consejo Nacional de Investigaciones Científicas y Técnicas, Santa Fe, Argentina

**Abstract.** Due to the growing popularity of the Internet of Things (IoT), the number of devices connected to the Internet has risen considerably, resulting in an increase in network traffic, which generates bottlenecks that can result in limitations in terms of communication latency, response times and bandwidth. Because traditional cloud-based infrastructures are insufficient for the current demands of such applications, the Fog Computing and Edge Computing paradigms have been proposed, which allow to alleviate these limitations by moving some processing capabilities closer to the network edges and away from central servers in the cloud.

Because of the heterogeneity that exists in the literature regarding the definitions associated with these distributed architectures, this article provides a conceptual review of the different layers that compose them: Fog, Edge, and End Devices. The scope of each of the layers is defined and the platforms and services that can be deployed in each of them are presented. An introductory analysis of types of applications and resilience strategies applied to different failure scenarios is also made.

**Keywords:** End Devices · Edge Computing · Fog Computing · Cloud Computing · Resilience · Internet of Things · Wireless Sensor Networks

## 1 Introduction and Motivation

In recent years, the technologies associated with the Internet of Things (IoT) have acquired great relevance, due to their characteristic of allowing the connection of a considerable number of sensor devices to the Internet [1]. These devices collect information from the environment and transmit it to cloud services for processing and storage. IoT is used to develop intelligent applications that interact with the environment, such as traffic management, smart homes, monitoring of natural events and human health [2].

M. Naiouf et al. (Eds.): JCC-BD&ET 2023, CCIS 1828, pp. 31–44, 2023.
https://doi.org/10.1007/978-3-031-40942-4_3

The Cloud Computing paradigm [3] makes available to Internet-connected applications and devices a large number of platforms and services to improve data processing, storage and analysis. The large growth of the IoT leads to a considerable dependency on Cloud capabilities, thus generating a bottleneck in network and resource utilization.

To address these problems, in recent years, the Fog Computing and Edge Computing paradigms have been proposed to alleviate these limitations by moving some processing capabilities closer to the edges of the network and away from the central servers in the cloud. In both cases, the goal is not to replace cloud computing, but to provide additional layers capable of complementing it [4, 5].

Within the literature, the Fog Computing paradigm arises mainly as a result of the bandwidth and communication latency limitations presented by the Cloud for IoT applications and is defined in different ways. In [6] the authors define Fog Computing as *"a promising complementary computing paradigm to cloud computing where computational, networking, storage and acceleration elements are deployed at the edge and network layers in a multi-tier, distributed and possibly cooperative manner"*, while in [7] it is stated that *"Fog computing bridges the gap between the cloud and end devices (e.g., IoT nodes) by enabling computing, storage, networking, and data management on network nodes within the close vicinity of IoT devices"*.

Meanwhile, Edge Computing is a paradigm that has been gaining relevance as a solution to the latency and real-time response problems specific to IoT applications. In different sources within the literature, it is defined as *"a new computing paradigm that performs computing at the edge of the network. Its core idea is to make computing closer to the source of the data"* [8], or, alternatively, *"Edge computing directs computational data, applications, and services away from Cloud servers to the edge of a network. The content providers and application developers can use the Edge computing systems by offering the users services closer to them. Edge computing is characterized in terms of high bandwidth, ultra-low latency, and real-time access to the network information that can be used by several applications"* [9]. On the industry side, IBM presents Edge Computing as *"a distributed computing framework that brings enterprise applications closer to data sources such as IoT devices or local edge servers. This proximity to data at its source can deliver strong business benefits, including faster insights, improved response times and better bandwidth availability"* [10]; meanwhile, Microsoft claims that *"Edge computing allows devices in remote locations to process data at the "edge" of the network, either by the device or a local server"* [11].

End Devices, also called sensor nodes or IoT nodes, are the components of the architecture that interact with the environment for data collection. Within the literature, there is a wide and varied analysis of these devices. For example, [12] highlights the importance in the selection of these devices *"The dynamic nature of the IoT devices, coupled with their stringent resource constraints and the availability of multiple communication modalities necessitate proper selection of communication architecture based on the application and corresponding resource constraints"*, while [13] classifies them into two large groups: *"High-end IoT devices have enough resources and adequate characteristics to run software based on traditional operating systems such as Linux or BSD"* and *"low-end IoT devices, which are too resource constrained to run these traditional OSs"*.

Motivated by the existing heterogeneity in the literature, the main objective of this work is to present the results of the research about the definitions, associated concepts, scopes and applications of Fog and Edge Computing within the current bibliography. It also proposes the integration of these two paradigms with End Devices to build a distributed architecture that allows the scalability of applications. Finally, an analysis of the types of applications that can take advantage of this type of architectures and an introduction to the resilience strategies that can be implemented to cope with different types of failures is provided.

The rest of the paper is organized as follows. Section 2 provides definitions and concepts associated with distributed architectures with different processing tiers. Section 3 describes different platforms and services that can be deployed in each tier. Section 4 discusses the different types of applications that can be used in these architectures and resiliency strategies to address different classes of failures. Finally, Sect. 5 presents conclusions and future work.

## 2  Definitions

Based on a variety of definitions found in the literature, this paper attempts to arrive at a homogeneous version of each concept, agreed upon by the research team, in order to provide a common framework for all future work (some of which is in progress) on this topic.

The diagram in Fig. 1 shows the structure of all the layers that make up the distributed architecture and schematizes the interactions and interconnections between them. Starting from the lower level, where the data is collected, private LANs are established between the end devices and an edge device (typically a router) that enables wireless communication with the IoT nodes. This router functions as an Edge node and also enables the access to the Internet to access the services provided by the upper layers.

### 2.1  Fog Computing

Fog Computing is a distributed architecture model that seeks to extend the characteristics of Cloud Computing to bring services, platforms, processing, and storage capabilities closer to the network edges and end nodes.

In this model, data is processed and stored in devices and servers located in peripheral or more distant networks, but always outside the boundaries of an organization's LAN (consisting of IoT nodes and edge devices). This provides an intermediate layer between the private edge network and the public cloud, which serves to obtain a faster and more efficient system response, due to the reduction of communication latencies.

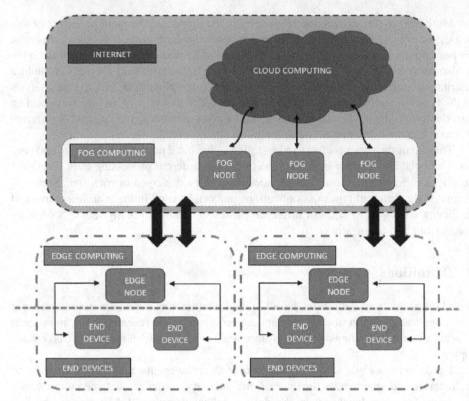

**Fig. 1.** Distributed Architecture based on Cloud, Fog, Edge, and End Devices

This layer is made up of the so-called Fog nodes, which typically consist of servers on which are deployed, alternatively, databases for storing the information generated by the edge networks, platforms that provide various services, intensive processing units, applications to generate dashboards for control and analytics, among other functionalities offered to the lower layers (Edge Computing and End Devices). The functions offered by the Fog nodes are schematized in Fig. 2.

The characteristics proposed by this model allow the deployment of an architecture that offers services and resources to distributed applications in a more flexible and scalable way. In addition, it enables a certain independence from the services of a public cloud, since an organization can use its own distributed hardware resources to generate a fog level that functions as a private cloud which provides services for its applications.

## 2.2  Edge Computing

The Edge Computing distributed architecture model seeks to leverage the computing power of devices at the edge of the network to collaborate with the end nodes that generate the data and alleviate the processing tasks of the upper layer servers. The ability of edge nodes to perform preprocessing avoids excessive latency and network congestion caused by constant transmissions to the fog and the cloud levels.

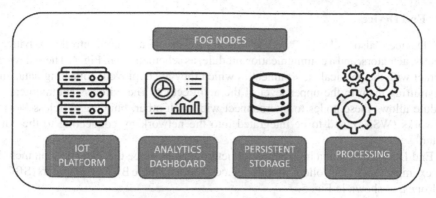

**Fig. 2.** Possible functions of Fog Nodes

According to this paradigm, nodes can offer processing capacity, networking solutions, security configurations, dashboards for data visualization and storage options, among other services, as schematized in Fig. 3.

Edge computing layer services are deployed and configured on routers, gateways, or servers. These devices, called Edge nodes, are located in the same private network of the organization or in a nearby network, no more than one network hop away from the edge router which is the access point where the End Devices are connected.

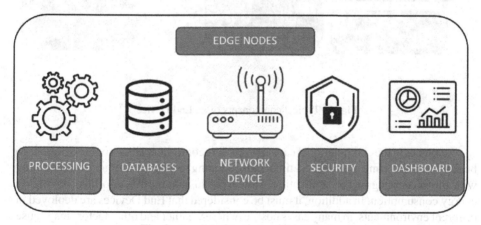

**Fig. 3.** Possible functions of Edge Nodes

## 2.3  End Devices

End Devices (also called IoT nodes) usually consist of a microcontroller, a battery, sensors, actuators, and a communication module, as schematized in Fig. 4. These devices interact with the physical environment in which they are deployed, collecting data, and transmitting them to the upper level of the architecture. The wireless communication module allows these nodes to interconnect with each other, building Wireless Sensor Networks (WSNs), and to be integrated into the network by connecting to the edge router.

End Devices present a high degree of heterogeneity, since this category can include (for example) microcontrollers, mobile devices, robots, Single Board Computers (SBC's) or drones, as shown in Fig. 5.

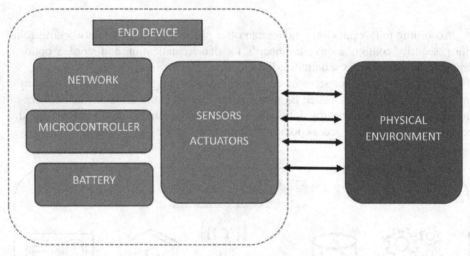

**Fig. 4.** Typical components of an End Device

Advances in the computational capacity of microcontrollers allow some operations to be solved on the same node, in real time, thus reducing response times and collaborating with the processing of the application. However, this alternative also involves higher energy consumption. In addition, it must be considered that End Devices are deployed in different environments, in many cases hostile, where weather and other factors may cause device failures. Moreover, the reliance on potentially unstable wireless communications can cause errors in connections to the network edge [2].

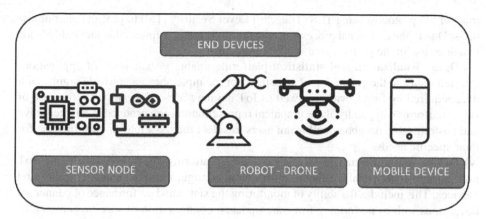

**Fig. 5.** Some examples of End Devices

# 3  Platforms and Services

The individual services provided by the Fog or Edge layers are often integrated into a single framework which aims to provide loosely coupled microservices to the upper and lower layers of the network, thus giving rise to a platform.

The main objective of the Fog and Edge Computing platforms is to provide a specialized environment for the management of tasks at different levels of the architecture. They centralize the main functionalities in order to improve operational efficiency and reduce complexity of use. The wide range of functionalities offered include storage, data visualization and statistics, security, device administration, network connectivity management and gateway functions, analysis, and real-time data processing [14]. The following is a brief description of the main functionalities of the platforms in general.

i) **Data processing and computational offloading:** the central service that a platform (both in Edge and Fog) provides to its lower layer is computation offloading, by means of which it is possible to transfer to the platform those tasks that require a higher processing capacity than the one available in that layer [8]. This is accomplished by migrating some or all the computationally intensive work that should be performed by lower-level devices to a nearby infrastructure that is richer in resources, thereby decreasing the bandwidth used in the central connection to the cloud as well as the latency of transmission. However, to achieve this, the platform must have the ability to make decisions such as the amount of computation that can be offloaded (and its selection) based on allowable power consumption and latency, the allocation of resources based on compute load and geographic location, and whether computation is performed in a centralized manner, or horizontally distributed.

ii) **Security, authentication, and authorization:** Since the transmissions of data and tasks are very frequent in these architectures, ensuring the confidentiality and integrity of the exchanged information is essential, especially when handling sensitive data, which is the case of medical or banking applications. In this context, platforms must allow data transfer via protocols using TLS (Transport Level Security [15]) to protect communications. Due to the additional processing cost required for encryption, this inevitably leads to a decrease in the performance of the architecture.

iii) **Data visualization and statistics:** platforms enable visualization of application-relevant data and the generation of statistics. For example, they can provide graphs with data acquired by End Devices, as well as IoT device status information (in the case of Edge platforms). Typically, these graphical representations are grouped in an interactive and customizable dashboard, allowing users to select the most relevant information for their specific needs.

iv) **Device management:** in Edge Computing platforms, the functionalities for IoT node administration enable efficient supervision, configuration, and management of End Devices. This includes the ability of monitoring the status and performance of connected devices, as well as performing firmware updates, configuration of specific parameters, diagnostics, and troubleshooting, among others.

Looking at the specifics of Edge and Fog platforms, there are some significant differences between them. Platforms operating at the Fog level must be able to handle larger scale infrastructures, computational power, and storage capacity than Edge platforms. In addition, the design of a Fog platform must consider that Fog nodes tend to be geographically distributed, so that a particular node is more likely to serve those requestors that are closer to it, in order to avoid excessive latency resulting from orders passing through several intermediate nodes.

### 3.1  Design Objectives

Listed below are the main design objectives for platforms which operate at the Edge and Fog Computing level [16].

- Latency: platforms must be oriented to guarantee low latency for the services they offer to users and end devices. Latency is affected by task transfer time, network resource search time, task execution time and decision-making speed, among other factors.
- Efficiency: unlike Cloud Computing scenarios, lower tiers have restricted computation, memory, and storage capacities (especially in Edge Computing). In addition, as already mentioned, most end nodes are battery powered (such as mobile devices and wireless sensors). Therefore, platforms must be oriented to efficiently manage these limited resources, also considering energy consumption.
- Generality: Because of the great heterogeneity of client nodes and devices in these paradigms, platforms must provide a common abstraction for upper-layer applications and services. For this purpose, they must provide general application programming interfaces (APIs) that are compatible with existing protocols and APIs, such as machine-to-machine (M2M) protocols and APIs for smart vehicles and appliances.

## 4  Application Types and Resilience

Depending on the particular needs regarding the use of the architecture resources, a first tentative classification of the applications is proposed in this work. From this point of view, a distinction is made between:

a) Applications with Heterogeneous Computing requirements - **type H**: require the computing power of the nodes of the different layers of the architecture. For these applications, the distribution of the processing to be performed at each level of the architecture is planned based on knowledge of the capabilities of the devices located at that level and the services available. The objective, for type H applications, is to complement the tasks performed at the different levels, in order to optimize the use of resources, reduce latency and congestion in the network and obtain higher response speeds. The data obtained from the Edge nodes can be synthesized and integrated in the cloud in order, on the one hand, to be able to perform more complex analysis and obtain more significant results a posteriori [17]; and on the other hand, to avoid transmitting large volumes without preprocessing, to save bandwidth. Applications of this type constitute the most typical scenario within the universe of IoT applications.

b) Applications with Redundant Computing requirements (or with Resilient Computing requirements) - **type R**: the criticality of the tasks they perform requires a degree of resilience, in which at least part of the computation is protected, to be able to provide results even in the presence of failures in certain components of the architecture. In these cases, the nodes in the different layers are planned to be used redundantly, totally or partially replicating in each level the processing performed in the others. Combining this with an adequate fault characterization and detection scheme, it is possible to achieve resilient applications that allow preserving a level of functionality while guaranteeing a minimum quality of service in the occurrence of faults.

The aforementioned propensity of wireless links and end-device power supply batteries to fail, coupled with the heterogeneity and complexity of the distributed architecture, makes the creation of fault-tolerant schemes, aimed at increasing system availability and robustness, a particularly challenging task [18].

It is important to note that this type of distributed architecture inherently presents a certain degree of redundancy at the hardware component level. This makes it possible to incorporate resiliency strategies into H-type applications in case it is necessary. For example, if a Fog server suffers an issue that causes a temporary service outage, the processing that was taking place there can be migrated to another node in the same tier, as is typically done in the fault-tolerance domain [19]. However, in the remainder of this section, the focus will be on the issues presented by R-type applications.

## 4.1 Critical Applications

In this work, critical (or R-type) applications are considered to be those that provide services with high availability requirements (such as patient monitoring or a safety-critical system) or demands for real-time or very low latency response (e.g., an autonomous vehicle). For these applications, it is essential to maintain the functionality of the system, even in case of failures, at least in a downgraded or reduced accuracy mode.

The aforementioned characteristics mean that these applications cannot rely exclusively on processing that is performed in the cloud, since they would not be able to provide service in case of connection loss; and if, in order to provide results of a certain accuracy, computation is required that can be performed only in the cloud (due to the power that only the cloud can provide), the design must provide for a reduced version of that computation that can be performed on edge devices.

## 4.2 Types of Failures and Detection

The failures that can occur in a layered distributed architecture can affect the tasks running on it. In this context, a distinction is made between component failures (or node failures), connection failures (or link failures) and service failures. In turn, each of these failures can be, depending on their duration, permanent, intermittent, or transient.

In node failures, the depletion of a power supply battery or a sensor failure, due to adverse conditions in the environment in which it is located, results in the component no longer functioning. If it is an End Device, the data acquired by it becomes unavailable, and it is also unable to perform any task previously assigned to it. The situation gets worse (although less likely) if the node that goes down belongs to the Edge or Fog layer; in these cases, simply put, the tasks and services for which that node is responsible are no longer available for the other layers. Meanwhile, intermittent node failures are also usually related to environmental conditions, and quite possibly foreshadow the next occurrence of a permanent crash of the affected component.

Connection failures are associated with link instability, especially wireless links, in environments with interference or obstacles that threaten signal strength and range. They are more likely to occur at lower layers (typically between End Devices and Edge layer nodes), as higher layers typically use more powerful and stable wired links. However, a drop in the internet connection between the Edge layer and the Fog or Cloud can result in the local network being isolated, so the system response will depend on the strategy adopted, which in turn depends on the criticality of the application. Again, intermittent connections may foreshadow an upcoming outage.

Finally, service failures are those in which the node is available and reachable but is temporarily unable to provide the service for which it was deployed. These failures are related to the configuration, or to the excess of workload for the requested service. In the absence of a physical failure, recovery is a priori simpler (and less costly); consequently, a permanent failure of this nature is less likely, but instead transient failures grow in relevance, producing errors in the processing results that may be difficult to detect (and with a high detection latency), or directly undetectable [20].

When addressing the issue of detection, it is important to determine in which layer the failure should be detected and in what way, depending on its type and location; this is a preliminary step to take the appropriate resilience strategy in each case.

Downtime of end nodes or edge layer devices must be detected from higher layers. One possible way is to set a maximum time to wait for communication from a given node, or, more directly, to send periodic keep-alive messages to monitor its status. Once the timeout period has elapsed without a response, the node in question is assumed to be down. This situation is equivalent to (and essentially indistinguishable from) link failure detection, if considered from a top-down approach.

The crash of a server at a higher layer can be detected from an Edge device as a lack of response, in a manner equivalent to the crash of a link to the Internet or to a private Fog infrastructure (bottom-up approach). If detection schemes based on message exchanges between devices at different layers are considered, a link failure could be detected from either of both ends, unlike a node crash, which can only be detected from the end that remains active. The drop of an Edge Node (or of the link between an Edge Node and an End Device) can also be detected from the End Device in a similar manner as described.

Finally, service failures can be detected by setting a maximum waiting time to obtain the response to the request made, so it is carried out by the node that requires the service.

## 4.3 Resilience Strategies

The problem of resilience in architectures especially based in Edge and Fog Computing has recently been addressed. Some interesting research that focuses on this issue can be found in [21–24].

As mentioned at the beginning of this section, it is necessary to consider resilience strategies for critical applications, which must keep responding even in the presence of failures; while H-type applications have lighter resilience requirements, and the infrastructure they use can be reconfigured without excessively strict time limits.

The resilience required to withstand a variety of failures must be contemplated from the design stage of the infrastructure on which critical applications run. Of course, the failure of an End Device or an Edge Node that collects and/or preprocesses critical information must be warned as soon as possible by the upper layer through an alarm to the user, so that the failed component is repaired or replaced in the short term; something similar happens if, in a top-down approach, the loss of connectivity with the edge level or with the end devices is detected from the upper layer.

However, while the failure of an Edge node or an End Device requires physical redundancy of components, the most interesting case occurs when the connection is lost between the IoT or Edge devices and a server outside the network, in the Fog layer, which they reached through that link. Although the drop can be detected by both layers, the Edge layer (which remains active) must be prepared to continue providing a basic service, being able to, at least, make decisions to change the state of actuators, based on a low-scale processing of the data acquired by the sensor nodes. For this, the same processing that is performed at higher levels must be replicated, albeit with lower precision, at the edge nodes, taking advantage of their computational capacity.

Similarly, a Fog server should be able to replicate, in a reduced version, the processing that is normally performed in the cloud, in case connection to the cloud is lost. The time-out in the response to keep-alive messages is the event that should trigger the lower-level processing to start with reduced precision. In this way, a resilient system would be achieved, which can maintain a degree of functionality even if the upper levels were unreachable for a certain period. Figure 6 depicts an example of an architecture that can behave in such a resilient way.

To accomplish resilience to service failures, services must be deployed on nodes other than those that provide the primary service; the temporary failure of the service would trigger the execution of its backup instance.

In all cases, resilience mechanisms can be applied either **reactively** or **preventively**. In the first case, resilience comes into play after the actual detection of the failure. The cost of detection is lower, but starting to act a posteriori means that a considerable amount of work time has been lost. On the other hand, if resilience is applied in a preventive manner, it is necessary to consider, at the system design stage, which parameters indicate that the probability of failure of a particular type is increasing, and to dedicate resources to monitor these parameters. In return, the system will be able to react more quickly, minimizing losses.

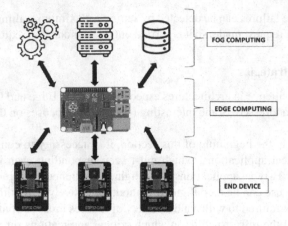

**Fig. 6.** An architecture that can behave resiliently

## 5   Conclusions and Future Work

Given the variety of concepts and notions found in the literature, regarding distributed architectures based on several processing levels and capable of providing different services, this article reviews several sources seeking to provide unified definitions for the Fog Computing and Edge Computing paradigms, which will serve as a stable and consensual theoretical basis for future research. The integration of the End Devices layer to the architecture is proposed, taking into account the computational capacity of IoT nodes to collaborate with application processing. The main functions of the platforms and services used in these architectures are reviewed and the applications are classified according to their reliability and availability requirements, describing the main types of failures to which they may be subjected and analyzing possible strategies to face these failures from the resilience point of view.

Regarding future work, the preliminary stages of the design of an image processing system for people detection are being carried out, incorporating redundancy in the processing, at lower levels, for possible connection failures that prevent the performance of the task in the upper layers. Another incipient line of work is oriented to the intelligent monitoring and control of various parameters, such as energy consumption and $CO_2$ concentration, in university buildings. Finally, an application is being designed to control robots that perform space or object recognition, incorporating resilience strategies to keep the robot's task under control even in the case of connection failures with the server.

## References

1. Mohan, N., Kangasharju, J.: Edge-fog cloud: a distributed cloud for internet of things computations. In: 2016 Cloudification of the Internet of Things (CIoT), pp. 1–6. IEEE (2016)
2. Tong, Y., Tian, L., Lin, L., Wang, Z.: Fault tolerance mechanism combining static backup and dynamic timing monitoring for cluster heads. IEEE Access **8**, 43277–43288 (2020)

3. Rucci, E., Naiouf, M., Chichizola, F., De Giusti, L.: Cloud computing, big data & emerging topics. In: 8th Conference, JCC-BD&ET 2020, La Plata, Argentina, September 8–10, 2020, Proceedings. Springer CCIS. ISBN: 978–3–030–61218–4, 2020

4. Bierzynski, K., Escobar, A., Eberl, M.: Cloud, fog and edge: cooperation for the future? In: 2017 Second International Conference on Fog and Mobile Edge Computing (FMEC), pp. 62–67. IEEE (2017)

5. Ren, J., Zhang, D., He, S., Zhang, Y., Li, T.: A survey on end-edge-cloud orchestrated network computing paradigms: transparent computing, mobile edge computing, fog computing, and cloudlet. ACM Comput. Surv. (CSUR) **52**(6), 1–36 (2019)

6. Habibi, P., Farhoudi, M., Kazemian, S., Khorsandi, S., Leon-Garcia, A.: Fog computing: a comprehensive architectural survey. IEEE Access **8**, 69105–69133 (2020)

7. Yousefpour, A., et al.: All one needs to know about fog computing and related edge computing paradigms: a complete survey. J. Syst. Architect. **98**, 289–330 (2019)

8. Cao, K., Liu, Y., Meng, G., Sun, Q.: An overview on edge computing research. IEEE Access **8**, 85714–85728 (2020)

9. Khan, W.Z., Ahmed, E., Hakak, S., Yaqoob, I., Ahmed, A.: Edge computing: a survey. Futur. Gener. Comput. Syst. **97**, 219–235 (2019)

10. https://www.ibm.com/cloud/what-is-edge-computing

11. https://azure.microsoft.com/en-us/resources/cloud-computing-dictionary/what-is-edge-com puting/

12. Chatterjee, B., Cao, N., Raychowdhury, A., Sen, S.: Context-aware intelligence in resource-constrained IoT nodes: opportunities and challenges. IEEE Des. Test **36**(2), 7–40 (2019)

13. Hahm, O., Baccelli, E., Petersen, H., Tsiftes, N.: Operating systems for low-end devices in the internet of things: a survey. IEEE Internet Things J. **3**(5), 720–734 (2015)

14. Hejazi, H., Rajab, H., Cinkler, T., Lengyel, L.: Survey of platforms for massive IoT. In 2018 IEEE International Conference on Future IoT Technologies (Future IoT), pp. 1–8. IEEE (2018)

15. Cynthia, J., Parveen Sultana, H., Saroja, M.N., Senthil, J.: Security protocols for IoT. Ubiquitous Comput. Comput. Secur. IoT, 1–28 (2019)

16. Yi, S., Hao, Z., Qin, Z., Li, Q.: Fog computing: platform and applications. In: 2015 Third IEEE Workshop on Hot Topics in Web Systems and Technologies (HotWeb), Washington, DC, USA, pp. 73-78 (2015).https://doi.org/10.1109/HotWeb.2015.22

17. Gomez D'Orazio, L., Medina, S., Montezanti, D.M.: Integración de una red de sensores con una plataforma IoT para control inteligente de aulas. In XXVIII Congreso Argentino de Ciencias de la Computación (CACIC)(La Rioja, 3 al 6 de octubre de 2022) (2023)

18. Medina, S., Montezanti, D.M., Gomez D'Orazio, L., Compagnucci, E., De Giusti, A.E., Naiouf, M.: Incorporating resilience to platforms based on edge and fog computing. In X Jornadas de Cloud Computing, Big Data & Emerging Topics (La Plata, 2022) (2022)

19. Castro-León, M., Meyer, H., Rexachs, D., Luque, E.: Fault tolerance at system level based on RADIC architecture. J. Parallel Distrib. Comput. **86**, 98–111 (2015)

20. Montezanti, D., Rucci, E., De Giusti, A., Naiouf, M., Rexachs, D., Luque, E.: Soft errors detection and automatic recovery based on replication combined with different levels of checkpointing. Future Gener. Comput. Syst. **113**, 240–25 (2020)

21. Shirazi, S.N., Gouglidis, A., Farshad, A., Hutchison, D.: The extended cloud: review and analysis of mobile edge computing and fog from a security and resilience perspective. IEEE J. Sel. Areas Commun. **35**(11), 2586–2595 (2017). https://doi.org/10.1109/JSAC.2017.276 0478

22. Harchol, Y., Mushtaq, A., Fang, V., McCauley, J., Panda, A., Shenker, S.: Making edge-computing resilient. In: Proceedings of the 11th ACM Symposium on Cloud Computing, pp. 253–266 (2020)

23. Prokhorenko, V., Babar, M.A.: Architectural resilience in cloud, fog and edge systems: a survey. IEEE Access **8**, 28078–28095 (2020)
24. Moura, J., Hutchison, D.: Fog computing systems: State of the art, research issues and future trends, with a focus on resilience. J. Netw. Comput. Appl. **169**, 102784 (2020)

# Resilience Analysis of an Emergency Department in Stressful Situations

Mariela Rodriguez[1]([⊠]), Francesc Boixader[2], Francisco Epelde[3], Eva Bruballa[2],
Armando De Giusti[4], Alvaro Wong[5], Dolores Rexachs[5], and Emilio Luque[5]

[1] Faculty of Engineering, National University of Jujuy, 4600 San Salvador de Jujuy, Argentina
mariela.rodriguez@fi.unju.edu.ar
[2] Escoles Universitaries Gimbernat (EUG), Computer Science School, Universitat Autonoma de
Barcelona, Sant Cugat del Vallès, 08174 Barcelona, Spain
{francesc.boixader,eva.bruballa}@eug.es
[3] Consultant Internal Medicine, University Hospital Parc Tauli, Universitat Autonoma of
Barcelona, 08208 Sadabell, Barcelona, Spain
[4] Faculty of Informatics, National University of La Plata, Calles 50 y 120 – La Plata,
1900 Buenos Aires, Argentina
degiusti@lidi.info.unlp.edu.ar
[5] Computer Architecture and Operating Systems Department, Universitat Autónoma of
Barcelona Campus UAB, Edificio, Bellaterra, 08193 Barcelona, Spain
{alvaro.wong,dolores.rexachs,emilio.luque}@uab.es

**Abstract.** The performance analysis an Emergency Department (ED) is fundamental and necessary to plan the service when it is affected by increasing number
of patients due to an external scenario multiple victims from accidents, disasters or
catastrophes. In order to perform this analysis, it is important to set up a simulated
scenario that allows this study. The proposal is to analyze the ED simulator developed by the HPC4EAS research group at UAB by taking it to a stress situation.
The work analyzes key performance indicator (KPI) that measure the performance
of an ED (length of stay, waiting queue length, service rate) and make it possible
to evaluate the percentage of patients that can be attended without altering the
available resources. Study allowed us to determine that the care box (area A - area
for the care of seriously ill patients) becomes congested when 40% more patients
than usual are received, and the next resource to become congested is the room for
the care of milder patients (area B). Analysis that will later allow us to investigate
what happens when there is an accident, natural disaster or pandemic.

**Keywords:** Emergency Department · length of stay · waiting queue length

## 1 Introduction

Emergency Department (ED) is a place that receives patients suffering from mild to
severe symptoms. Number of patients that are received daily has average numbers that
depend a time a week, months of the year, holidays; situations that the ED administration
foresees and plans the care of patients. There are particular situations that alter the daily

M. Naiouf et al. (Eds.): JCC-BD&ET 2023, CCIS 1828, pp. 45–54, 2023.
https://doi.org/10.1007/978-3-031-40942-4_4

flow of incoming patients, such as major traffic accidents, building fires, natural disasters, epidemic or pandemics diseases. In these cases, it is important to evaluate the number of patients that an ED can receive so that the service is not impaired.

Evaluating a critical situation allows planning and preparing for these events. The agent-based model (ABM) developed by research group HPC4EAS at UAB [1] in collaboration with the Sabadell hospital [2] will be used to recreate the ED.

In the course of life, disruptive events occur that require the intervention of primary care entities such as health and safety. These events are classified as accidents, emergencies and disasters according to their magnitude. There are different definitions throughout history that describe these concepts. To establish the difference between the concepts, Britton [2, 3] details three criteria: number and people type involved, the degree of involvement, the amount of destruction caused in the social system. These criteria generate collective stress in society, ranging from the least stressful, such as in the case of an accident, to the most stressful, such as in case of a disaster. A disaster is the event that causes the greatest collective stress and is defined by the United Nations Office for Disaster Risk Reduction as follows "*Serious disruption of the functioning of a community or society at any scale due to hazardous events interacting with conditions of exposure, vulnerability and capacity, resulting in one or more of the following losses and impacts: human, material, economic and environmental*" [4].

Disturbances are categorized from accidents to catastrophes that can be natural or provoked and influence people's lives. The occurrence of these events activates the EDs in order to attend to the injured persons. It is necessary to size up the type of event that occurs so that ED management can plan patient care. Then, in Table 1. below shows how an ED acts according to the severity of the situations that arise. Three types of situations can be distinguished in this environment: Situation 1 involves accidents, where several people are involved, for example traffic accidents, fires or similar, where the number of injured does not affect the care service in an ED. Situation 2 is when there are emergencies that disrupt normal flow of care in an ED and for this scenario, lower priority should be given to minor and more seriously injured persons. Situation 3 is when a major disaster occurs, in which case only patients with serious injuries are treated as a priority. Cases 2 and 3 are determined according to the location and the response capacity of the hospitals involved.

**Table 1.** Emergency Situations.

| Injury kind | Situation 1 | Situation 2 | Situation 3 |
|---|---|---|---|
| Not injured | Yes | | |
| Simple fractures | Yes | Yes | |
| Multiple and severe fractures | Yes | Yes | Yes |
| Shortness of breath | Yes | Yes | Yes |
| Rib cage hemorrhages | Yes | Yes | Yes |
| Severe organ involvement | Yes | Yes | |
| Death | | | |

This paper objective is analyzed the performance indicators of the care service in the face of incremental patient admissions when disruptive situations occur that alter patients' daily flow in an ED.

For the experimental phase we worked with the ED simulator developed by the HPC4EAS research group at UAB. Patients were introduced incrementally in order to evaluate the performance of the service, so that in future works it will be possible to act in each of the situations mentioned in the previous section.

The key performance indicators (KPI used to evaluate the performance of the emergency care service are as follows: care box queue length, care queue length for patients with mild symptoms, average length of stay (LoS) and the percentage of doctor and nurse occupancy. The Care box waiting queue length is related to the KPI bed occupancy percentage, it is given when the occupancy percentage is 100% and the waiting queue for a care box is formed.

The document is organized as follows: Sect. 2 shows the description of the ED Simulator of the project; Sect. 3 details the configuration of the incoming patients and resources necessary to carry out the stress simulation model; Sect. 4 shows the results obtained from the simulations carried out; and finally, Sect. 5 details the conclusions obtained.

## 2   ED Simulator

Decision-making in systems in which there is a structure in which processes and people interact cannot always be represented in reality, so the representation through agent-based simulation (ABM) is useful. ABM combines elements of game theory, complex systems, emergence, computational sociology, multi-agent systems and evolutionary programming [8]. Agent-based modeling is a computational method for building models consisting of agents that interact with each other within an environment to carry out virtual experiments. Agent-based simulation allows dealing in a simple way with the complexity, emergence and non-linearity typical of social phenomena, which make a researcher create, analyze and experiment with models composed of agents interacting within an environment [9].

The ED is simulated using ABM in which patients, doctors, nurses and care staff interact was developed in NetLogo v 5.3. Simulator in which this work was carried out has six defined areas: admission area, triage area, patient waiting area and laboratory, staff quarters, Zone A and Zone B [1, 10] (see Fig. 1).

Admission zone: this is the area where administrative staff attend to patients when they arrive at the ED, register their entry and then transfer them to the waiting area for further attention.

Triage zone: This is where the patient's priority level is identified. This is where patients interact with nurses. Here the staff classifies the patient according to Manchester triage [6] in five levels: 1-reanimation, 2-emergent, 3-urgent, 4-less urgent and 5-non-urgent.

Wait patient zone and Laboratory: In this area there are X-ray, computed tomography and ultrasound laboratories. In addition, there is a waiting area for patients in traige 4 and 5.

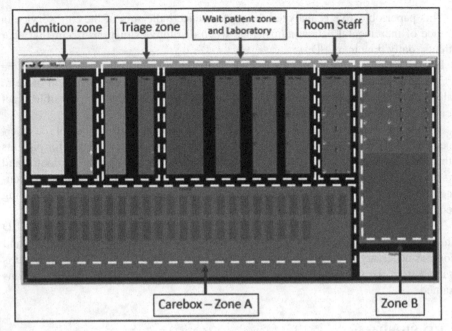

**Fig. 1.** ED Simulator

Room staff: Room where doctors and nurses stay while they are not attending any patient.

Carebox - Area A: The most urgent patients arrive in this area. Each patient remains in each care box during the entire diagnosis and treatment.

Area B: here patients with traige 4 and 5 arrive, there are several boxes in which doctors and nurses interact with patients.

Doctors and nurses in zone A and zone B are different.

Figure 2 shows that when an incident occurs (accident, emergency or major disaster), patients are referred to the hospital's ED. Once in the ED, the patient is first admitted to the admission area, then goes through the triage area and from there, if necessary, goes to the laboratory and the waiting room to be assigned to a care box (area A) or to care in area B, as appropriate according to the triage.

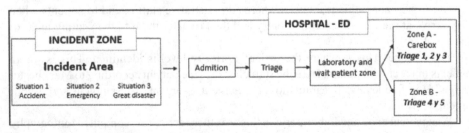

**Fig. 2.** Patient pathway from incident area to ED care

# 3    Simulation Setup

The initial configuration of the ED simulator and the staff and infrastructure resources available in each area detail the resources available to the ED of Sabadell hospital [2] and are as follows:

- Staff distribution: Table 2. shows the distribution of personnel, with a total of 99 people in different roles. The staff is divided into three shifts per day; the first shift begins at 6:00 am, the second at 2:00 pm and the third at 10:00 pm.
- Area A capacity: there are 49 service boxes available, and in the event that all the service boxes are occupied, there are 10 backups available.
- Area B capacity: 52 patients can be attended simultaneously.

**Table 2.** Distribution of staff in ED.

| Staff | 6 am | 2 pm | 10 pm | Total |
|---|---|---|---|---|
| Admission junior | 3 | 3 | 2 | 8 |
| Admission senior | 0 | 0 | 0 | 0 |
| Triage junior nurse | 1 | 1 | 0 | 2 |
| Triage senior nurse | 2 | 2 | 2 | 6 |
| Area A junior nurse | 2 | 2 | 2 | 6 |
| Area A senior nurse | 2 | 2 | 2 | 6 |
| Area B junior nurse | 5 | 5 | 5 | 15 |
| Area B senior nurse | 7 | 7 | 7 | 21 |
| Area A junior doctor | 2 | 2 | 1 | 5 |
| Area A senior doctor | 3 | 3 | 2 | 8 |
| Area B junior doctor | 5 | 5 | 5 | 15 |
| Area B senior doctor | 3 | 2 | 2 | 7 |

The number of patients admitted to the ED varies depending on the time and day of the week as shown in Fig. 3, which generates a daily average of 261 patients.

The development of the simulation consisted of increasing the number of patients the ED receives daily to analyze the behavior of the ED in a stressful situation. The increase was carried out progressively, varying in each simulation iteration by 10% more according to the initial value (261 patients), table 3. shows the number of patients that entered for each simulation to be evaluated.

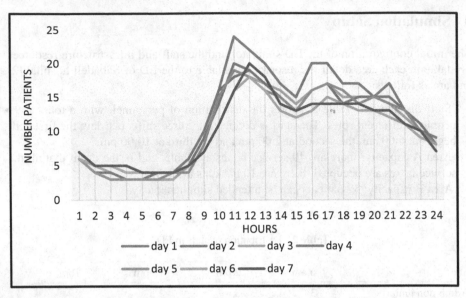

**Fig. 3.** Number of patients admitted to the ED per day

**Table 3.** Average number of patients per day.

| Percentage Increase | 1 | 10 | 20 | 30 | 40 | 50 | 60 | 70 | 80 | 90 | 100 | 110 | 120 | 130 | 140 | 150 |
|---|---|---|---|---|---|---|---|---|---|---|---|---|---|---|---|---|
| Average Patients | 261 | 288 | 315 | 341 | 365 | 398 | 417 | 446 | 468 | 499 | 522 | 549 | 576 | 602 | 626 | 659 |

## 4   Results

ED simulator initially receives, on average, 261 patients per day in this experiment; when this number is increased by external situations, the increase may occur in a short period of time or it may be extended according to the severity of the events. For this analysis, two weeks of work have been carried out, the rate of increase is reflected in Table 3. in the average number of patients. The first increase was 10%, receiving a total of 288 patients per day. The second increase was 20% over the initial value, with a total of 315 patients on average. In each iteration, the average number of patients received per day was increased in order to evaluate the evolution of indicators This is achieve objetive (see Fig. 4), the waiting queues for care (see Fig. 5) and the percentage utilization of doctors and nurses (see Fig. 6).

Figure 4 shows the length of stay of patient in the ED classified according to triage. In general, the average length of stay increases slowly according to increase in the number of patients. It is noteworthy that, unlike the others, the patients who are more critical triage 1 have fluctuations in the iterations analyzed and the patients who have triage 3, after 40% more patients increase, grow considerably, with an average LoS between 15 to 20 h.

Figure 5 shows the increase in the waiting queue for patients in zone A and in zone B. On typical day, there is no waiting queue in the care box or for care in zone B.

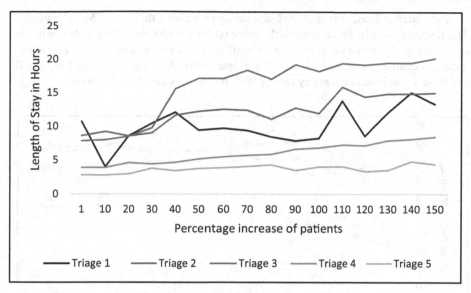

**Fig. 4.** Percentage increase of patients by triage.

However, after a 40% increase (365 patients), the waiting queue in the care box averages 24 patients; from then on, the increase is constant. Regarding patients waiting to be seen in zone B when number of patients is 50% more (398 patients) the queue is 8 people waiting to be attended.

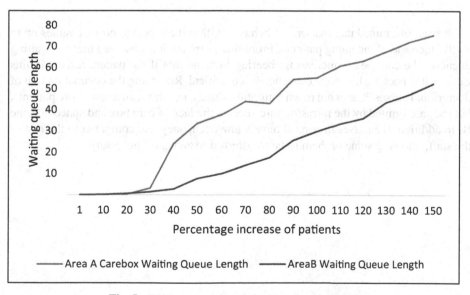

**Fig. 5.** Waiting queue length in Area A and Area B.

If resource utilization is analyzed, according to queuing theory and Markov models [7], a resource is said to be saturated if the value is close to 100% occupancy. Accordingly, we can see in Fig. 6 that the percentage of staff occupancy in area A: doctors and nurses reach an occupancy rate of 80% and 90% respectively. As for the personnel in area B, they have a maximum occupancy rate of 90% for doctors and 56% for nurses.

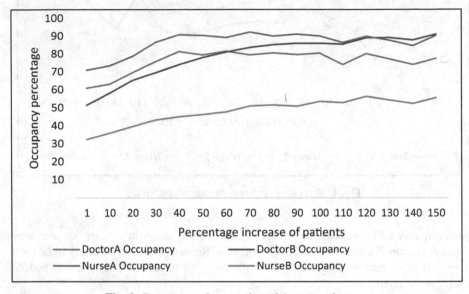

**Fig. 6.** Percentage of occupation of doctors and nurses.

It was determined that the service behaves within the expected normal values up to a 40% increase of incoming patients. From that point on, it is observed that the waiting queue in the care box is increasing, bearing in mind that if the patient arrives in this Zone A it is because his triage classification is critical. Regarding the occupation rate of doctors and nurses, it does not reach saturation values, i.e., they can attend more patients, but they are limited by the infrastructure such as the lack of care box and space in Zone B. In addition, the nurses in zone B have a low occupancy rate compared to the rest of the staff, allowing some of them to be transferred to zone A if necessary.

# 5    Conclusions

Research is framed within the development of the project that studies the resilience analysis of an ED in order to plan the service in case of accidents, disasters and catastrophes framed in the fulfillment of Sustainable Development Goals 3, 5 and 9.

Developed job consisted of the percentage increase of patients admitted to the ED in order to evaluate the performance of the service. The LoS, waiting queue length and service rate were used for the evaluation.

It can be concluded that several factors influence patient care, and in this analysis, it is possible to increase the number of patients by up to 40% without modifying other areas of care. From there, it is necessary to reallocate resources, increase care box, decrease the time of care in certain areas, procedures based on disaster situations, which were analyzed by organizations dedicated to health care.

Analysis carried out allows us to open three avenues of investigation: to analyze the resources in case of accidents (situation 1), to analyze and allocate the necessary resources in case of disasters (situation 2) such as earthquakes or tsunamis, and finally, to evaluate the resources in case of catastrophes (situation 3) such as pandemics.

**Acknowledgment.** This research has been supported by the Agencia Estatal de Investigacion (AEI), Spain and the Fondo Europeo de Desarrollo Regional (FEDER) UE, under contracts PID2020- 112496GB-I00 and partially funded by the Fundacion Escue- las Universitarias Gimbernat (EUG).

# References

1. Liu, Z., Rexachs, D., Luque, E., Epelde, F., Cabrera, E.: Simulating the micro-level behavior of emergency departments for macro-level features prediction. In: Proceedings of the 2015 Winter Simulation Conference, pp. 171–182 (2015)
2. Britton, N.R.: Developing an understanding of disaster. Aust. New Zealand J. Sociol. **22**, 254–271 (1986)
3. Joya Rincón, L.P., Jaimes Barajas, G.P.: Revisión documental de la conceptualización del desastre. University Autonomous University of Bucramanga (2009). http://hdl.handle.net/20.500.12749/17589
4. UNDRR United Nations Office for Disaster Risk Reduction. https://www.undrr.org/terminology. Accessed 22 Apr 2023
5. Lopéz Jaramillo, J.I.: Clasificación de las víctimas en emergencia y catástrofes (TRIAGE). Civil Hospital of Ipiales Empresa Social del Estado. https://hospitalcivilese.gov.co/site/images/guiasyprot/GUIASAMPH/3%20clasificacion%20de%20victimas.pdf. Accessed 20 Apr 2023
6. Mackway-Jones, K. (ed.): Emergency Triage: Manchester Triage Group, 1st edn. BMJ Publishing Group, London (1997)
7. Taha, H.A.: Operations Research. 9 edición. Pearson Educación, México (2012). ISBN: 978–607–32–0796–6
8. Academialab homepage, "Modelo basado en agentes". https://academia-lab.com/enciclopedia/modelo-basado-en-agentes/. Accessed 25 Apr 2023

9. García-Valdecasas, J. I.: Agent-based simulation: a new way of exploring social phenomena. Socialogical Res. Center. Span. J. Sociological Res., Num. **136**, 91–109 (2011)
10. Eduardo, C., Manel, T., Ma, L.I., Francisco, E., Emilio Luque, E.: Hospital emergency department simulation: an approach developed using individual oriented modeling techniques. Procedia Comput. Sci. **4**, 1880–1889 (2011)

# Big Data

# CoVaMaT: Functionality for Variety Reuse Through a Supporting Tool

Líam Osycka[1][✉], Alejandra Cechich[1], Agustina Buccella[1], Ayelén Montenegro[2], and Angel Muñoz[2]

[1] GIISCO Research Group - Departamento de Ingeniería de Sistemas, Facultad de Informática, Universidad Nacional del Comahue, Neuquen, Argentina
{liam.osycka,alejandra.cechich,agustina.buccella}@fi.uncoma.edu.ar
[2] Instituto Nacional de Tecnología Agropecuaria (INTA), Alto Valle de Río Negro y Neuquén, Buenos Aires, Argentina
{montenegro.ayelen,munoz.angel}@inta.gob.ar

**Abstract.** Developing reusable Big Data Systems (BDSs) implies dealing with modeling variety as reusable assets. Conceptually speaking, these assets might be similar to reusable software artifacts built under software product line (SPL) engineering; however, similar does not imply they are the same. Variety identification in BDSs is more related to collecting and preparing data, and of course, analytics; meanwhile SPLs model reusable pieces of software. Although in the end all it is about software, its nature differs as treatment for its reuse does. In this paper, we introduce our proposal for modeling reusable variety by describing the way it is processed by our supporting tool CoVaMaT (Context-Based Variety Management Tool). We exemplified its functionality through two case studies in the precision agriculture domain.

**Keywords:** Big Data Systems · Variety · Software Product Lines

## 1 Introduction

As a result of the increasing demand to obtain and generate useful information from the huge volume of data inside and outside organizations, the academy and industry are continually putting forward novel techniques, methodologies and strategies. In particular, the growth of Big Data Systems technologies is a clear example of this. BDSs include a wide set of activities, techniques and supported technologies to face to 5V's requirements including volume, value, variety of data, and velocity of data growth. Each of these 5 Vs needs special attention to be addressed; as for example, *volume* and *velocity* need new repository capabilities to store large amounts of data with undefined and changing structure, new mechanisms for query data in a feasible time, etc.

At the same time, in the last years an important work is coming from the engineering area. In particular the Artificial Intelligence Engineering (AIE) is an emergent discipline that combines software engineering principles for developing

M. Naiouf et al. (Eds.): JCC-BD&ET 2023, CCIS 1828, pp. 57–74, 2023.
https://doi.org/10.1007/978-3-031-40942-4_5

AI systems[1]. In one of its pillars, the AIE *examines how AI infrastructure, data, and models may be reused across problem domains and deployments*. In this sense, in our work we are focused on BDS developments based on reusability within particular domains. However, as in traditional software developments, reaching reusability is far from trivial, requiring well-defined mechanisms and agreed processes of the involved stakeholders.

Thus, in a previous work [12], we proposed to extend the *variety* requirement (of the 5 Vs) to identify and model common and variant software artifacts during the development of BDSs in a domain. We redefined variety by categorizing it over four diversities (source, content, process and context) in order to allow software/AI engineers/developers to create similar BDSs. We proposed a variety identification process for carrying out big data developments *with* and/or *for* reuse, which rely on documenting domain assets. In this work, as an extension of the previous one, we describe the functionality of our *Context-based Variety Management Tool (CoVaMaT)* that supports the variety identification/reuse process. Therefore, the tool implements the two sides of reusability by allowing users to develop domain assets (assets for reuse) and/or use them for new BDS developments (assets with reuse).

There exist in the literature some works focused on designing reusability in BDSs. For example, in [10] a reference architecture is mapped to use cases (strategic geospatial information analysis and visualization, signal analysis, etc.). From these cases, relevant requirements are identified, including categories such as data types (unstructured text, geospatial, audio, etc.), data transformation (clustering, correlation), data visualization (images, networks), etc. The architecture is organized as a collection of modules representing functions or capabilities of a set of aspects. However, to the best of our knowledge, there is no proposal of a methodology together with a software tool to identify, model and implement domain assets that can be reused in the context of a BDS developments. Thus, our main contribution here is based on the definition of three main functionalities, supported by a software tool, for variety documentation, case instantiation and case reuse. These functionalities are the basis for reusability in our proposal, and they will be introduced as services of the tool.

This article is organized as follows. The next section analyzes related works focused on reusability in Big Data Systems. Next, in Sect. 3 we briefly describe the variety identification process presented in previous works. In Sect. 4 we describe the base functionalities of CoVaMaT for defining domain variety and create and/or use reusable domain assets. In Sect. 5 we show the use of the functionalities in two case studies in the precision agriculture domain. Finally, we address conclusions and future work.

## 2  Related Work

In Big Data Systems (BDSs), reusability has been approached from various angles. For example, in [13] some concepts are discussed in the context of data

---

[1] https://www.sei.cmu.edu/our-work/artificial-intelligence-engineering/index.cfm.

analytics distinguishing between data use and reuse. Various open research questions on reuse are proposed, such as tradeoffs between collecting new data and reusing existing ones; the needs to distinguish between use and reuse; etc. More specifically, but in the same sense, the work in [5] deepens privacy aspects in the context of data reusability. Here, a data reuse taxonomy is proposed, which may be useful in determining to what extent that reuse should be allowed and under what conditions to preserve privacy. Other proposals address reuse issues in terms of increasing collaboration in the development of BDSs through the use of new technologies (i.e. cloud computing). For example, the work in [17] proposes a management approach for BDSs by using storage and processing capabilities of a public cloud. Additionally, the different support platforms for the development of BDSs are also approached from the point of view of reuse; more specifically, the work in [1] analyzes the improvement in the efficiency of tools such as Apache Hadoop[2] and Spark[3] due to the reuse of artifacts among different projects. To do so, common aspects are analyzed to provide a workflow implemented in a scalable and extensible way.

On the reuse management side, in [8] an exploratory analysis is carried out through interviews with Microsoft scientists, to collect information about which tasks within the life cycle are reused and, along with them, strategies for sharing and reusing previous works.

In addition to managing reuse across different teams, reusability was also addressed in terms of how architectures can be composed. In this sense, the work in [10] incorporates the detection of common and variable aspects within the development of BDSs as families of systems. This work presents a reference architecture that allows system designers to: (1) define requirements – the reference architecture identifies significant requirements and shows variations depending on the type of requirement; (2) develop and evaluate solutions – the architecture identifies modules that must be developed in order to enable certain required capabilities; and (3) integrate systems – existing systems can be mapped to modules of the reference architecture, resulting in easy identification of points of conflict where interoperability between systems must be worked on. Components of the Component Off-The-Shelf (COTS) paradigm, or other reusable technologies, can be mapped to particular modules within this architecture, which allows to evaluate how different technologies may contribute to the development of the solution.

Finally, there are some reference architectures for BDSs that propose the addition of semantics to their components to expand domain and design knowledge. For example, the work in [6] compares different architectures concluding that three proposals (*Bolster, Solid, and Polystore*) add semantics, so that the underlying data schema is understood by a machine; that is, when describing data and their characteristics/relations. For instance, *Bolster* [11] adds a semantic layer that contains a metadata management system, which is responsible for providing information to work on data governance and description, and modeling of raw data. It includes a repository where all relevant annotations can

---

[2] https://hadoop.apache.org/.
[3] https://spark.apache.org/.

be machine readable by using an RDF ontology (Resource Description Framework[4]). This ontology contains characteristics of the input data, such as their attributes and sources. Differently, *Solid* [4] aims to integrate heterogeneous data under the same data model. Using RDF in conjunction with OWL (Web Ontology Language[5]), semantics can be associated to individual schemes facilitating their integration. The data layer of Solids can be seen as storing large batches of RDF data, where triplets are manipulated using a binary representation of RDF. The index layer, which sits on top of the data layer, provides efficient queries to these batches using typically SPARQL[6]. Finally, *Polystore* [7] unifies queries when there are multiple heterogeneous storage engines with different data and query models. It organizes data in different islands, where each one represents a category of storage engines that provide a single data model and appropriate query languages to manipulate data found in that island. For example, a relational island can be a collection of traditional database management systems, such as MySQL[7] or Postgres[8]. It is also possible for an engine to appear in multiple categories and therefore on multiple islands. The idea is that a user can consult an island through its corresponding query language.

Although all these efforts are addressing reusability and/or semantics during SBDs development, their integration is scarce. In this sense, novelty of our proposal relies on the use of a supporting tool to manage variety (and consequently reuse possibilities) during SBDs developments by adding contextual semantics through cases. Services of our tool support the process, and they will be introduced as functionalities in the following sections.

## 3    A Variety Identification Process

In a previous work [12], we have proposed a variety identification process based on bottom-up and top-down approaches. In Fig. 1 we can see how these two approaches determine the way a BDS development can be performed:

– *Top-down (T-VIP) approach:* In this approach, left hand side of Fig. 1, (1) given a domain problem, an expert user elaborates one or more hypotheses that should be tested through data analysis (i.e. Are data supporting this?); (2) then, the hypotheses are taken by data analysts who proceed to carry out the activities included in a Big Data Process (3); finally, results are returned to verify the hypotheses (4) possibly visualizing data in different ways, and allowing hypothesis reformulation or process ending, alternatively (5).
– *Bottom-up (B-VIP) approach:* In this approach, right hand side of Fig. 1, (1) given a domain problem, an expert user decides to launch an exploratory study to find out what data can reveal for this problem (i.e. What do data say?);

---

[4]    https://www.w3.org/RDF/.
[5]    https://www.w3.org/OWL/.
[6]    https://www.w3.org/TR/rdf-sparql-query/.
[7]    https://www.mysql.com/.
[8]    https://www.postgresql.org/.

(2) then, the study is carried out by data analysts (2), again by applying the activities included in a Big Data Process (3); and finally, results (findings) are returned to be validated with experts (4), alternately ending the process or reformulating the search (5).

In the middle of the figure, we can see the activities of the Big Data Process including *collection* of source data, *preparation* and *transformation* of these source data, *analytics* of data for analyzing prepared data and determining the processing type (batch, real-time, etc.), *visualization* of the resulting analysis, and *access* of data consumers to these results. Following, the left side of the figure shows how the variety can influence design decisions. We define four varieties: (1) *source variety* during *collection*, helps to detect different data structures, acquisition techniques, etc., (2) *content variety* is focused on the way data should be transformed according to relevant variables for the business goals to be achieved, mostly considering source variations during *preparation*, (3) *process variety* helps detect variations in data analysis techniques and it is particularly involved in *analytics* and visualization, and (4) *context variety* allows developers to identify domain variations that may constrain or affect the results of the analysis during the whole Big Data system development.

Finally, highlighted components in the figure are the *knowledge-based assets* (in green in the figure). These components represent the repositories that software/AI engineers/developers can use to develop BD systems, reducing the need to re-create components that provide similar functionalities. In particular, in this work we describe CoVaMaT that acts as a *domain asset repository*, which is focused on allowing the definition of domain assets (for variety and case definitions), and reuse previous experiences of use in the same or similar domains/subdomains.

## 4   Context-Based Variety Management Tool (CoVaMaT)

CoVaMaT is developed for assisting in the variety identification process (top-down and/or bottom-up) showed in Fig. 1. Specifically, it allows stakeholders (software/AI engineers, developers, data scientists and expert users) to define, document and query the variety of a domain and represent it as *domain assets*. In Fig. 2 we can see the way the requirements (defined as a domain problem) are the starting point to define a bottom-up or top-down approach in order to identify the four types of possible varieties found while implementing the big data activities. Each execution of the five activities of the Big Data Process constitutes a *domain case* that is documented as one (or more) domain assets. Therefore, before describing functionality supported by CoVaMaT, it is necessary to introduce the following concepts.

- **Case Instantiation**: It consists of the description of a domain case through the selection of variations. For example, in the domain of water resources, the water bodies can be rivers, lakes, etc.; and the case may correspond to one of these values (e.g. rivers). In addition, for that particular river, specific

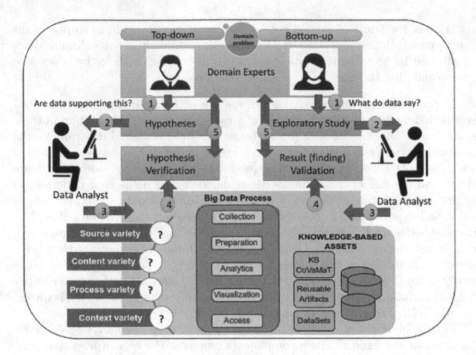

**Fig. 1.** Top-down and bottom-up approaches for variety identification process

water quality values may be relevant, such as dissolved oxygen, pH, etc. The set of values selected for all the variables that are relevant in the domain will constitute the instantiated case.

– **Case Reuse**: it is used to compose a query, which retrieves those cases already instantiated in the repository that have similar characteristics. This query is composed of a context determined by the selected variations (e.g. river with water quality variables focused on determining turbidity). The objective is to analyze previous work performed under specified conditions for the reuse case.

CoVaMat includes three main functionalities (F1, F2 and F3) supported by three services, three business processes, and three events. They are functionalities for variety documentation, case instantiation and case reuse, respectively. Following we describe each of these functionalities showing the conceptual level by using the ArchiMate modeling language[9].

---

[9] https://www.opengroup.org/archimate-forum/archimate-overview.

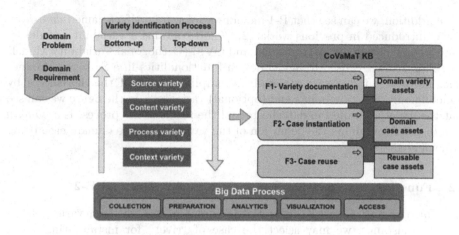

**Fig. 2.** Functionalities of CoVaMaT

## 4.1 Functionality for Variety Documentation: S-1, P-1 and E-1

This functionality allows to specify domain variety of a case as hierarchies of variety types, which may be identified through domain analysis (usually T-VIP) or exploratory studies (usually B-VIP). For instance, the different possibilities for water bodies, water quality parameters, etc., are candidates for specifying domain variations of hydrology systems. Thus, variety types are detected when developing domain cases and attended by a service (S-1), which is supported by a process (P-1: *Documenting domain variety*) when a searching requirement occurs (event E-1: *Start looking for varieties*), as Fig. 3 shows.

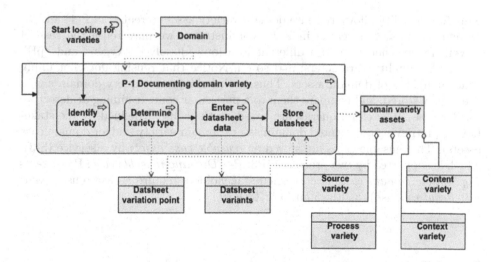

**Fig. 3.** P-1 Documenting domain variety

In addition, we can see that P-1 includes a software artifact named *datasheet*. It was introduced in previous works [2,3], and contains a variability model by using a combination of UML notation and OVM (Orthogonal Variability Model) [15]. This artifact is used to model design functionalities in a Software Product Line; however, in this case we apply a simplified view of the datasheets by modeling only variation points and (optional) variants[10]. In the figure we can see that the variety is stored in datasheets and the result of the process is a *domain variety asset* containing the definition of the varieties for the domain case being implemented.

### 4.2   Functionality for Case Instantiation: S-2, P-2 and E-2

This functionality allows to instantiate a domain case through variety selection. For instance, we may select the case of "river" for instantiating water body variety; "dissolved oxygen" for quality parameters, and so on. Notice that possible variety instances were previously created by P-1. Thus, domain case instantiations are created and stored as domain assets by a service (S-2), which is supported by a process (P-2: *Defining domain case*) when an invocation to CoVaMaT occurs (event E-1: *Require the use of case instantiation*), as Fig. 4 shows.

We can see the main activities of P-2, which retrieve documented varieties in P-1 and instantiate them for a specific domain case. That is, the variability models defining the possible varieties of a domain case, are here selected to create the specific case to be implemented. Finally, the domain case is also stored as a *domain case asset*.

### 4.3   Functionality for Case Reuse: S-3, P-3, P-4 and E-3

This functionality allows to reuse domain variety assets (created in P-1) and/or domain case assets (created in P-2). For instance, we may reuse the case of "river" for another river in a different location; "dissolved oxygen" and "pH" as relevant quality parameters; and so on. Notice that reusing does not imply exact matching of domain assets. Thus, stakeholders may query domain assets previously stored, and compare them to a particular context aiming at detecting similar cases. Therefore, queries are based on the context defined by the stakeholders, retrieving any related domain asset (domain variety and/or domain case assets). The reusable cases are stored as *reusable case assets* by a service (S-3), which is supported by two processes (P3: *P-3 Defining reusable case*; P4: *Querying similar domain case assets*) when stakeholders require a case reuse (event E3: *Require Reuse*), as Fig. 5 and Fig. 6 show.

---

[10] A variation point is used to specify that a variable can change, and the variants are the concrete variations that can/must be selected for each variation point.

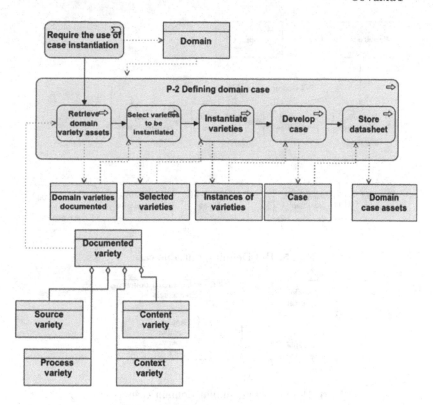

**Fig. 4.** P-2: Defining the case

In Fig. 5, we can see that varieties (created in P-1) are firstly retrieved and then instantiated for the specific case under development. Finally, P-4 is invoked to retrieve similar domain case assets; and once they are obtained, the final task creates the new instantiated case, which is also stored by CoVaMaT as a *reusable case asset*.

As a summary of the four processes defined, Fig. 7 shows all of them along with their generated/queried domain assets. Green arrows in the figure denote the specific domain asset the process generates, and orange ones denote the queries to the previously generated assets. Bidirectional arrows (between P-2 and P-3 and the domain variety assets) denote the fact that the definition of domain varieties is an incremental task, which can be firstly defined during P-1, but extended in successive case developments in order to be used in future BDSs.

## 5    Case Studies in the Agriculture Domain

Our case studies were performed in the agriculture domain, which includes activities focused on the process of developing land and coastal/aquatic areas for farming, animal husbandry, and fishing. It includes not only the specific activities and actors involved, but also the ecosystems and environments that these

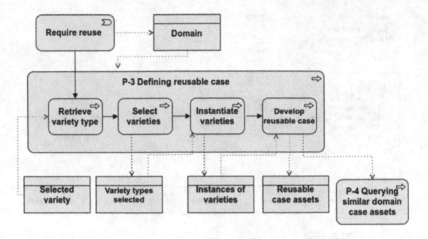

**Fig. 5.** P-3 Defining reusable case

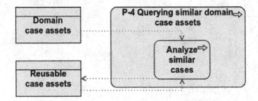

**Fig. 6.** P-4 Querying similar domain case assets

activities modify and transform. In particular, in this work, we are interested in a more-specific domain (or subdomain) within the agriculture one, called *precision agriculture*. According to [14], *precision agriculture is the application of technologies and principles to manage spatial and temporal variability associated with all aspects of agricultural production for the purpose of improving crop performance and environmental quality*. This subdomain, which is related also to the *digital agriculture* subdomain, includes the use and application of modern information and communication technology in agriculture. Agricultural data and their uses for better decision-making and innovation are at the center of the digital transformation of agriculture [9].

We are currently collaborating with expert users of the National Institute of Agricultural Technology (INTA) belonging to an experimental station in Alto Valle of Río Negro and Neuquén[11]. The Alto Valle is a productive area of approximately sixty thousand hectares, with an estimated annual production of seven hundred thousand tons of pears and apples, destined mainly for export and for the concentrated juice industry. In particular, the institute analyzes and researches areas such as plant entomology and therapeutics, plant nutrition, plant pathology, irrigation and drainage, post-harvest, crop management, etc. (see footnote 11).

---

[11] https://inta.gob.ar/altovalle/sobre-812000.

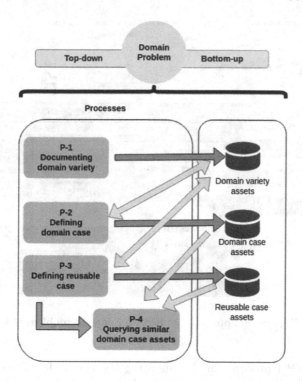

**Fig. 7.** Summary of the interaction between processes and domain assets

Part of the institute's research is focused on determining factors that affect the health of the crops, in order to define policies and mechanisms that maximize productivity and profits. In particular, here we show an example of the creation of domain cases starting from a domain problem: *determining factors affecting the NDVI index*. This index describes the health of vegetation by measuring the difference between near infrared and visible red light (what vegetation reflects).

In Fig. 8 we show the bottom-up approach addressing our domain problem, where the five steps (Fig. 8a)) have been applied for developing two domain cases. These cases describe an implementation of a context variety situation, in which processes and assets created for the first case are documented and reused in the second one. Thus, the *Domain case 1* creates *Domain variety assets* and *Domain core assets* in the context of the analysis of an area labeled as *Area 1*; and the *Domain case 2*, in the context of the analysis of an new *Area 2*, reuses core assets already generated and/or eventually creates new ones.

Following, we describe these two cases in detail.

## 5.1    Domain Case 1: P1 and P2

We started from scratch, without previous cases stored in CoVaMaT; therefore, in this first domain case we used the *functionality for variety documentation*,

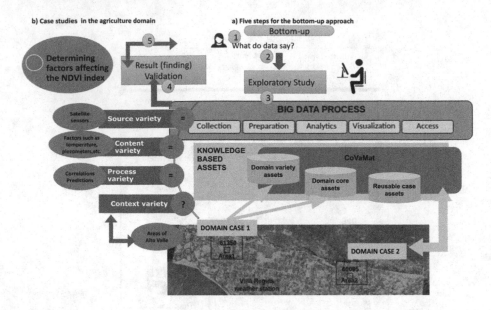

**Fig. 8.** Bottom-up approach applied to a domain problem of INTA

specifically the P-1 process, for documenting the variety for this domain problem (Fig. 9). The B-VIP approach means that we looked into existing datasets to identify different sources, variables, and values, arranging them as variety hierarchies. Then, variety was defined as follows:

– *Source variety*: information was collected by the Villa Regina weather station (X:663742, Y:5666849)[12], which registers information each ten minutes. The data generated are semi-structured in a text format; and included temperature, atmospheric pressure, humidity, wind speed, wind direction, precipitations, and evapotranspiration (ET). Another source considered here was the *water table*, registering different measures of underground water level. For registering these data, INTA has installed more than fifty piezometer[13] in Villa Regina subregion. Data are collected manually once a month and registered in a structured file (as a spreadsheet file). Finally, the last source included the values of the NDVI index within specific areas of Villa Regina subregion. The period considered for populating the sources was 2015–2022. The documentation of this variety, in a datasheet model, can be seen in Fig. 9 labeled with number 1. As we can see, there are two types of sources linked to the name of their respective repositories as references.
– *Content variety*: For this variety we followed a zig-zag approach by combining T-VIP and B-VIP. Firstly, we worked with expert users and also researched

---

[12] Coordinate system WGS 84 UTM ZONE 19S.
[13] A piezometer is used to measure underground water pressure and level. It converts water pressure to a frequency signal via a diaphragm and a tensioned steel wire.

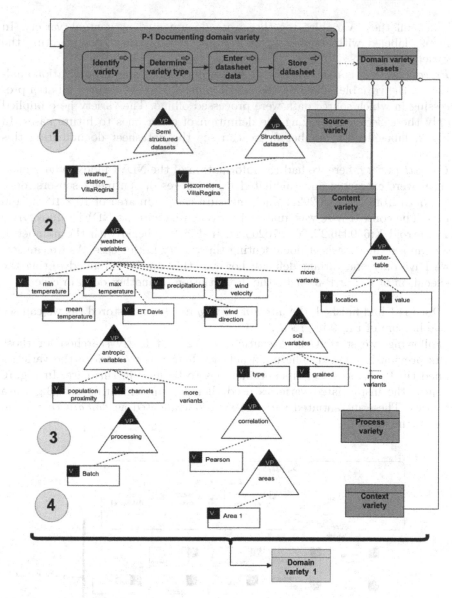

**Fig. 9.** Variety definition during the execution of P-1 for the problem domain (Color figure online)

works in the literature to determine factors or variables influencing the NDVI index (top-down). In [16] we described a characterization of these factors that included both natural and artificial resources, such as rivers, channels, soil and subsoil types, soil uses, proximity to populations, etc. Then, we searched the datasets for identifying variables that may influence the index, and their availability to be used during analysis (bottom-up).

Thus, all these variables together were documented as content variety. In Fig. 9, labeled with number 2, we can see the datasheet documenting the variety.

– *Process variety*: For this variety we began performing simple correlation analyses of the variables affecting the NDVI values. Also, we defined a batch processing in which source data were processed offline. The variety here implied only these decisions, leaving the definition of other ones to future cases. In Fig. 9, labeled with number 3, we can see the datasheet documenting this variety.

– *Context variety*: here we had the information of the NDVI index, whose measures were extracted and calculated from images of Sentinel-2 sensors, once a month from 2015 to 2022. Each measure covers an area of $10 \times 10$ m (100 m$^2$). The context here was analyzed for one area with its NDVI values (*Area 1* centroid X:659946.27, Y:5670205.4). In Fig. 9, labeled with the number 4, we can see the datasheet documenting the variety in this case. As we can see, we have only one variant defined; however this can be extended during the execution of P-2 or P-3, or by the instantiation of another domain case.

Once P-1 had finished, the *domain variety asset 1* was stored (as we can see at the bottom of Fig. 9 in green).

Following, we started the execution of P-2 that firstly searched for those assets previously created. The main activity here was to retrieve the varieties defined (in P-1) and select the specific ones to be used in this case. In Fig. 10 we show the instantiated varieties used then for implementing the Big Data activities. These instantiated varieties were documented as *domain case 1* (in green in the figure).

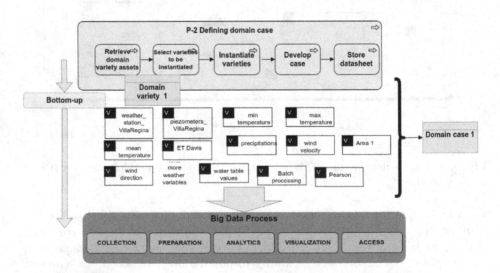

**Fig. 10.** Variety instantiation during the execution of P-2 according to the domain variety asset created in P-1

## 5.2    Domain Case 2: P3 and P4

In this case, we considered that there was information already documented in CoVaMaT (stored as *domain case 1*). This stored case had the same domain problem as the new one: (*determining factors affecting the NDVI index*), but domain experts were interested in a different area of Villa Regina subregion (*Area 2* centroid X:676845.02, Y:5666654.85).

Thus, we started running P-3 to search for similar domain variety assets (Fig. 11). In this case, CoVaMaT retrieved the *domain variety 1* (Fig. 11 labeled with number 1) and showed it to us. At this point, we could analyze all the variants defined, and determine if they were enough for this new case. Here, we realized that we needed a new variant for the context definition, because only *Area 1* was previously defined. So, we detected that we were in a *context variety case*, and we had to create a new variant, named *Area 2*. Therefore, the domain variety asset was changed to contain two variants, *Area 1* and *Area 2* (Fig. 11 labeled with number 2).

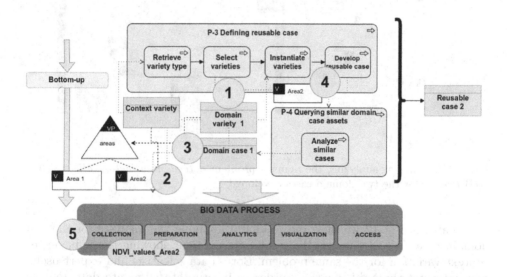

**Fig. 11.** Reusable case domain generation for domain case 2

Following, P-4 was invoked to search for a similar domain case asset; and as a result, the *domain case 1* (Fig. 10) was retrieved (Fig. 11 labeled with number 3). Here, we again analyzed the instantiations in order to see if we needed a different configuration. In this case, we had only to change the instantiation of the context variety by choosing the *Area 2* (Fig. 11 labeled with number 4). Then, we performed the activities of the Big Data Process but in a simplified manner. That is, as the sources (weather_station_VillaRegina and piezometers_VillaRegina) and the variables were the same, it was not necessary to redo the collection and preparation activities for them. These activities had to be performed only for the new source (the NDVI values for *Area 2*) and rerun the analytics (correlation) and visualization activities (Fig. 11 labeled with number 5). The domain case 2 was finally stored as *reusable case 2*. As a conclusion, the development of the second case in the domain was simplified thanks to the domain assets already stored in CoVaMaT.

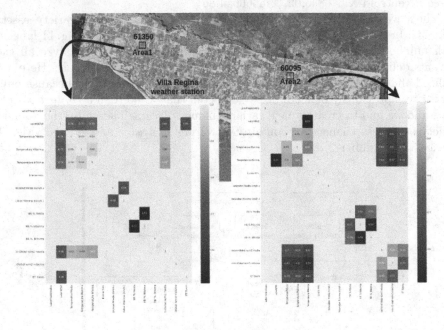

**Fig. 12.** Results of analyzing the domain problem *determining factors affecting the NDVI index* for the two domain cases developed

Finally, in Fig. 12 we show the results of applying the analyses for the two domain cases. As we can see, the results are different showing the influence of context variation for the same problem. Both, data scientists and expert users, may interpret these differences in order to incorporate/eliminate data sources according to their significance. For example, the analyses correlated content from climatology and underground water information; however, climate is similar for the whole Villa Regina region, meanwhile other not considered influencing factors might be decisive, such as the soil type of Area 1 and Area 2 (a more porous soil might influence irrigation and consequently the NDVI results). Therefore, we could iterate by building a new domain case, which reuse some domain assets and incorporate new ones again. The iterative cycle is benefited by less effort because of reuse.

# 6   Conclusion and Future Work

We have introduced functionality of CoVaMaT[14] as processes that support variety reuse during BDSs development. Although the tool is continuously updated and its processes empirically tested, there is still a huge amount of work to do.

Currently, since the first prototype only showed the applicability, we are extending CoVaMaT to incorporate a more friendly and graphic interface. In the same sense, similarity for detecting reusable domain assets is using simple algorithms in this first prototype. More intelligence is needed to become CoVaMaT into a more accurate recommender system.

At the same time, we continue empirically testing the process (T-VIP and B-VIP), as well as CoVaMaT, for different agriculture domain problems in cooperation with INTA Alto Valle.

**Funding Information.** This paper has been supported by Universidad Nacional del Comahue, Project 04/F019-Modelado de Variedad en Sistemas Big Data.

# References

1. Borrison, R., Klöpper, B., Chioua, M., Dix, M., Sprick, B.: Reusable big data system for industrial data mining - a case study on anomaly detection in chemical plants. In: Yin, H., Camacho, D., Novais, P., Tallón-Ballesteros, A.J. (eds.) IDEAL 2018. LNCS, vol. 11314, pp. 611–622. Springer, Cham (2018). https://doi.org/10.1007/978-3-030-03493-1_64
2. Buccella, A., Cechich, A., Pol'la, M., Arias, M., Doldan, S., Morsan, E.: Marine ecology service reuse through taxonomy-oriented SPL development. Comput. Geosci. **73**, 108–121 (2014)
3. Buccella, A., Cechich, A., Porfiri, J., Diniz Dos Santos, D.: Taxonomy-oriented domain analysis of GIS: a case study for paleontological software systems. ISPRS Int. J. Geo-Inf. **8**(6) (2019). https://www.mdpi.com/2220-9964/8/6/270
4. Cuesta, C.E., Martínez-Prieto, M.A., Fernández, J.D.: Towards an architecture for managing big semantic data in real-time. In: Drira, K. (ed.) ECSA 2013. LNCS, vol. 7957, pp. 45–53. Springer, Heidelberg (2013). https://doi.org/10.1007/978-3-642-39031-9_5
5. Custers, B., Uršič, H.: Big data and data reuse: a taxonomy of data reuse for balancing big data benefits and personal data protection. Int. Data Privacy Law **6**(1), 4–15 (2016)
6. Davoudian, A., Liu, M.: Big data systems: a software engineering perspective. ACM Comput. Surv. **53**(5), 1–39 (2020)
7. Duggan, J., et al.: The bigdawg polystore system. ACM SIGMOD Rec. **44**(2), 11–16 (2015)
8. Epperson, W., Yi Wang, A., DeLine, R., Drucker, S.M.: Strategies for reuse and sharing among data scientists in software teams. In: Proceedings of ICSE-SEIP 2022, Pittsburgh, PA, USA. Association for Computing Machinery (2022). https://willepperson.com/papers/reuse-sharing-DS-icse22.pdf

---

[14] Current version of CoVaMaT can be accessed at https://github.com/liamosycka/CoVaMaT.

9. Jouanjean, M.A., Casalini, F., Wiseman, L., Gray, E.: Issues around data governance in the digital transformation of agriculture (146) (2020). https://www.oecd-ilibrary.org/content/paper/53ecf2ab-en

10. Klein, J.: Reference architectures for big data systems, Carnegie Mellon University's software engineering institute blog (2017). http://insights.sei.cmu.edu/blog/reference-architectures-for-big-data-systems/. Accessed 9 June 2021

11. Nadal, S., et al.: A software reference architecture for semantic-aware big data systems. Inf. Softw. Technol. **90**, 75–92 (2017)

12. Osycka, L., Buccella, A., Cechich, A.: Data variety modeling: a case of contextual diversity identification from a bottom-up perspective. In: Pesado, P., Gil, G. (eds.) CACIC 2021. CCIS, vol. 1584, pp. 124–138. Springer, Cham (2022). https://doi.org/10.1007/978-3-031-05903-2_9

13. Pasquetto, I., Randles, B., Borgman, C.: On the reuse of scientific data. Data Sci. J. **16**(8) (2017)

14. Pierce, F.J., Nowak, P.: Aspects of precision agriculture. Adv. Agron. **67**, 1–85 (1999). https://www.sciencedirect.com/science/article/pii/S0065211308605131

15. Pohl, K., Böckle, G., Linden, F.J.: Software Product Line Engineering: Foundations, Principles and Techniques. Springer, New York (2005). https://doi.org/10.1007/3-540-28901-1

16. Villegas, C., Buccella, A., Cechich, A.: Caracterización de variables para el análisis del Índice de vegetación. In: Memorias del XXVIII Congreso Argentino de Ciencias de la Computación (CACIC) - Workshop Alumnos, pp. 978–982 (2022)

17. Xie, Z., Chen, Y., Speer, J., Walters, T., Tarazaga, P.A., Kasarda, M.: Towards use and reuse driven big data management. In: Proceedings of the 15th ACM/IEEE-CS Joint Conference on Digital Libraries, pp. 65–74. Association for Computing Machinery (2015)

# Local Pluralistic Homophily in Networks: A New Measure Based on Overlapping Communities

Fernando Barraza[1,4]([✉]) [iD], Carlos Ramirez[1] [iD], and Alejandro Fernández[2,3] [iD]

[1] Pontificia Universidad Javeriana de Cali, Cali, Colombia
[2] LIFIA, FI, Universidad Nacional de La Plata, La Plata, Argentina
[3] Comisión de Investigaciones Científicas de la Provincia de Buenos Aires, Tolosa, Argentina
[4] Universidad de San Buenaventura Cali, Cali, Colombia
fbarraza@usbcali.edu.co

**Abstract.** Pluralistic homophily is an important phenomenon in social network analysis as nodes tend to associate with others that share their same communities. In this work, we present the concept of local pluralistic homophily of a node in a network, along with a method to measure it. It is based on the assortativity index proposed by other authors. We analyze the distribution of local pluralistic homophily in different networks using publicly available datasets. We identify patterns of behavior of the proposed measure that relate to various structural and topological characteristics of a network. These findings are significant because they help better understand how pluralistic homophily affects communities. Furthermore, our results suggest possible applications of local pluralistic homophily in future research.

**Keywords:** Local Pluralistic Homophily · Networks · Communities

## 1 Introduction

In the field of social network analysis, homophily is known as *assortativity* or *assortative mixing*. Assortative mixing is the tendency of a node to link with nodes similar to it. The similarity between nodes can be defined based on a common characteristic, such as the node degree [4], but other features can also be used. Social networks have shown a high assortativity, contrary to biological and technological networks where a low assortativity is observed (i.e., *disassortativity*) [5]. The study of homophily and communities is essential to understand the structure and dynamics of social networks.

In network science, we call a community a group of nodes that have a higher likelihood of connecting to each other than to nodes from other communities [2]. To detect these groups, several techniques are used, such as differential equations, random walks, spectral clustering, and modularity maximization. In some cases, the network can be partitioned into disjoint communities, while in others,

© The Author(s), under exclusive license to Springer Nature Switzerland AG 2023
M. Naiouf et al. (Eds.): JCC-BD&ET 2023, CCIS 1828, pp. 75–87, 2023.
https://doi.org/10.1007/978-3-031-40942-4_6

the structure can be viewed as communities where some nodes belong to two or more of them. In these cases, it's said that the network has overlapping communities. In a study conducted by Yang and Leskovec [12], it was found that overlapping community areas in networks exhibit a higher density of connections compared to non-overlapping ones. Furthermore, the authors noted a noteworthy pattern where nodes belonging to multiple communities tend to connect with similar nodes based on their community memberships. This phenomenon, termed as *pluralistic homophily*, highlights the tendency of nodes to exhibit preference towards nodes with similar attributes across multiple communities.

In this article, we introduce the concept of local pluralistic homophily as the tendency of a specific node to link with others with the same overlap. Our measures are based on the already-established concept of assortativity and provide a more suitable way to measure the phenomenon of pluralistic homophily. We define an extended measure of homophily based on the similarity of nodes that share community memberships. Our measures reveal how much nodes from a network with overlapping communities prefer to attach to others with similar membership quantities. We validate the measure using six datasets from social networks and collaboration networks. Our results suggest the likely application of local pluralistic homophily in node attribute prediction and other tasks common in the network analytics field.

## 2 Theoretical Framework

In social networks, individuals often exhibit a strong tendency to associate with others who share similar attributes, such as political beliefs and social status. This phenomenon is referred to as *assortativity*. However, in certain networks, such as dating networks, an opposite pattern can be observed, where the majority of links exist between nodes with dissimilar attributes. This is known as disassortativity. An assortativity metric, as defined in [5], captures the inclination of nodes to form direct links with others who possess similar properties. The properties of nodes can be categorized as enumerative or scalar. Enumerative properties have a finite set of possible values, such as gender, nationality, and profession in the context of a social network composed of individuals. On the other hand, a common example of assortative mixing based on scalar properties is mixing by degree, where nodes with high degrees tend to connect with other highly connected nodes, while nodes with low degrees are primarily linked to nodes with few connections.

The formal structure of network analysis models is based on the concept of graphs. In this work, we will use the standard concept of a simple graph, where a set of nodes is connected to other nodes through edges. More formally:

*Definition.* Let a graph be an ordered pair $G = (V_G, E_G)$ where $V_G$ is the vertex set whose elements are the vertices denoted by $v$ (or nodes of the graph), and $E_G$ is the edge set whose elements are the edges, denoted by $e$ (or links between vertices of the graph), such that $V(G) \equiv V_G = \{v_1, v_2, \ldots, v_n\}$, and $E(G) \equiv E_G = \{e = (v_x, v_y) \mid v_x, v_y \in V_G\}$. Since the analysis carried out in this paper is done on a static network, any discussion around the network assumes that it is built on the basis of the definition presented above, so no explicit reference will be made to this concept in the following of this paper.

## 2.1 Pluralistic Homophily

The concept of pluralistic homophily is introduced in [11]. Previous studies on community detection have typically assumed that nodes within the same community share similar properties. However, the authors of this paper argue that nodes can also be considered similar based on the number of shared memberships they have across multiple communities. This phenomenon is known as pluralistic homophily.

To illustrate this concept, consider a community of students who all play football. In this case, the similarity between two individuals could be based on their shared interest in football. However, if those same individuals also play basketball, we might hypothesize that they share an even stronger similarity than if they only had one shared activity. This is an example of pluralistic homophily, where the similarity between two individuals is based on their shared memberships across multiple communities.

While homophily has received significant attention in research, the concept of pluralistic homophily remains under-explored. To address this research gap, we propose a novel measure of assortativity that specifically considers overlapping community memberships. In our measure, we extend the commonly used correlation coefficient for quantifying homophily by incorporating the degree of overlap in community memberships. This overlap refers to the number of communities to which each node belongs in the network. By introducing this measure, we aim to gain a deeper understanding of the role of pluralistic homophily in community detection and other network analysis tasks.

Based on Eq. 3 in [4], we define a coefficient denoted by $h$ that measure the pluralistic homophily of a network as,

$$h = \frac{1}{\sigma_q^2} \sum_{xy} m_x m_y (e_{m_x m_y} - q_{m_x} q_{m_y}) \tag{1}$$

where $m_x, m_y$ are the number of membership of the nodes $x$ and $y$ in a link, $e_{m_x m_y}$ is the joint probability for the memberships values $x$ and $y$, and $q$ is the quantity membership distribution of the network. Note that Eq. 1 uses the number of memberships of each node as the scalar value to calculate the assortativity as defined in [5]. Under this equation, the assortativity value must be interpreted according to the nearing of the result to zero. If the result is near $-1$ means that, in general, nodes trends to link with others having a different scalar number. On the contrary, if it nears 1, the nodes tend to link with others with a similar scalar number. A result near zero means that nodes tend to link randomly. To avoid subjectivity in the interpretation of the results on how much $h$ is nearest or farthest to zero, we define a $\varepsilon$-value to establish clear limits in such appreciation. In general, a $|h| < \varepsilon$ means a network non-assortative by node membership, $h < -\varepsilon$ is a disassortativity one, while $h > \varepsilon$ exhibits assortativity mixing, in other words, is pluralistic *homophilically* speaking.

## 2.2  Local Pluralistic Homophily

It is common to find cases where some nodes tend to link differently than most other nodes on the network. This is, despite a network that can exhibit an overall positive or negative assortativity, some individual nodes could have an opposite tending. For these cases, [7] introduces the concept of local assortativity, making a comparative analysis between the assortativity of a node and the network's assortativity. This distinction has allowed some works [8,9] to understand the composition of patterns found throughout the network structure, as well as to observe the different assortative mixing throughout the hierarchical levels of the networks. From this perspective, the local assortativity can then be seen as the contribution that each node makes to the network's assortativity or also a group of them (for example, a partition, a community, etc.).

Local assortativity can also be observed when thinking in terms of pluralistic homophily. This means that it is possible that a specific node with a high quantity of memberships links to others with also high memberships, even when the pluralistic homophily of the entire network is near $-1$. Based on this behavior, the local pluralistic homophily can be defined as the tendency of a specific node to link to other nodes with similar overlapping quantities.

We examine several works about local assortativity as reviewed in [6], looking for a reasonable way to compute the local pluralistic homophily. Finally, we based on Eq. 4.10 on [10] to define the local pluralistic homophily $h$ of a node $v$ as,

$$
h_v = \frac{\sum\limits_{i \in N(v)} (m_v - \mu_q)(m_i - \mu_q)}{2M\sigma_q^2} \tag{2}
$$

where $i$ iterates over all the neighbors of node $v$, $m_v$ is the number of communities to which node $v$ belongs, while $m_i$ is the number of communities to which node $i$ belongs. $M$ is the total number of nodes in the network, and $\mu_q$ and $\sigma_q$ are the mean and standard deviation of the probability distribution of node memberships in the network. The resulting value of $h_v$ represents numerically the trend of a specific node $v$ to link to other nodes with near memberships number. The summation of $h_v$ values for all nodes is congruent with the results obtained using Eq. 1 for the pluralistic homophily of the entire network.

Figure 1 shows an example of calculating the assortative mixing by the number of memberships of the network nodes, i.e. the pluralistic homophily $h$ of the entire network. Taking $\varepsilon$ as 0.1, the value of $h = -0.032$ show a non-assortative mixing due to $|h| < \varepsilon$. This is consistent with the result of $h_v$ for most of the nodes ($v_1, v_3, v_4, v_5, v_7$). However, a node is disassortative $h_{v_6} < -\varepsilon$, and other assortative $h_{v_2} > \varepsilon$. This behavior can be explained, for instance, by node $v_2$ being more assortative than the others because it connects more frequently with nodes that have a similar number of memberships. Node $v_6$, on the other hand, is the most disassortative because it links to nodes with dissimilar numbers of memberships. In the following sections, we will show this behavior in real networks with a different number of nodes, links, and communities.

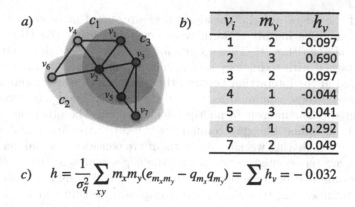

a)

b)

| $v_i$ | $m_v$ | $h_v$ |
|---|---|---|
| 1 | 2 | -0.097 |
| 2 | 3 | 0.690 |
| 3 | 2 | 0.097 |
| 4 | 1 | -0.044 |
| 5 | 3 | -0.041 |
| 6 | 1 | -0.292 |
| 7 | 2 | 0.049 |

c) $$h = \frac{1}{\sigma_q^2} \sum_{xy} m_x m_y (e_{m_x m_y} - q_{m_x} q_{m_y}) = \sum h_v = -0.032$$

**Fig. 1.** Calculus of pluralistic homophily of a network and its nodes. $a$) A network with 7 nodes (filled with different colors to differentiate the number of memberships of each node) and 3 detected communities in shaded colors ($c_1$:green, $c_2$:sky blue, $c_3$:brown). $b$) A table that calculates the pluralistic homophily $h_v$ for every node $v_i$ in the network with its respective number of memberships $m_v$. $c$) Calculus of the pluralistic homophily for the entire network. We can see the result is equal to the sum of all local pluralistic homophily $h_v$ from the table. (Color figure online)

## 3   Methodology

We performed a series of experiments to analyze the behavior of pluralistic homophily in six datasets containing networks and communities related to them. To calculate pluralistic homophily, we used the Eq. 1 presented above. In addition, we calculated the local pluralistic homophily of each node in the networks using the Eq. 2. We used these resulting measures to generate complementary cumulative continuous distribution (CCDF) plots that allowed us to analyze what distribution follows these data for each dataset. We also compare the behavior of pluralistic homophily with what we have called simple homophily, which is based on the degree of the nodes. This comparison is relevant as it allows us to understand better the role of pluralistic homophily in network structure and how it differs from other measures of homophily. In particular, we expect to find that pluralistic homophily highlights clustering patterns in communities that are not evident in simple homophily. We also expect evidence of the behavior of local pluralistic homophily versus the node membership and node degree. This is useful to understand how pluralistic homophily behaves in some hubs (nodes with high degrees) and in peripherical nodes (nodes with low degrees).

### 3.1   Datasets

For our study, we selected six data sets of real-world networks and their respective communities: Stackoverflow (SO), DBLP, Amazon Product, Livejournal, Youtube, and Orkut. SO is a collaborative network for questions and answers on programming and related topics. The SO network is reconstructed by users as nodes, and the edges are the questions that are asked or answered between them. Communities in this network were generated using the HLC community detection algorithm [1]. These communities reflect, through questions that have been tagged with technology topics, common and correlated interests that are addressed in the interaction between the members of said communities. An overlap between those communities occurs when a user belongs to several communities, given their interest in multiple technologies. The other networks are Livejournal, an online blogging community; Orkut, an online social network; Youtube, a video-sharing website; All of them are considered social networks in which users are represented as nodes, and the edges represent the explicit relationships established between them. These networks allow users to form groups that other members can then join. These groups are the communities, and overlapping happens when a user belongs to more than one group. The two last networks are Amazon and DBLP. In the former, every product is a node, and the edges are formed between them when they are bought together. Product categories define the communities. And latter is DBLP, where authors are the nodes, edges mean coauthoring between them, and each magazine and conference where they publish defines a community. All network datasets[1], except SO, with their respective ground-truth communities, are publicly available at [3]. The choice of these datasets and their source provides high reliability in the data to be used in our experiments as well as the possibility of comparing them with the works of other authors who have also been using them extensively.

Table 1 shows basic characteristics and measures for the datasets. In summary, we include three networks considered collaborative and the other three considered social networks, each with different characteristics in terms of size, structure, and methods used to define their communities. This will help us gain a better understanding of pluralistic homophily behavior across diverse contexts.

The table presents the characteristics of the networks. Generally, we observe that these datasets differ in size, i.e. in the number of all nodes, links, and communities they exhibit. Also, we present the values of pluralistic homophily $h$ and homophily by degree $r$ (also known as degree assortativity) on which we will go into more depth in the next section. According to the size of the networks, SO, DBLP, and Amazon could be considered medium-sized. The rest are large-size. Values of average degree $\langle d \rangle$ are consistent with the size of the networks, except for the Youtube network where there is a low $\langle d \rangle$ compared with the others of similar size. With respect to the properties of the communities, we can observe three kinds of community sizes: Small ones such as DBLP and Youtube, medium as SO and Amazon, and large ones such as Livejournal and Orkut. These community sizes are consistent with the size of the networks, except again for the Youtube network where the community size is more like that of small networks. The average number of community memberships per node $\langle m \rangle$, a value intrinsically related to the pluralistic homophily seems not to be directly related to

---

[1] Dates from datasets are shown on the SNAP web page except for SO which was downloaded from the site https://archive.org/details/stackexchange and communities generated until 2021.

**Table 1.** Comparison of network and community properties, as well as assortativity measures, for six different datasets. $N$: number of nodes, $E$: number of edges, $\langle d \rangle$: average node degree, $K$: number of communities, $\langle m \rangle$: average number of community memberships per node, $h$: pluralistic homophily coefficient, $r$: degree assortativity coefficient.

| Dataset | Network Properties | | | Community Properties | | Assortativity Measures | |
|---|---|---|---|---|---|---|---|
| | $N$ | $E$ | $\langle d \rangle$ | $K$ | $\langle m \rangle$ | $h$ | $r$ |
| StackOverflow | 790.458 | 1.872.715 | 4.76 | 115.969 | 1.85 | 0.0332 | −0.0381 |
| DBLP | 317.080 | 1.049.866 | 6.62 | 13.477 | 2.27 | 0.2166 | 0.2665 |
| Amazon | 334.863 | 925.872 | 5.53 | 75.149 | 6.78 | 0.4887 | −0.0588 |
| LiveJournal | 3.997.962 | 34.681.189 | 17.35 | 664.414 | 1.79 | 0.2132 | 0.0451 |
| Youtube | 1.134.890 | 2.987.624 | 5.26 | 16.386 | 0.11 | 0.0647 | −0.0369 |
| Orkut | 3.072.441 | 117.185.083 | 76.28 | 6.288.363 | 34.85 | 0.2335 | 0.0158 |

network size. For example, while Amazon's network has the second largest $\langle m \rangle$, Livejournal network has one of the smallest, despite the latter having a network size ten times the former. We then have different values of $\langle m \rangle$ independent of the size of the network, which provide us with a solid base in the data sets to explore the behavior of pluralistic homophily in the conducted experiments.

## 4    Results

We present the results of the local pluralistic homophily analysis conducted on each of the six datasets described earlier. We calculated the entire pluralistic homophily of each network and the local pluralistic homophily for all nodes belonging to any related community. Notably, as we can see in Table 1 pluralistic homophily $h$ displays positive values across all datasets, contrasting with the mixing results of assortativity by the degree $r$ that show some negative ones. DBLP, Amazon, Livejournal, and Orkut show pluralistic homophily $h > \varepsilon$, while the other networks, SO and Youtube do not, $|h| < \varepsilon$, having as $\varepsilon$ the same value defined for the toy example above. Relating to assortativity by degree $r$, only the DBLP network shows assortative mixing, the others non-assortative. This is the only network that shows assortative mixing in both $h$ and $r$ as we have shown in the Table 1. None shows disassortativity in both measures for the entire network. These very varied results in the correlation between $h$ and $v$, suggest that overall at the level of the entire network, there may not be a uniform direct relationship between the tendency of nodes to connect with nodes of the same degree with the tendency of those nodes to connect with nodes that share the same communities. Regarding that both the quantities related to the size of the input data sets ($N$, $E$ and $K$) and also to the average values ($\langle d \rangle$ and $\langle m \rangle$) influence the value of $h$ and $r$ respectively, we can see that there is no obvious correlation either.

Results at the entire network level contrast with the results at the local level. To visualize the results of how is the tendency of nodes to link with others with the same $m$ we calculate the distribution of local pluralistic homophily. Before interpretation of when a node exhibits pluralistic homophily or not, we set $\varepsilon = 0.1 \cdot 10^{-5}$, a very small value. We must take into account as noted above that $h = \sum h_v$, so given the significant difference in the number of nodes $v$ between the toy example (shown above) and the real networks, it is necessary to apply a scaling factoring to $\varepsilon$ of $-5$ which is related to the size difference between the networks. The rationale behind applying a scaling factor to $\varepsilon$ of $-5$ is related to the difference in network size. As the magnitude of $\varepsilon$ values varies with the network size, we need to adjust $\varepsilon$ to account for this difference and ensure meaningful comparisons between networks. When scaling up or down the network size by an order of magnitude of 10 (e.g., from a small network to a large network), $\varepsilon$ values need to scale proportionally to maintain consistency in measuring pluralistic homophily. Applying a scaling factor of $-5$ means dividing the original value of $\varepsilon$ by $10^5$, ensuring that the adjusted value of $\varepsilon$ is suitable for the scale of the network under consideration. This scaling procedure allows us to compare the local pluralistic homophily values across different-sized networks effectively, enabling a fair assessment of the tendencies of nodes to exhibit pluralistic homophily. By considering the scaling factor, we account for the size discrepancy and ensure that the interpretation of pluralistic homophily remains consistent across diverse network sizes.

We show then, the complementary cumulative probability distribution function (CCDF) of the local pluralistic homophily for each network (see Fig. 2). The "S" shaped curves present in all CCDF figures indicate a distribution with a high probability of low values, followed by a decreasing probability as values increase, and then a long tail to the right that indicates the presence of extreme values. The initial part of the curve indicates that there are many nodes in the network with low local pluralistic homophily, while the final part of the curve indicates that there are a small number of nodes with high local pluralistic homophily. The abrupt decrease in probability close to zero indicates an inflection point in the distribution, which coincides with the value determined for $\varepsilon$ and can be interpreted as a threshold from which local pluralistic homophily begins to increase significantly. The presence of extreme values may be indicative of nodes or groups of nodes in the network (hubs) that have extremely high or low local pluralistic homophily, which may be important for understanding the overlap of communities and their relationship with the structure of the network. Note for instance that, in the case of DBLP and Amazon such a decrease at a certain threshold is not so pronounced, maybe there are additional factors at play that influence the distribution as the node degree. In order to approach a better understanding of these patterns, we present the next figure.

We created scatter plots showing the relationship between a node's degree $d$ and its local pluralistic homophily $h_v$, as well as between $d$ and the number of communities it belongs to, denoted as $m_v$. Each dot in the scatter plot represents a node $v$ in the network (see Fig. 3). We colored the dots according to whether the $m_v$ value is low or high. At first glance, the figures show different patterns but looking in detail there are similarities between some of them that can reveal

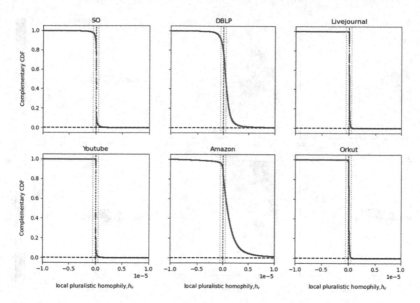

**Fig. 2.** CCDF local pluralistic homophily for each dataset. The x-axis range in each subplot is deliberately narrow, from $-1 \cdot 10^{-5}$ to $1 \cdot 10^{-5}$, to provide a close-up view of the $h_v$ values at that level. It is important to note that the narrow x-axis range does not necessarily indicate a low tendency of nodes to be linked but rather serves the purpose of zooming in on the figure for better visualization of the localized $h_v$ values. The red vertical dotted lines denote the range value of $h_v$ to be considered as non-assortative as $|\varepsilon| < 0.1 \cdot 10^{-5}$.

interesting findings. For instance, the dispersion of points looks much larger in some networks as $d_v$ increases. This is most evident at DBLP and Amazon. It can also be noted that this dispersion is marked by the value of $h_v$ taking the zero value on the y-axis as the initial point of said dispersion, which is less accelerated in Livejournal and Orkut, and a little less observable in SO.

We observed that, as the degree of the node $d_v$ increases, the points become more dispersed. However, it is important to note that these observations are based on a sample rather than the entire population. While we did not observe a significant trend in the proportion of low and high values of $m_v$ across all figures, suggesting that the distribution of $m_v$ may not be strongly correlated with the degree of the node, further statistical analysis is needed to establish a conclusive relationship. It is worth noting that in the DBLP dataset, there appears to be a potential trend of more high values of $m_v$ beyond a certain value of $d_v$, while in the SO dataset, the opposite trend is observed, with lower values of $m_v$ after a certain point. For now, this is an initial analysis that requires going further to determine the statistical significance of the relationships.

In our analysis, we aim to examine the relationship between $h_v$ and $m_v$ and identify patterns in the distribution of nodes across the scatter plots. Specifically, we investigate the concentration of nodes with high $h_v$ and low $h_v$ values

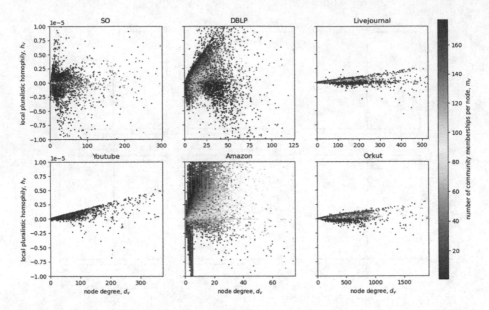

**Fig. 3.** A scatter plot of node degree $d_v$ versus pluralistic homophily $h$, with the number of community memberships per node $m_v$ represented by dot colors. A random sample of 100,000 nodes is plotted. In this representation, darker shades of blue indicate higher values of $m_v$, while brighter shades of red indicate lower values of $m_v$. Please note that the x-axis limits vary in each figure, with the range set from 0 to $\sigma_{d_v} + 10$ standard deviations of $d_v$. The sample selection is based on a random sampling approach, ensuring an unbiased representation of nodes in the network. (Color figure online)

and how they relate to $m_v$. We examine the behavior of average $m_v$ values in relation to $h_v$ and how these values are represented in the scatter plots. To better understand this relationship, we analyze different regions of the scatter plots. We observe that, on average, $m_v$ values rise until reaching a certain point, which corresponds to the average values of $m_v$. This behavior occurs similarly at low values of $h_v$. However, in this case, an inverse behavior seems to emerge, indicating a different relationship between $h_v$ and $m_v$. By conducting a thorough analysis and examining the scatter plots, we aim to gain insights into the specific trends and relationships between $h_v$, $m_v$, and the distribution of nodes. This analysis will provide a more comprehensive understanding of the interplay between these variables and their implications within the network. The patterns in the figure show similarities between a group of networks comprising SO, DBLP, and Amazon, versus a second group comprising the Livejournal, YouTube, and Orkut networks. In the first group, the nodes with the highest pluralistic homophily start at the first values of $d_v$, but as we move along their x-axis, these values tend to decrease. However, at some point on the said axis, the high values of $h_v$ begin to appear rapidly in nodes with low $m_v$, and then surprisingly rise again until reaching the average values of $m_v$. This behavior occurs similarly at low values of $h_v$. However, in this case, it seems an inverse behavior, that is, they start with low values of $m_v$ first and then increase as the degree of the node increases. In the second group of networks, the patterns are different from the networks in the first one. In this case, the high values of pluralistic homophily are in nodes with low $m_v$ while the low ones are in higher proportion in nodes with high values of $m_v$. This is maintained along the x-axis however with a greater spread of points as $d_v$ increases, forming a kind of "comet" going left to right on such axis. In general, the networks in the first packet exhibit a great dispersion on the pluralistic homophily of the nodes with a relatively low degree $d_v$, while the second one show that the dispersion along moves all the node degrees. Also, it could be said that the areas with a high density of values of $h_v$ under the $\varepsilon$ range indicate that the nodes have a greater diversity in terms of connections with nodes of a different number of community membership, i.e. they link to other nodes indistinctly if share the same number of community memberships. On the other side, nodes with higher or lower values of $\varepsilon$ indicate a greater homogeneity in the connections. We follow to discuss these findings according to the type and characteristics of the networks analyzed.

# 5  Discussion

Our findings reveal interesting patterns in the behavior of local pluralistic homophily values across the analyzed networks. The distribution of these values exhibits a bimodal shape, with two modes representing assortative and non-assortative connections between nodes. However, in the Amazon and DBLP networks, we observe a slightly higher number of nodes connecting with others who share a similar number of community memberships. This suggests that areas with the highest and lowest overlapping of communities exhibit a comparable density of nodes. This behavior may be influenced by the network type, as both Amazon and DBLP networks are informational in nature. In contrast, social networks display different behavior. The most connected nodes, or hubs, in these networks, exhibit high and low levels of overlap, belonging to multiple or few communities. Interestingly, this does not seem to significantly affect the proportion of nodes belonging to many or few communities.

The shape of the local pluralistic homophily distribution provides insights into the presence or absence of specific homophily patterns in the network. In information or collaboration networks, nodes are more likely to connect with others who share their interests or work areas, resulting in a greater similarity in the number of communities they belong to. In social networks, on the other hand, the diversity of interests and connections tends to be higher, explaining the concentration of the cumulative distribution around zero. The greater heterogeneity in the number of community memberships in social networks leads to a wider dispersion of local pluralistic homophily values. Surprisingly, we did not find a clear relationship between network size and the local pluralistic homophily exhibited by its nodes. Instead, our results indicate that this relationship depends more on the network type and its structural characteristics. Different patterns emerge, indicating a varying tendency for nodes to connect with others having the same level of overlap. We also observed distinct patterns between the number of connections and memberships of nodes in specific areas of the networks.

These observations highlight the unique behavior of pluralistic homophily and its potential applications in network analysis. It is evident that the behavior of pluralistic homophily carries significant value in understanding network dynamics and uncovering underlying social phenomena. However, further research is needed to delve deeper into the specific mechanisms driving these observations and explore their implications in different contexts.

## 6    Conclusions and Future Work

We have presented a measure that serves to estimate the tendency of nodes to connect with others that share a similar level of overlap, that is when they are members in similar numbers of various communities. Our experiments have shown what is the relationship between the said level of overlap with the degree of the nodes in the network. Likewise, despite the fact that networks can exhibit a general behavior in this sense, this is different from what is presented at the level of each node, and this varies depending on where such node is located in the network structure. A measure is then presented which allows us to consistently estimate the pluralistic homophily of an entire network and at the level of each node present in it. We consider this as an important contribution to the discussion of assortativity in general since assortativity based on the overlapping of communities allows for analysis different from the widely explored assortativity based on the degree of nodes. This leads us to think about possible future works, such as the use of the local pluralistic homophily measure in methods for various applications, such as the prediction of the properties of a given node or the prediction of links between nodes in a network. These methods range from the use of distance-based algorithms as a weight in the similarity between nodes and links, as well as the construction of feature representation vectors to be used in machine-learning models to make such predictions.

## References

1. Ahn, Y.-Y., Bagrow, J.P., Lehmann, S.: Link communities reveal multiscale complexity in networks. Nature. **466**(7307), 761–764 (2010). https://doi.org/10.1038/nature09182
2. Barabási, A.-L.: Network Science. Cambridge University Press, USA (2016). http://networksciencebook.com/chapter/9
3. Leskovec, J., Krevl, A.: SNAP Datasets: Stanford Large Network Dataset Collection (2014). http://snap.stanford.edu/data
4. Newman, M.E.J.: Assortative mixing in networks. Phys. Rev. Lett. **89**, 1 (2002). https://doi.org/10.1103/PhysRevLett.89.208701
5. Newman, M.E.J.: Mixing patterns in networks. Phys. Rev. E. **67**(2), 5–7 (2003). https://doi.org/10.1103/PhysRevE.67.026126

6. Noldus, R., Mieghem, P.V.: Assortativity in complex networks. J. Complex Netw. **3**(4), 507-542 (2015). ISSN: 2051-1310. https://doi.org/10.1093/comnet/cnv005, https://academic.oup.com/comnet/article-pdf/3/4/507/2328341/cnv005.pdf, https://doi.org/10.1093/comnet/cnv005

7. Piraveenan, M., Prokopenko, M., Zomaya, A.Y.: Local assortativeness in scale-free networks. EPL. **84**(2), 1–2 (2008). https://doi.org/10.1209/0295-5075/84/28002

8. Sendiña-Nadal, I., et al.: Assortativity and leadership emerge from antipreferential attachment in heterogeneous networks. Sci. Rep. **6**(1), 21297 (2016). https://doi.org/10.1038/srep21297. ISSN: 2045–2322

9. Tan, F., Xia, Y., Zhu, B.: link prediction in complex networks: a mutual information perspective. PLOS ONE. **9**(9), 6 (2014). https://doi.org/10.1371/journal.pone.0107056

10. Thedchanamoorthy, G.: New approaches and their applications in measuring mixing patterns of complex networks. Ph.D. thesis. (2014). http://hdl.handle.net/2123/13211

11. Yang, J., Leskovec, J.: Community-affiliation graph model for overlapping network community detection. In: 2012 IEEE 12th International Conference on Data Mining, p. 1179 (2012). https://doi.org/10.1109/ICDM.2012.139

12. Yang, J., Leskovec, J.: Overlapping communities explain core-periphery organization of networks. Proc. IEEE. **102**(12), 1897–1898 (2014). https://doi.org/10.1109/JPROC.2014.2364018

# Machine and Deep Learning

# The Implementation of the RISE Algorithm for the Captum Framework

Oscar Stanchi[1,3]($\boxtimes$) (iD), Franco Ronchetti[1,2] (iD), and Facundo Quiroga[1] (iD)

[1] Instituto de Investigación en Informática LIDI - Universidad Nacional de La Plata, La Plata, Argentina
[2] Comisión de Investigaciones Científicas de la Pcia. de Bs. As. (CIC-PBA), Tolosa, Argentina
[3] Becario Doctoral UNLP, La Plata, Argentina
ostanchi@lidi.info.unlp.edu.ar

**Abstract.** This paper introduces an implementation of the RISE method, using the Captum library in PyTorch. RISE is an algorithm that generates explanations for the predictions of a deep learning model by randomly masking parts of the input image and observing the changes in the model's output. Our focus is on the implementation and its performance, rather than on the RISE method itself. Through a series of experiments, we have obtained results that demonstrate the importance of the number of masks used in the RISE method. We found that the number of masks can have a significant impact on the interpretability of the outcome. Additionally, we conducted tests to determine the effect of mask size on the interpretability of the results. Our findings indicate that the size of the masks, whether larger or smaller, is also a decisive factor in achieving a good interpretable outcome. Furthermore, we demonstrate how tuning RISE parameters can yield in different results, making RISE effective for several tasks and neural network architectures. Overall, our implementation of RISE over Captum provides a powerful tool for interpreting deep learning models in PyTorch.

**Keywords:** Black Box · Computer Vision · Deep Learning · Interpretability · RISE

## 1 Introduction

Machine Learning is a branch of Artificial Intelligence that studies systems capable of learning to perform a task from example data [2,4]. In recent years the processing of text, sound, video and other signals has experienced great progress through the use of a Machine Learning technique called Deep Neural Networks or Deep Learning [11], which extends previous models of artificial neural networks with architectures and optimization algorithms that allow training networks with millions of parameters, based on large amounts of training data [2,4]. In Computer Vision the state-of-the-art has currently been achieved using

M. Naiouf et al. (Eds.): JCC-BD&ET 2023, CCIS 1828, pp. 91–104, 2023.
https://doi.org/10.1007/978-3-031-40942-4_7

Deep Learning, with a combination of Convolutional Neural Network (CNN) for visual feature extraction, combined with Recurrent Neural Networks (RNN) and Transformers, for temporal information processing [2].

However, Deep Learning models are currently classified as black box models due to their low level of interpretability, large number of parameters, and use of nonlinear functions [12]. While their interpretability is a task that has been in continuous progress in recent years, there are still many advances to be made to reveal the gap between the goals of Deep Learning models and the costs of putting them into real-world runs [19]. For this reason, the interpretability of a model is becoming increasingly important in this area. This field of AI research aims to study techniques to understand the causes and behaviors by which models generate certain outputs, and thus provide a way to understand and analyze them in human terms, thus enabling stakeholders to trust their use [6,12]. If people or user communities do not trust the model or its output, they will not use it [18]. Therefore, interpretability is now becoming a requirement, especially for systems that make high-risk decisions [12,19].

Some models have intrinsic or transparent interpretability [19], such as decision trees or linear/logistic regression. These methods are also known to be explainable at times [5,19]. In contrast, other models are not explainable on their own, for which post-hoc analysis is required to try to understand what they learned [6,12]. Post-hoc interpretability can also be classified as local, when applied to individual model outputs, or global, when applied to the entire output domain. Interpretability methods can also be classified based on whether they are model-specific, or model-agnostic [15]. Interpretability can be used in a diagnostic role to discover what the contribution of each of these different hidden layers in the models is, since without a correct understanding of how these networks work internally, the development of better models is limited to "trial and error" processes [7]. At the same time, understanding how a model works internally can also be useful in providing feedback to end users regarding how the model output was generated [3,7].

In this work we present an implementation of a technique called RISE (Randomized Input Sampling for Explanation) for the Captum model interpretability library, built on top of PyTorch, which improves the interpretability of black box neural networks [17]. RISE is a post-hoc and local method, focused on black box models (it does not require access to the internal parameters of the models) which generates an importance map (when its applied to images) that allows to visualize the regions of the image that were important for the prediction of a certain class. An importance map is a visualization technique used in interpretability methods for deep learning models. It is a heatmap that highlights the areas of an input image that are most important for the model's decision-making process.

RISE uses a technique similar to occlusion to generate masks and compute masked inputs within the neural network. A value is obtained for each mask and weighted with the corresponding mask importance to obtain an importance map. In Fig. 1, we can see some examples of importance maps generated by the algorithm RISE for a hare, a Siamese cat, a king penguin and an orangutan. RISE uses Monte-Carlo integration to approximate the integral value using random numbers. Monte-Carlo is a numerical integration technique that consists of writing the integral as an expected value, and then approximate it using the method of moment estimator.

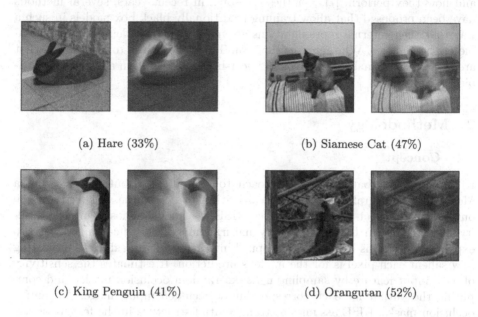

(a) Hare (33%)    (b) Siamese Cat (47%)

(c) King Penguin (41%)    (d) Orangutan (52%)

**Fig. 1.** Importance Maps generated by our RISE implementation.

## 1.1 Related Work

Some of the first specific techniques to emerge in this area were LIME [18] and SHAP [13], which offer a simple explanation without limiting the power of the original models. However, these techniques ignore the existence of the hidden layers, thus ignoring the exact performance of the model [7,15].

Other widely used interpretability methods are Occlusion and Grad-CAM. Occlusion systematically occludes different parts of the input image and observes the effect on the model's output [23]. On the other hand, Grad-CAM uses the gradients of the target class flowing into the final convolutional layer to produce a coarse localization map highlighting important regions in the image for predicting the target class [20].

Additional gradient-based solutions for interpreting models are Saliency Maps and Integrated Gradients. Saliency Maps is a method for computing the spatial support of a given class in a given image (image-specific class saliency map) using a single back-propagation pass through a classification CNN. This technique is based on computing the gradient of the class score with respect to the input image [21]. Meanwhile, Integrated Gradients requires no modification to the original network and uses only a few gradient computations. The method is based on two fundamental axioms: Sensitivity and Implementation Invariance that attribution methods ought to satisfy [22].

Despite the progress that has been made under the interpretability of CNNs and RNNs, there is still uncertainty in the internal behavior of these models and how they perform [7]. For these reasons, in recent years, several methods have been proposed that allow training traditionally black box models in such a way that their internal representations are more interpretable; a notable example of the Concept Whitening method [5]. Thus, the aim is to use models that are directly explainable, and avoiding post-hoc interpretation as much as possible [10].

## 2    Methodology

### 2.1    Concept

RISE is a perturbation-based approach to compute attribution, involving a Monte-Carlo integral approximation algorithm to detect the sensitivity of the output with respect to features. Since RISE is a model-agnostic interpretability method, it can be used in every natural images classification network to explain its decisions by generating a pixel importance map (saliency) indicating how salient each pixel is for the model's prediction. It estimates the sensitivity of each input feature by sampling `n_masks` random occlusion masks, and computing the output for each correspondingly occluded input image. To sample occlusion masks, RISE assumes a strong spatial structure in the feature space, so that features that are close to each other are more likely to be correlated. Each mask is assigned a score based on the output of the model. Afterwards, masks are averaged, using the score as a weight.

### 2.2    Technologies

In this work we chose to implement RISE within the Captum framework. Captum is a model interpretability library for PyTorch that makes it easier to implement interpretability algorithms that can interact with PyTorch models because it provides researchers and developers an easy way to understand which features are contributing to a model's output [9].

On the other hand, PyTorch is an open-source deep learning framework based on the Torch library that is known for its flexibility and ease-of-use [16]. PyTorch was designed to provide good flexibility and high speeds for deep neural network implementation, and this is enabled in part by its compatibility with the popular Python high-level programming language. In this paper we also used the torchvision package which provides many useful functions for computer vision tasks [14].

## 2.3 Background

Using RISE, the parameters required to set to calculate the importance map are the followings:

- $I$: input of size $H \times W$ in the space of color images $\mathcal{I} = \{I | I : \Lambda \to \mathbb{R}^3\}$ with $\Lambda = \{1, \ldots, H\} \times \{1, \ldots, W\}$.
- $M : \Lambda \to [0, 1]$: random binary bilinear upsampled mask set of $N$ elements.
- $f : \mathcal{I} \to \mathbb{R}$: black box model that for a given input produce a scalar confidence score (or a probability of some class in the present input).

The equation for the output of RISE for a given input pixel position $\lambda$ is:

$$S_{I,f}(\lambda) \overset{MC}{\approx} \frac{1}{\mathbb{E}[M] \cdot N} \sum_{i=1}^{N} f(I \odot M_i) \cdot M_i(\lambda)$$

$S_{I,f}$ is the importance map, explaining the decision of model $f$ on input image $I$, normalized to the expectation of $M$. The importance of a pixel $\lambda \in \Lambda$, is the score over all possible masks $M$ conditioned on the event that pixel $\lambda$ is observed, i.e., $M(\lambda) = 1$. Finally, $f(I \odot M_i)$ is a random variable that represents the model's output for the target class by performing the inference over the masked input, where $\odot$ denotes the Hadamard product (element-wise multiplication). Figure 2 shows the model overview with an example of how it works.

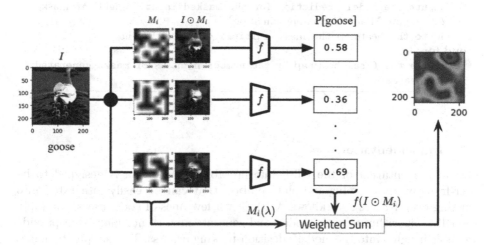

**Fig. 2.** RISE Model Overview & Example with input image. The algorithm generates a saliency map from a linear combination of random masks sub-sampled to the input images, where each weight is calculated as the output probability for the target class predicted by the model for each masked input image.

## 2.4  Pseudocode

We describe the steps to generate a set of masks and create the importance map in Algorithm 1 and Algorithm 2 respectively. Our formal implementation in Captum with full code from its development can be found in the project's repository[1].

---

**Algorithm 1.** Mask Generation

---

**Require:** input_shape = $(H \times W) \wedge$ initial_mask_shape = $(h \times w)$
**Ensure:** upsample_shape = $(((h + 1) \cdot \text{ceil}(H/h)) \times ((w + 1) \cdot \text{ceil}(W/w)))$
   for $i := 0 \to N$ do
      Create a binary mask$_i$ of size initial_mask_shape
      {//Convert Binary Mask to Smooth Mask}
      Apply bilinear interpolation with size upsampled_shape to mask$_i$
      Crop mask$_i$ randomly to it have a size of input_shape
      Store the resulting mask$_i$ inside the masks array or list
   end for
   return masks

---

**Algorithm 2.** Importance Map Generation

---

   for $i := 0 \to N$ do
      Compute the model prediction for the masked input (weight$_i$ of mask$_i$)
      {//Compute Monte Carlo approximation}
      Add to the heatmap the mask$_i$ multiplied by its weight$_i$
   end for
   Normalize the final heatmap by the number n_masks of masks generated
   return heatmap

---

## 2.5  Implementation

Our implementation of the RISE interpretability algorithm is designed to be user-friendly. It is a plug-and-play solution that can be easily integrated into existing deep learning workflows. With just a few lines of code, users can apply the RISE algorithm to their models and generate importance maps that provide valuable insights into the model's decision-making process. This simplicity makes it easy for researchers and practitioners to incorporate interpretability into their work and gain a better understanding of their models.

To use our implementation, simply import RISE from Captum's Attribution module and create an instance of it with the black box model forward function as an argument[2].

---

[1] https://github.com/indirivacua/captum-rise/tree/main.
[2] This is consistent with all other attribution constructors in Captum.

```
from captum.attr import RISE
#...
rise = RISE(forward_func)
heatmap = rise.attribute(inputs,
            n_masks=n_masks,
            initial_mask_shapes=(initial_mask_shape,),
            target=pred_label_idx,
            show_progress=True)
```

The `attribute` method from RISE class expect the following arguments and returns a Tensor or a tuple of Tensors:

```
def attribute(
    self,
    input_set: TensorOrTupleOfTensorsGeneric,
    n_masks: int,
    initial_mask_shapes: TensorOrTupleOfTensorsGeneric,
    baselines: BaselineType = None,
    target: TargetType = None,
    additional_forward_args: Any = None,
    show_progress: bool = False,
) -> TensorOrTupleOfTensorsGeneric:
```

Where the `input_set` are the inputs for which RISE attributions are computed. Depending if `forward_func` takes a single or multiple tensors as input, a single or a tuple of the input tensor should be provided. It is assumed that for all given input tensors, dimension 0 corresponds to the number of examples (batch size), and if multiple input tensors are provided, the examples must aligned appropriately.

Also `initial_mask_shapes` must be a Tensor or a tuple of Tensor which represent the initial mask shapes for each input of the model. A custom class named `MaskSetConfig` is in charge of computing the generation of the set of masks for the preconfigured input shapes, types and initial mask shapes. By default, it assumes each input is of shape `[B,C,D1,D2,D3]`, where B and C are the batch and channel dimensions which are ignored, and the final mask sizes are extracted as `[D1,D2,D3]`. Dimensions D2 and D3 are optional[3].

## 3    Experiments and Results

### 3.1    Experiments

We conducted an evaluation of our implementation through the use of ImageNet over an architecture of a Residual Network of 50 layers (ResNet50) for image

---

[3] Because of PyTorch's "interpolate" limitations, this only supports 5D inputs (3D masks) at most.

classification tasks. All images were cropped to 224 × 224 (the common input size for ImageNet). To the input images we applied a z-score normalization with mean = [0.485, 0.456, 0.406] and std = [0.229, 0.224, 0.225].

We also applied the method on FGR-NET, a state-of-the-art model that automatically assesses and interprets the quality of fundus images with high accuracy and F1-score [1]. The extracted features are then used to distinguish between gradable and ungradable fundus images. This is used in conjunction with another model to detect diabetic retinopathy. To evaluate RISE with FGR-NET model we used the EyeQ dataset, a subset ($\sim$ 25%) of EyePACS data [8]. The same normalization used for the tests on ImageNet was applied in this particular case, but the images were cropped to a size of 640 × 640 pixels.

The hardware used to compute the tests was a NVIDIA GTX 1060 6 GB for the first model (ResNet50, 25557032 parameters) and a NVIDIA Titan X Pascal 12 GB for the second (FGR-NET, 48019613 parameters). The Table 1 shows the runtimes for different numbers of masks on each configuration. The runtime increases significantly with the number of masks on the first one. Since each masked input needs to be evaluated, the algorithm requires a larger number of full inferences. However, the size of the mask does not significantly affect the computational time.

**Table 1.** Runtimes for different models, numbers and sizes of masks.

| Model | Number of masks | Size of masks | Runtime (min) |
|---|---|---|---|
| ResNet50 | 128 | 8 × 8 | 00:14 |
| ResNet50 | 8192 | 4 × 4 | 05:15 |
| ResNet50 | 8192 | 8 × 8 | 05:17 |
| ResNet50 | 8192 | 15 × 15 | 05:20 |
| FGR-NET | 8192 | 5 × 5 | 11:22 |

### 3.2   Results

In the following sub-sections we show a comparison between tuning the n_mask and initial_mask_shape arguments and how affect the RISE-generated importance maps. In the last sub-section, we also show how our implementation of RISE method perform with the FGR-NET model for gradability of fundus images.

**Sensitivity to the Number of Masks.** Figure 3 shows the results of applying the RISE interpretability method to a ResNet50 model trained on ImageNet. The experimental results show the areas of the image that were most important for the model's decision-making process. We notice that using a larger number of masks implies that the algorithm converges to a more reliable result.

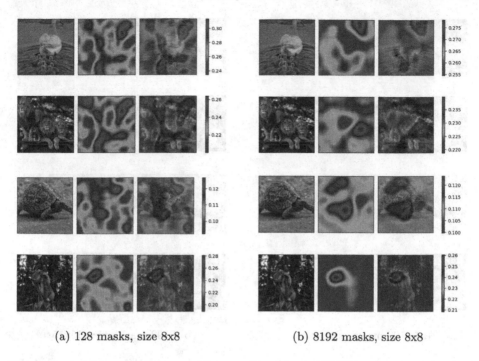

(a) 128 masks, size 8x8          (b) 8192 masks, size 8x8

**Fig. 3.** Comparison of importance maps generated by our RISE implementation using different numbers of masks.

Note that increasing the number of masks can significantly slow down its computation. As we mentioned in Sect. 2, the RISE method involves generating random masks and applying them to the input image to compute the importance of each pixel. The more masks used, the more computations are required, which can increase the time it takes to run the algorithm. The relation between the execution time and the convergence of the algorithm is directly proportional to the number of masks used.

**Sensitivity to Mask Size.** On the other hand, Fig. 4 shows the explanations generated by the RISE algorithm over a ResNet50 using weights from ImageNet. In this case we observe how the mask size affects the results. Bigger mask size cause more concentrated importance patches, which impact the efficacy of the method depending on the size of the objects in the image.

Therefore, the size of the masks determines the level of detail that the algorithm can capture in its importance maps. For example, if the problem involves identifying small objects or fine details in an image, larger masks may be more appropriate to accurately capture the relevant information. On the other hand, if the problem involves identifying larger objects or patterns, smaller masks may be more appropriate. Ultimately, the choice of mask size should be guided by the specific characteristics of the problem being addressed.

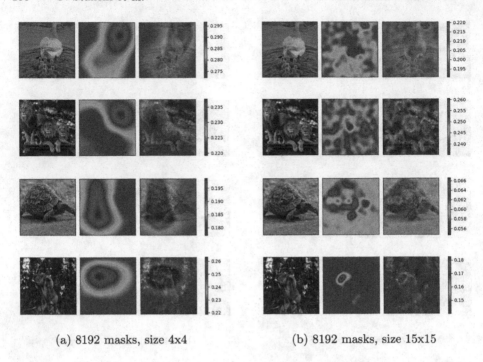

(a) 8192 masks, size 4x4                    (b) 8192 masks, size 15x15

**Fig. 4.** Comparison of importance maps generated by our RISE implementation using different mask sizes.

**Interpretability of Fundus Image Gradeability.** Finally, Fig. 5 shows a fundus image with multiple plots of interpretability algorithms applied to it. These algorithms include Saliency Maps (Gradient), Grad-CAM, Occlusion and RISE. Each plot provides a visualization of the areas in the image that the algorithm has determined to be most relevant for the model's decision-making process. By comparing the results of these different algorithms, we can gain a better understanding of how the model is evaluating the quality of the fundus image.

We can notice that all algorithms gave a similar result: the macula and the fovea are more important than the optic disc and the blood vessels. Similar results from multiple interpretability algorithms can indicate the correctness of the model used for a certain task.

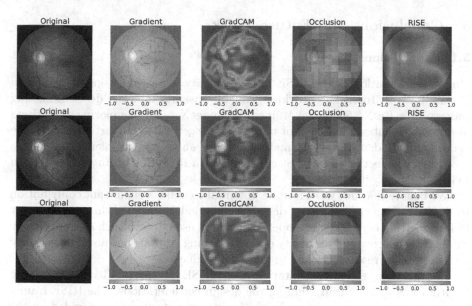

**Fig. 5.** Comparison of attribution methods computed over a gradable fundus images. RISE was computed with 8192 masks of size $5 \times 5$.

## 4    Discussion

When comparing RISE with Occlusion, it is notable that both methods are very similar. Their main differences are based on the generation of masks and the use of a reference score (accuracy) [23]. Occlusion generates masks that only hide one patch of the image at a time, similar to convolution operator, with a fixed window size and step. RISE, on the other hand, hides several patches at once, in addition to doing it with continuous (soft) masks. In Occlusion, the attribution is computed by the change in the output score when some part of the input example is "occluded" (i.e. set to zero), that score responds to the equation $\sigma = \|f(I) - f(I_{masked})\|$, where if $\sigma$ is large, then the patch must be important since removing it generates a great change in the output (an example of this technique can be seen in Fig. 6). In RISE, a score is not taken into consideration.

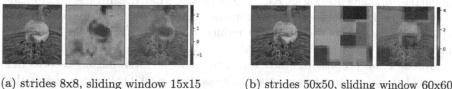

(a) strides 8x8, sliding window 15x15                (b) strides 50x50, sliding window 60x60

**Fig. 6.** Importance Maps generated by Occlusion using different parameters.

# 5   Conclusions and Future Work

## 5.1   Conclusions

Our implementation of the RISE interpretability algorithm using the Captum library from PyTorch has provided valuable insights into the decision-making process of a ResNet50 model trained on ImageNet. By comparing the effects of different numbers and sizes of masks on the generated importance maps, we can be able to identify the optimal settings for an specific problem. Also, it has proved to be effective in two distinct domains: a ResNet50 on ImageNet and an FGR-NET on EyeQ.

We believe that our work has the potential to make a significant contribution to the field of interpretability of deep learning models. By providing another way to indicate the correctness of models in a widely used library such as Captum, we can help to improve the reliability of deep learning systems for model developers, interpretability researchers and application engineers.

In conclusion, the implementation of the RISE interpretability method using Captum was successful in fulfilling the design considerations. The RISE framework proved to be very generic for the input and output shape provided by the user, and the return is an importance map that is ready to use. This implementation provides a valuable tool for understanding and validating machine learning models.

## 5.2   Future Work

In our future work, we plan to explore the use of different normalization techniques in the calculation of importance maps (output) or during execution (training). Normalization is a crucial step in the generation of importance maps, as it ensures that the values in the map are comparable and interpretable.

We also plan to investigate the potential benefits of changing the size of the masks used in the RISE algorithm during execution, using an adaptive solution which varies them based on objects on the input image. Our hypothesis is that this could improve the accuracy and interpretability of the generated importance maps. Additionally, we are working on a method to automatically select the best parameters for the algorithm in different scenarios and tasks.

Similarly, we found that there are problems and limitations associated with the current implementation of RISE. One issue is that it can take a significant number of masks to compute the importance maps. To address this, we propose implementing a stopping criteria to reduce the number of masks needed for convergence.

Moreover, we propose to study how black patches from masks, used to hide regions of an image, affect the output score of the model. Our proposition is that instead of using black patches, we could blur that region of the image, or average the colors of the masked section. The goal in this task is to explain if black patches filter classes, thus positively influencing the expected class prediction.

# References

1. AL Khalidy, S.K.M., Rashwan, H.A., Abdulwahab, S., Mohamed, M.A., Puig Valls, D.S., Quiroga, F.M.: Fgr-Net: interpretable fundus image gradeability classification based on deep reconstruction learning. Expert Syst. Appl. (2023)
2. Bragg, D., et al.: Sign language recognition, generation, and translation: an interdisciplinary perspective. In: Proceedings of the 21st International ACM SIGACCESS Conference on Computers and Accessibility, pp. 16–31 (2019)
3. Broniatowski, D.A., et al.: Psychological foundations of explainability and interpretability in artificial intelligence. Technical Report NIST (2021)
4. Carreira, J., Zisserman, A.: Quo vadis, action recognition? A new model and the kinetics dataset. In: Proceedings of the IEEE Conference on Computer Vision and Pattern Recognition, pp. 6299–6308 (2017)
5. Chen, Z., Bei, Y., Rudin, C.: Concept whitening for interpretable image recognition. Nat. Mach. Intell. **2**(12), 772–782 (2020)
6. Doshi-Velez, F., Kim, B.: Towards a rigorous science of interpretable machine learning. arXiv preprint: arXiv:1702.08608 (2017)
7. Escalante, H.J., et al.: Explainable and Interpretable Models in Computer Vision and Machine Learning. Springer, Cham (2018). https://doi.org/10.1007/978-3-319-98131-4
8. Fu, H., et al.: Evaluation of retinal image quality assessment networks in different color-spaces. In: Shen, D., et al. (eds.) MICCAI 2019, Part I. LNCS, vol. 11764, pp. 48–56. Springer, Cham (2019). https://doi.org/10.1007/978-3-030-32239-7_6
9. Kokhlikyan, N., et al.: Captum: a unified and generic model interpretability library for pytorch (2020)
10. Laugel, T., Lesot, M.J., Marsala, C., Renard, X., Detyniecki, M.: The dangers of post-HOC interpretability: unjustified counterfactual explanations. arXiv preprint: arXiv:1907.09294 (2019)
11. LeCun, Y., Bengio, Y., Hinton, G.: Deep learning. Nature **521**(7553), 436–444 (2015)
12. Lipton, Z.C.: The mythos of model interpretability: in machine learning, the concept of interpretability is both important and slippery. Queue **16**(3), 31–57 (2018)
13. Lundberg, S.M., Lee, S.I.: A unified approach to interpreting model predictions. In: Advances in Neural Information Processing Systems, vol. 30 (2017)
14. Maintainers, T., et al.: TorchVision: PyTorch's computer vision library, November 2016. https://github.com/pytorch/vision
15. Molnar, C., Casalicchio, G., Bischl, B.: Interpretable machine learning – a brief history, state-of-the-art and challenges. In: Koprinska, I., et al. (eds.) ECML PKDD 2020. CCIS, vol. 1323, pp. 417–431. Springer, Cham (2020). https://doi.org/10.1007/978-3-030-65965-3_28
16. Paszke, A., et al.: PyTorch: an imperative style, high-performance deep learning library. In: Wallach, H., Larochelle, H., Beygelzimer, A., d'Alché Buc, F., Fox, E., Garnett, R. (eds.) Advances in Neural Information Processing Systems 32, pp. 8024–8035. Curran Associates, Inc. (2019). http://papers.neurips.cc/paper/9015-pytorch-an-imperative-style-high-performance-deep-learning-library.pdf
17. Petsiuk, V., Das, A., Saenko, K.: Rise: randomized input sampling for explanation of black-box models. In: Proceedings of the British Machine Vision Conference (BMVC) (2018)
18. Ribeiro, M.T., Singh, S., Guestrin, C.: "why should i trust you?" Explaining the predictions of any classifier. In: Proceedings of the 22nd ACM SIGKDD International Conference on Knowledge Discovery and Data Mining, pp. 1135–1144 (2016)

19. Rudin, C.: Stop explaining black box machine learning models for high stakes decisions and use interpretable models instead. Nat. Mach. Intell. **1**(5), 206–215 (2019)
20. Selvaraju, R.R., Cogswell, M., Das, A., Vedantam, R., Parikh, D., Batra, D.: Grad-Cam: visual explanations from deep networks via gradient-based localization. In: Proceedings of the IEEE International Conference on Computer Vision, pp. 618–626 (2017)
21. Simonyan, K., Vedaldi, A., Zisserman, A.: Deep inside convolutional networks: visualising image classification models and saliency maps. arXiv preprint: arXiv:1312.6034 (2013)
22. Sundararajan, M., Taly, A., Yan, Q.: Axiomatic attribution for deep networks. In: International Conference on Machine Learning, pp. 3319–3328. PMLR (2017)
23. Zeiler, M.D., Fergus, R.: Visualizing and understanding convolutional networks. In: Fleet, D., Pajdla, T., Schiele, B., Tuytelaars, T. (eds.) ECCV 2014, Part I. LNCS, vol. 8689, pp. 818–833. Springer, Cham (2014). https://doi.org/10.1007/978-3-319-10590-1_53

# Drug Repurposing Using Knowledge Graph Embeddings with a Focus on Vector-Borne Diseases: A Model Comparison

Diego López Yse[1](✉) ⓘ and Diego Torres[1,2,3] ⓘ

[1] Universidad Austral, Buenos Aires, Argentina
diego.lopezyse@gmail.com
[2] LIFIA, CIBPBA-Facultad de Informática, UNLP, La Plata, Argentina
[3] Depto. CyT., Universidad Nacional de Quilmes, Bernal, Argentina

**Abstract.** Vector-borne diseases carried by mosquitoes, ticks, and other vectors are among the fastest-spreading and most extensive diseases worldwide, mainly active in tropical regions. Also, in the context of the current climate change, these diseases are becoming a hazard for other climatic zones. Hence, drug repurposing methods can identify already approved drugs to treat them efficiently, reducing development costs and time. Knowledge graph embedding techniques can encode biological information in a single structure that allows users to operate relationships, extract information, learn connections, and make predictions to discover potential new relationships between existing drugs and vector-borne diseases. In this article, we compared seven knowledge graph embedding models (TransE, TransR, TransH, UM, DistMult, RESCAL, and ERMLP) applied to Drug Repurposing Knowledge Graph (DRKG), analyzing their predictive performance over seven different vector-borne diseases (dengue, chagas, malaria, yellow fever, leishmaniasis, filariasis, and schistosomiasis), measuring their embedding quality and external performance against a ground-truth. Our analysis found that no single predictive model consistently outperformed all others across all diseases and proposed different strategies to improve predictive performance.

**Keywords:** Machine Learning · Knowledge Graphs · Knowledge Graph Embeddings · Drug repurposing · Vector-borne diseases · Biotechnology

## 1 Introduction

Vector-borne diseases are infections spread by the bite of infected arthropod species, such as mosquitoes and ticks. Additionally, certain vectors will have climate change as an ally for their habitat to grow even more, extending their habitable regions beyond the current ones [38]. This phenomenon seems to have materialized recently with autochthonous cases of chikungunya in Italy (2007) and France (2010 and 2014) and dengue in Spain, France, and Italy (2019 and 2020) [41].

M. Naiouf et al. (Eds.): JCC-BD&ET 2023, CCIS 1828, pp. 105–117, 2023.
https://doi.org/10.1007/978-3-031-40942-4_8

For these reasons, the inability to continue responding to such dynamic diseases with traditional drug development methods becomes clear. The traditional drug discovery path is a lengthy and expensive process, estimated to take 14 years, and cost approximately USD 1.8 billion to develop one drug [39]. As a consequence, the process of drug repurposing appears as an alternative to face this challenge.

Drug repurposing refers to identifying new indications for existing, discontinued, or under-development drugs as a way to maximize return on assets that were initially designed with different patient populations in mind. Repurposing drugs is attractive since, generally, drugs approved for an indication are more likely to be safe in a new indication and different patient population [6]. However, this process presents difficulties since, in biomedical research, the data is mainly fragmented and stored in databases that are generally not linked, hampering progress [23]. One way to tackle this problem is by using knowledge graphs, which can exploit diverse, dynamic, large-scale collections of data [24].

A Knowledge graph represents a network of real-world entities-i.e., objects, events, situations, or concepts, and illustrates their relationships [35]. Any object, place, or person can be an entity (or node), and an edge defines the relationship between entities. Knowledge graphs are represented as a collection of "head entity" - "relation" - "tail entity" triples (h, r, t), where entities correspond to nodes and relations to edges between them [48]. This representation can help to gain a contextualized understanding of data, helping to drive automation and process optimization, improve predictions, and enable an agile response to changing environments [5]. In this regard, knowledge graphs can support many biomedical applications [34] by representing diseases, compounds, genes, side-effects, and other related concepts as nodes (or entities), and establishing relationships between them, like for example "Ibuprofen, treats, Fever". Here, "Ibuprofen" and "Fever" are entities that are connected by the relationship "treats". The link or relationship is directed from the entity "Ibruprofen" to the entity "Fever", and is labeled as "treats". Entities can have types that further describe them and group them into categories. Following the example, "Ibuprofen" is a type of Compound, whereas "Fever" is a type of Disease. This conceptualization allows data integration from various domains, making knowledge graphs a highly flexible data structure [18]. Many biomedical knowledge graphs exist, systematically curating information and facilitating the discovery of new knowledge. Moreover, open-access knowledge graphs like Hetionet [23], PharmKG [49], and DRKG [26] integrate data from genes, drugs, and diseases.

In knowledge graphs terms, drug repurposing can be stated as a link prediction problem. This way, the aim is to predict unknown links between drug and disease entities, where a link between a drug-disease entity suggests that the drug treats the disease [17]. But traditional machine learning approaches applied to solving these challenges have many constraints, including dimensionality and incompleteness, sparsity, and heterogeneity [1].

While the native representation of a knowledge graph is high-dimensional, bringing high computation and space costs, there are methods to project the information into a lower-dimensional latent space that best preserves the graph structure [18] to perform tasks like link prediction more efficiently. Graph embedding methods convert graph data into a low dimensional space where the structural information and properties are maximumly preserved [10], allowing us to state the drug repurposing problem as a link prediction challenge in a vectorized space.

Differences between the various embedding algorithms are related to three aspects: (i) how they represent entities and relations, (ii) how they define the scoring function, and (iii) how they optimize the ranking criterion that maximizes the global plausibility of the existing triples [16]. Some of the embedding models that show state-of-the-art performance in knowledge graph completion relate to translation-based models that treat relations as translation operators over the entities in an embedding space [42] (e.g., TransE, TransR, TransH, UM). Alternatively, semantic matching models that use semantic similarity between entities and relations in the embedding space are commonly used for the task (e.g., DistMult, RESCAL, and ERMLP).

In recent years, embedding methods on knowledge graphs have been mainly focused on accelerating the drug repurposing process for Covid-19 [48], working retrospectively after the health crisis materialized. Reacting in hindsight over these challenges and developing solutions to face an individual disease instead of multiple or groups of diseases limit the impact these technologies might have on saving and improving human lives. Still, few efforts anticipate future health threats in a systematic way, particularly those that will be brought by climate change. Vector-borne diseases are becoming a worldwide hazard since climate alteration is the primary driver of the activity and migration of these vectors.

This paper analyzes the predictive performance of seven popular knowledge graph embedding models (TransE, TransR, TransH, UM, DistMult, RESCAL, and ERMLP) over seven different vector-borne diseases (dengue, chagas, malaria, yellow fever, leishmaniasis, filariasis, and schistosomiasis), measuring their embedding quality and external performance against a ground-truth. Our goal is not to develop the best overall model but to examine the differences in performance between models and diseases to identify gaps, trends, and opportunities in building a comprehensive drug repurposing system. We also validate all predictions against ground truth, analyzing the overall results and exploring further options to enhance our proposal.

This article is structured as follows: Sect. 2 describes related studies focused on drug repurposing using knowledge graphs. Section 3 introduces the main characteristics of knowledge graphs and the most promising ones related to our research. Section 4 describes our methodological approach to evaluate knowledge graph embedding models. Section 5 details our evaluation method to validate the predictions generated in Sect. 4. Section 6 analyzes and interprets our findings, explaining the significance of our results. Finally, Sect. 7 summarizes our work and establishes routes to enhance our proposal even further.

## 2   Related Work

Link prediction on knowledge graphs is the task of predicting unseen relations between two existing entities. Recent approaches to this activity rely on knowledge graph embedding methods [47], which learn a mapping from nodes and edges to a continuous vector space, preserving the proximity structure of the knowledge graph to run machine learning algorithms.

Some of the most popular translation-based embedding models used for drug repurposing include (i)TransE [31], which embeds entities and relations in the same vector space, and variants like (ii)TransH and (iii)TransR [13], designed to differently project entities depending on each relation type, meaning that they assign an entity with different representations when involved in various relation types.

Some of the main semantic matching embedding models for drug repurposing include (i)RESCAL [18], which applies a tensor to express the inherent structure of a knowledge graph and uses the rank-d factorization to obtain its latent semantics, (ii)DistMult [16], which simplifies the computational complexity of RESCAL and improves performance, (iii)UM [9], which models relation types similarly as entities and requires less parameters when the number of relation types grows, and (iv)ERMLP [2], a multi-layer perceptron based approach that uses a single hidden layer and represents entities and relations as vectors.

Regarding model predictions validation, while several studies [19] compare predicted drugs against a ground truth like ClinicalTrials.gov [46], others add validation steps (e.g., gene set enrichment analysis to further validate the predicted drug candidates [47]).

Most of the latest efforts in this field focus on predicting drug candidates for individual diseases, specially Covid-19 [17], without extending the analysis to other types of diseases. These approaches not only limit the scope of the proposals (can the predictive models perform well on other diseases?) but also misses identifying potential dynamics between diseases (do the predictive models respond similarly to related diseases?).

Additionally, most studies concentrate on validating the top-n predicted drugs against ground truth [14] for an apparent reason: since only a limited number of compounds can be experimentally screened, knowledge graph embedding models that achieve a high accuracy for the top predicted drug-disease combinations are preferred over models that might achieve a better overall precision but exhibit a lower accuracy among the top predictions [37]. But not analyzing the model's behaviors below those thresholds prevents us from understanding if predictive models that perform similarly within the threshold outperform others below it. Whatsmore, analyzing those patterns can help us to ensemble models that maximize predictive performance among top predictions.

## 3   Biomedical Knowledge Graphs

Knowledge graphs organize data from multiple sources, capturing information about entities of interest in a given domain or task, using a graph-structured data model or topology to integrate data. Contrary to relational databases, they store nodes and relationships instead of tables or documents. Find next some of the main publicly available biomedical knowledge graphs that can be used for drug repurposing:

- **Hetionet v1.0** [23] is an integrative network encoding knowledge from millions of biomedical studies. It consists of 47,031 nodes of 11 types and 2,250,197 relationships of 24 types. Data were integrated from 29 public resources to connect compounds, diseases, genes, anatomies, pathways, biological processes, molecular functions, cellular components, pharmacologic classes, side effects, and symptoms. The edges represent relationships between these nodes. It uses compiled information from databases for the following entity types: diseases from Disease Ontology [40], symptoms from Medical Subject Headings (MeSH) [30], compounds from DrugBank [45], side effects from SIDER [28], pharmacologic classes from DrugCentral [44], genes from Entrez Gene [32], anatomies from Uberon [33], pathways from WikiPathways [29], and biological processes, cellular components, and molecular from the Gene Ontology [4].
- **PharmKG** [49] is composed of more than 500,000 individual interconnections between genes, drugs, and diseases, with 29 relation types over a vocabulary of approximately 8,000 disambiguated entities. It was constructed based on 6 public databases that offered high-quality structured information, including OMIM [20], DrugBank, PharmGKB [22], Therapeutic Target Database (TTD) [11], SIDER and HumanNet [25], in combination with GNBR [36].
- **Drug Repurposing Knowledge Graph (DRKG)** [26] is a comprehensive biological knowledge graph relating genes, compounds, diseases, biological processes, side effects, and symptoms. It includes information from 6 existing databases: DrugBank, Hetionet, GNBR, String [43], IntAct [21] and DGIdb [15]. It consists of 97,238 entities belonging to 13 entity types; and 5,874,261 triples belonging to 107 edge types. For representing entities, DRKG uses an entity type identifier followed by a unique ID of the specific entity, e.g., Compound::DB00107, refers to the drug "Oxytocin" from the DrugBank database. For representing relations, DRKG uses a naming convention that combines the name of the data source, the name of the relation, and the types of head and tail entities involved, e.g., GNBR::J::Gene:Disease, refers to "a gene that has a role in the pathogenesis of a disease" from the GNBR database.

## 4   Methodological Approach for Evaluation

To perform a comparison of knowledge graph embedding models for drug repurposing on vector-borne diseases, we follow the protocols used in other works [48] and propose the following evaluation pipeline:

- **Select a knowledge graph.** Since the embedding models that will be evaluated must be run on top of a knowledge graph, the first step is to select a knowledge graph in line with the target problem. Because our target challenge is drug repurposing for vector-borne diseases, a knowledge graph covering those diseases with an adequate volume of triples should be selected.

- **Train and test embedding models on the knowledge graph**. After selecting a knowledge graph, we can train and test different embedding models. By doing so, we map the knowledge graph nodes and edges to a low-dimensional representation (preserving the proximity structure of the knowledge graph) to exploit it for applications like link prediction.
- **Perform link prediction on knowledge graph embeddings**. The embedding models are subsequently used for link prediction tasks to predict new triples or infer missing ones between non-connected nodes within the knowledge graph [37]. The result of this step is a ranked list of predictions.
- **Define a ground truth to validate predictions**. Besides measuring the internal performance of the embedding models, it becomes essential to validate the predicted results against some ground truth. For this reason, a proper source for external validation must be selected, covering the target diseases and an adequate volume of compounds that treat them.
- **Evaluate model predictions against ground truth**. Next, we validate the accuracy of each model prediction for all target diseases by measuring at which ranked position a predicted compound matches a ground truth one. An embedding model that hits all compounds existing on the ground truth source for a given disease using fewer predictions is considered better than another model that needs more predictions to hit the same number of ground truth compounds.

## 5   Evaluation

Knowledge graph embedding models are usually evaluated based on link prediction. For example, for a given query of the form "X, treats, dengue", the capability of a link predictor to predict the correct entities that answer the query, i.e. "metformin, treats, dengue" is measured. Nevertheless, since true negative examples are not available in our study (both the training and the test set contain only true facts), the evaluation procedure is defined as a ranking task in which the capability of the embedding model to differentiate corrupted triples from known true triples is assessed [2].

### 5.1   Metrics

For evaluating embedding models, we analyzed the ranking results of each one: (a)intrinsically, within the scope of the knowledge graph and its defined triples, and (b)externally against a ground truth to understand their predictive power over real-world information.

Following prior studies [8], we used two standard rank-based metrics to measure each embedding model's intrinsic performance on link prediction: Adjusted Mean Rank (AMR) and hits@k.

- **Adjusted Mean Rank(AMR)** [7] is the ratio of the Mean Rank to the Expected Mean Rank, assessing a model's performance independently of the underlying set size. It lies on the open interval (0,2), where lower is better.
- **Hits@k** measures the fraction of times when the correct or "true" entity appears under the top-k entities in the ranked list. The value of hits@k is between 0 and 1. The larger the value, the better the model works [12]. For our work, we estimated hits@1, hits@3, hits@5, and hits@10 metrics, which were calculated using Python's PyKEEN library [3].

To validate the embedding models externally, we analyzed the predicted ranked compound list against the actual treatment drugs defined in ground truth for those diseases using the following metrics:

- **First hit** is the ranking position at which compounds proposed by an embedding model match one from the ground truth database for a given disease.
- **Median hit** is the ranking position at which compounds proposed by an embedding model match 50% of the compounds from the ground truth database for a given disease.
- **Last hit** is the ranking position at which compounds proposed by an embedding model match all the compounds from the ground truth database for a given disease.

For all these metrics, the smaller the value, the better, meaning that a model with lower "first", "median", or "last hit" values compared to another one, matches real-world compounds using fewer predictions.

## 5.2 Data

Although several embedding models were identified in literature review [16], only a subset was selected due to computational constraints related to high training costs. For this reason, we evaluated seven popular knowledge graph embedding models, covering both translational distance (TransE, TransR, TransH, and UM) and semantic matching (DistMult, RESCAL, and ERMLP). These models were applied to seven vector-borne diseases (dengue, chagas, malaria, yellow fever, leishmaniasis, filariasis, and schistosomiasis) on DRKG dataset. We used ClinicalTrials.gov as our source of ground truth and evaluated each model's performance. All the code for this study is available via open-source licensing on GitHub at: https://github.com/dlopezyse/Drug-Repurposing-using-KGE

Following the methodological approach described in Sect. 4, first, we selected DRKG as our knowledge graph due to the volume of triples and the high representation of compound-disease interactions.

Next, we used PyKEEN 1.10 pipeline to train, test and validate all embedding models with 50 epochs, Marging Ranking as the loss function, and random seed = 1234 as the only predefined parameters. We configured Google Colab GPUs to run the models, and no hyperparameter optimization was performed due to computational constraints. All models were evaluated using Adjusted Mean Rank(AMR) and hits@k measures.

Within DRKG, we focused on the GNBR database (the most extensive for our target problem) and defined "GNBR::T::Compound:Disease" as the target relation to predict compounds that treat the mentioned diseases. We performed link predictions for each target disease using all previously-mentioned embedding models, resulting in seven different compound predictions by disease. The result of all embedding model predictions for each disease (49 in total) was a ranked list of the 97,238 DRKG entities, ordered by their predicted effectiveness in treating the target disease. Afterward, all predicted compound IDs were mapped to their original data sources to identify their names.

We used ClinicalTrials.gov as an external validation point to measure the quality of our predictions. After extracting all compounds used in ClinicalTrials.gov for the seven target diseases, compound names were normalized against those from our model's predictions. For example, in the case of malaria, "Paracetamol" (defined as a compound in ClinicalTrials.gov to treat the disease) was mapped to "Acetaminophen" (which exists in DRKG).

## 5.3   Results

As detailed in Table 1, performance metrics results were compared across all models, with the best outcomes highlighted in light blue.

**Table 1.** Embedding models metrics table.

| Model | AMR | Hits@1 | Hits@3 | Hits@5 | Hits@10 |
|---|---|---|---|---|---|
| TransE | 0.023 | 0.008 | 0.066 | 0.091 | 0.132 |
| TransH | 0.062 | 0.006 | 0.013 | 0.021 | 0.039 |
| TransR | 0.019 | 0.012 | 0.063 | 0.088 | 0.131 |
| DistMult | 0.039 | 0.015 | 0.035 | 0.049 | 0.076 |
| RESCAL | 1.000 | 0.000 | 0.000 | 0.000 | 0.000 |
| UM | 0.044 | 0.000 | 0.034 | 0.049 | 0.074 |
| ERMLP | 0.018 | 0.027 | 0.079 | 0.109 | 0.163 |

Results show that ERMLP was the best performer both on AMR (scoring the lowest value of 0.018) and hits@k metrics (exhibiting the highest values on all measures) from the seven embedding models, while RESCAL was the worst on all of them (scoring 1.000 on AMR and 0.000 on all hits@k measures).

We also collected all reported compounds for treating the seven target diseases from the ClinicalTrials.gov database to test the embedding model results against ground truth. Next, we validated whether the previously mentioned metrics represented real-world performance.

To evaluate the performance of this method, we reported the position at which compounds proposed by the models matched the ones from the ClinicalTrials.gov database for a given disease. Since we used DRKG, the best possible

position for a single predicted compound would be 1 (meaning that the first predicted compound by the model matched one defined in ClinicalTrials.gov for the
same disease), and the worst one 97,238 (the total number of entities in DRKG).
We also considered the number of compounds identified in ClinicalTrials.gov for
a given disease that existed in DRKG (matching compounds). This way, if we
had 5 compounds that existed both in DRKG and ClinicalTrials.gov for a given
disease, the best possible model would predict those compounds from positions
1 to 5, and the worst one, from positions 97,234 to 97,238.

Table 2 details the results for one of the seven targeted diseases (filariasis),
highlighting the best results in light blue.

**Table 2.** Filariasis metrics table.

| Filariasis - matching compounds: 11 | | | |
|---|---|---|---|
| Model | First hit | Median hit | Last hit |
| TransE | 117 | 716 | 6,798 |
| TransH | 1,048 | 29,513 | 61,479 |
| TransR | 1 | 238 | 5,381 |
| DistMult | 37 | 474 | 22,054 |
| RESCAL | 8,703 | 44,404 | 64,470 |
| UM | 19 | 4,448 | 86,238 |
| ERMLP | 164 | 894 | 58,562 |

Following these outcomes, we observed that 11 compounds were identified in
ClinicalTrials.gov to treat filariasis that also existed in DRKG. TransR was the
best-performing model by reaching a first hit ("albendazole") at position 1 of
its 97,238 ranked predictions, a median hit using 238 predictions, and matching
all 11 compounds with 5,381 ranked predictions.

We also present in Table 3 the top 5 drug repurposing candidates for filariasis,
predicted by their best-performing models as identified in Table 2. We detail the
compound name, its ranked position according to the model, and highlight in
green compounds that were learned during the model training process:

**Table 3.** Filariasis predicted compounds.

| Filariasis: top 5 predictions | | | |
|---|---|---|---|
| TransR | | DistMult | |
| Drug | Position | Drug | Position |
| Albendazole | 1 | Doxycycline | 37 |
| Azithromycin | 12 | Praziquantel | 177 |
| Praziquantel | 17 | Azithromycin | 230 |
| Rifampicin | 37 | Albendazole | 245 |
| Ivermectin | 153 | Ivermectin | 373 |

Results show that from the 11 matching compounds between DRKG and ClinicalTrials.gov for filariasis, the TransR model identified the first 5 using 153 ranked compounds, while DistMult did it using 373. Interestingly, while DistMult needed 37 ranked compounds to get the first hit, TransR got 4 matching compounds with the same number of predictions.

## 6   Discussion

When measuring internal model predictions using hits@k and AMR metrics, ERMLP was identified as the best-performing model. Nevertheless, when comparing model predictions against an external ground truth, results were diverse, except for the RESCAL model showing the worst performance consistently on all diseases.

Several models matched partial compounds against ground truth using less than 100 ranked predictions (e.g., TransE for dengue, TransR for malaria and filariasis). What's more, these matchings include compounds that were not learned during the model's training processes.

For diseases with a low or zero percentage of ground truth compounds in DRKG available for training (e.g., yellow fever), embedding models significantly underperformed and required thousands of ranked predictions to reach first matches against ground truth.

The methodological approach described in Sect. 4 can be easily tested for enhancements incorporating techniques like hyperparameter optimization, graph filtering, and different loss functions for model training. From a modeling perspective, additional embedding models should be explored, and different combinations of dataset splits and loss functions to identify their impact on performance.

Additionally, it is possible to restrict model performance evaluation to our relations of interest (e.g., "Compound treats Disease") to identify models more appropriate for drug repositioning during hyperparameter optimization instead of good ones at predicting all types of relations.

Finally, expanding the ground truth to other databases besides ClinicalTrials.gov might help to identify additional hits and potential drugs for repurposing.

## 7   Conclusions and Further Work

This article compared seven knowledge graph embedding models applied to DRKG, focusing on seven specific vector-borne diseases. We introduced an evaluation pipeline to assess the embedding models for drug repurposing tasks, measuring their performance using internal metrics and a ground truth source.

Ensembling strategies should be explored by combining multiple knowledge graphs embedding models to exploit their complementary aspects.

Alternative performance evaluation metrics like AUROC, Precision-Recall curve, F1 score, Mean Reciprocal Rank, NDCG, or Average Precision should be considered for broader model comparison and understanding.

Lastly, developing additional evaluation criteria (e.g., molecular analysis [27]) could further increase the success rate of drug-repurposed candidates in laboratory validation.

# References

1. Abbas, K., et al.: Application of network link prediction in drug discovery. BMC Bioinform. **22**(1), 1–21 (2021). https://doi.org/10.1186/s12859-021-04082-y
2. Ali, M., et al.: Bringing light into the dark: a large-scale evaluation of knowledge graph embedding models under a unified framework. IEEE Trans. Pattern Anal. Mach. Intell. **44**(12), 8825–8845 (2022). https://doi.org/10.1109/tpami.2021.3124805
3. Ali, M., et al.: PyKEEN 1.0: a python library for training and evaluating knowledge graph embeddings. J. Mach. Learn. Res. (2021)
4. Ashburner, M., et al.: Gene ontology: tool for the unification of biology. Nat. Genet. **25**(1), 25–29 (2000). https://doi.org/10.1038/75556
5. Barrasa, J., Hodler, A.E., Webber, J.: Knowledge Graphs. O'Reilly Media (2021)
6. Barratt, M.J., Frail, D.: Drug Repositioning: Bringing New Life to Shelved Assets and Existing Drugs. John Wiley & Sons, Hoboken (2012)
7. Berrendorf, M., Faerman, E., Vermue, L., Tresp, V.: On the ambiguity of rank-based evaluation of entity alignment or link prediction methods (2020)
8. Bonner, S., et al.: Understanding the performance of knowledge graph embeddings in drug discovery. Artif. Intell. Life Sci. **2**, 100036 (2022). https://doi.org/10.1016/j.ailsci.2022.100036
9. Bordes, A., Glorot, X., Weston, J., Bengio, Y.: A semantic matching energy function for learning with multi-relational data. Mach. Learn. **94**(2), 233–259 (2013). https://doi.org/10.1007/s10994-013-5363-6
10. Cai, H., Zheng, V.W., Chang, K.C.C.: A Comprehensive Survey of Graph Embedding: Problems, Techniques and Applications (2018). http://arxiv.org/abs/1709.07604, number: arXiv:1709.07604arXiv:1709.07604 [cs]
11. Chen, X.: TTD: therapeutic target database. Nucl. Acids Res. **30**(1), 412–415 (2002). https://doi.org/10.1093/nar/30.1.412
12. Chen, Z., Wang, Y., Zhao, B., Cheng, J., Zhao, X., Duan, Z.: Knowledge graph completion: a review. IEEE Access **8**, 192435–192456 (2020). https://doi.org/10.1109/access.2020.3030076
13. Choi, W., Lee, H.: Inference of biomedical relations among chemicals, genes, diseases, and symptoms using knowledge representation learning. IEEE Access. **7**, 179373–179384 (2019). https://doi.org/10.1109/ACCESS.2019.2957812, https://ieeexplore.ieee.org/document/8931752/
14. Cohen, S., et al.: Improved and optimized drug repurposing for the SARS-COV-2 pandemic (2022). https://doi.org/10.1101/2022.03.24.485618
15. Cotto, K.C., et al.: DGIdb 3.0: a redesign and expansion of the drug–gene interaction database. Nucl. Acids Res. **46**(D1), D1068–D1073 (2017). https://doi.org/10.1093/nar/gkx1143, https://doi.org/10.1093/nar/gkx1143
16. Dai, Y., Wang, S., Xiong, N.N., Guo, W.: A survey on knowledge graph embedding: approaches, applications and benchmarks. Electronics. **9**(5), 750 (2020). https://doi.org/10.3390/electronics9050750, https://www.mdpi.com/2079-9292/9/5/750
17. Doshi, S., Chepuri, S.P.: A computational approach to drug repurposing using graph neural networks. Comput. Biol. Med. **150**, 105992 (2022). https://doi.org/10.1016/j.compbiomed.2022.105992

18. Ratajczak, F., et al.: Task-driven knowledge graph filtering improves prioritizing drugs for repurposing. BMC Bioinform. **23**, 84 (2022). https://doi.org/10.1186/s12859-022-04608-y, https://bmcbioinformatics.biomedcentral.com/articles/10.1186/s12859-022-04608-y

19. Gao, Z., Ding, P., Xu, R.: KG-predict: A knowledge graph computational framework for drug repurposing. J. Biomed. Inform. **132**, 104133 (2022). https://doi.org/10.1016/j.jbi.2022.104133

20. Hamosh, A.: Online mendelian inheritance in man (OMIM), a knowledgebase of human genes and genetic disorders. Nucl. Acids Res. **33**(Database issue), D514–D517 (2004). https://doi.org/10.1093/nar/gki033

21. Hermjakob, H.: IntAct: an open source molecular interaction database. Nucl. Acids Res. **32**(90001), 452D–455 (2004). https://doi.org/10.1093/nar/gkh052

22. Hewett, M.: PharmGKB: the pharmacogenetics knowledge base. Nucl. Acids Res. **30**(1), 163–165 (2002). https://doi.org/10.1093/nar/30.1.163

23. Himmelstein, D.S., et al.: Systematic integration of biomedical knowledge prioritizes drugs for repurposing. eLife **6**, e26726 (2017). https://doi.org/10.7554/eLife.26726

24. Hogan, A., et al.: Knowledge graphs. ACM Comput. Surv. **54**(4), 1–37 (May 2022). https://doi.org/10.1145/3447772

25. Hwang, S., et al.: HumanNet v2: human gene networks for disease research. Nucl. Acids Res. **47**(D1), D573–D580 (2018). https://doi.org/10.1093/nar/gky1126

26. Ioannidis, V.N., et al.: DRKG - Drug Repurposing Knowledge Graph for Covid-19 (2020)

27. Islam, M.K., et al.: Molecular-evaluated and explainable drug repurposing for COVID-19 using ensemble knowledge graph embedding. Sci. Rep. **13**(1), 3643 (2023). https://doi.org/10.1038/s41598-023-30095-z

28. Kuhn, M., Letunic, I., Jensen, L.J., Bork, P.: The SIDER database of drugs and side effects. Nucl. Acids Res. **44**(D1), D1075–D1079 (2015). https://doi.org/10.1093/nar/gkv1075

29. Kutmon, M., et al.: WikiPathways: capturing the full diversity of pathway knowledge. Nucl. Acids Res. **44**(D1), D488–D494 (2015). https://doi.org/10.1093/nar/gkv1024

30. Lipscomb, C.E.: Medical subject headings (MeSH). Bull. Med. Libr. Assoc. **88**(3), 265–266 (2000)

31. Ma, C., Liu, H., Zhou, Z., Koslicki, D.: Predicting drug repurposing candidates and their mechanisms from a biomedical knowledge graph. bioRxiv (2022). https://doi.org/10.1101/2022.11.29.518441, https://www.biorxiv.org/content/early/2022/12/02/2022.11.29.518441

32. Maglott, D., Ostell, J., Pruitt, K.D., Tatusova, T.: Entrez gene: gene-centered information at NCBI. Nucl. Acids Res. **39**(Database), D52–D57 (2010). https://doi.org/10.1093/nar/gkq1237

33. Mungall, C.J., Torniai, C., Gkoutos, G.V., Lewis, S.E., Haendel, M.A.: Uberon, an integrative multi-species anatomy ontology. Genome Biol. **13**(1), R5 (2012). https://doi.org/10.1186/gb-2012-13-1-r5

34. Nicholson, D.N., Greene, C.S.: Constructing knowledge graphs and their biomedical applications. Comput. Struct. Biotechnol. J. **18**, 1414–1428 (2020). https://doi.org/10.1016/j.csbj.2020.05.017, https://linkinghub.elsevier.com/retrieve/pii/S2001037020302804

35. What is a Knowledge Graph? — IBM — ibm.com. https://www.ibm.com/topics/knowledge-graph. Accessed 14 Mar 2023

36. Percha, B., Altman, R.B.: A global network of biomedical relationships derived from text. Bioinformatics **34**(15), 2614–2624 (2018). https://doi.org/10.1093/bioinformatics/bty114
37. Rivas-Barragan, D., Domingo-Fernández, D., Gadiya, Y., Healey, D.: Ensembles of knowledge graph embedding models improve predictions for drug discovery. Brief. Bioinform. **23**(6), bbac481 (2022). https://doi.org/10.1093/bib/bbac481
38. Ryan, S.J., Carlson, C.J., Mordecai, E.A., Johnson, L.R.: Global expansion and redistribution of Aedes-borne virus transmission risk with climate change. PLOS Negl. Trop. Dis. **13**(3), e0007213 (2019). https://doi.org/10.1371/journal.pntd.0007213
39. Sang, S., et al.: GrEDeL: a knowledge graph embedding based method for drug discovery from biomedical literatures. IEEE Access. **7**, 8404–8415 (2019). https://doi.org/10.1109/ACCESS.2018.2886311, https://ieeexplore.ieee.org/document/8574025/
40. Schriml, L.M., et al.: Disease ontology: a backbone for disease semantic integration. Nucl. Acids Res. **40**(D1), D940–D946 (2011). https://doi.org/10.1093/nar/gkr972
41. Semenza, J.C., Paz, S.: Climate change and infectious disease in Europe: impact, projection and adaptation. The Lancet Reg. Health - Europe. **9**, 100230 (2021). https://doi.org/10.1016/j.lanepe.2021.100230, https://linkinghub.elsevier.com/retrieve/pii/S2666776221002167
42. Song, H.J., Kim, A.Y., Park, S.B.: Learning translation-based knowledge graph embeddings by n-pair translation loss. Appl. Sci. **10**(11), 3964 (2020). https://doi.org/10.3390/app10113964, https://www.mdpi.com/2076-3417/10/11/3964
43. Szklarczyk, D., et al.: STRING v11: protein–protein association networks with increased coverage, supporting functional discovery in genome-wide experimental datasets. Nucl. Acids Res. **47**(D1), D607–D613 (2018). https://doi.org/10.1093/nar/gky1131
44. Ursu, O., et al.: DrugCentral: online drug compendium. Nucl. Acids Res. **45**(D1), D932–D939 (2016). https://doi.org/10.1093/nar/gkw993
45. Wishart, D.S., et al.: DrugBank 5.0: a major update to the DrugBank database for 2018. Nucl. Acids Res. **46**(D1), D1074–D1082 (2017). https://doi.org/10.1093/nar/gkx1037
46. Zarin, D.A., Tse, T., Williams, R.J., Califf, R.M., Ide, N.C.: The ClinicalTrials.gov results database — update and key issues. New England J. Med. **364**(9), 852–860 (2011). https://doi.org/10.1056/nejmsa1012065
47. Zeng, X., et al.: repurpose open data to discover therapeutics for COVID-19 using deep learning. J. Prot. Res. **19**(11), 4624–4636 (2020). https://doi.org/10.1021/acs.jproteome.0c00316
48. Zhang, R., Hristovski, D., Schutte, D., Kastrin, A., Fiszman, M., Kilicoglu, H.: Drug repurposing for COVID-19 via knowledge graph completion. J. Biomed. Inform. **115**, 103696 (2021). https://doi.org/10.1016/j.jbi.2021.103696, https://www.sciencedirect.com/science/article/pii/S1532046421000253
49. Zheng, S., et al.: PharmKG: a dedicated knowledge graph benchmark for bomedical data mining. Brief. Bioinform. **22**(4), bbaa344 (2020). https://doi.org/10.1093/bib/bbaa344

# An Analysis of Satellite-Based Machine Learning Models to Estimate Global Solar Irradiance at a Horizontal Plane

Paula Iturbide[1]([✉]) [iD], Rodrigo Alonso-Suarez[2] [iD], and Franco Ronchetti[3,4] [iD]

[1] Grupo de Estudios de la Radiación Solar (GERSolar), Instituto de Ecología y Desarrollo Sustentable (INEDES), Univ. Nacional de Luján, 6700 Buenos Aires, CP, Argentina
paula.iturbide@sas.com
[2] Laboratorio de Energía Solar, Facultad de Ingeniería, Universidad de la República, Montevideo, Uruguay
[3] Instituto de Investigación en Informática LIDI, Universidad Nacional de la Plata, Buenos Aires, Argentina
[4] Comisión de Investigaciones Científicas de la Pcia. de Buenos Aires (CICPBA), Buenos Aires, Argentina

**Abstract.** Accurate solar resource information is a fundamental requirement for solar energy ventures. The lack of precision in solar radiation data can significantly affect the success of the projects. Argentina has solar radiation ground measurement networks. The information obtained through this method is limited due to its spatial sparsity, since it is only possible to measure with appropriate quality in some sites across the territory. To overcome this limitation, it is common to generate models capable of estimating solar radiation through satellite images, which provide spatial resolution. This work develops and validates an empirical model for this purpose based on Machine Learning (ML), demonstrating that it is a useful and accurate tool to be considered. This allows ventures that make use of this type of energy to have greater certainty in the availability of the resource, and therefore in the decision-making process. Variables obtained from images of the geostationary meteorological satellite GOES-16, McClear clear-sky model estimates, and geometrically calculated information are used as input to the algorithms. The results of the ML models are compared with estimates from pre-existing models for the region that incorporate physical modelings, such as Heliosat-4 and CIMESRA. The evaluation shows a higher performance of the ML methods when multi-scale satellite information is used as input. The incorporation of multi-scale satellite data is not yet implemented in solar radiation physical modeling, which is an advantage of ML modeling.

**Keywords:** First keyword · Second Keyword · Third Keyword

## 1 Introduction

There are different ways to estimate solar radiation from satellites. One type of model, called physical models, attempts to solve the radiative transfer equations of solar radiation through the atmosphere. To do this, they use the information on atmospheric components

M. Naiouf et al. (Eds.): JCC-BD&ET 2023, CCIS 1828, pp. 118–128, 2023.
https://doi.org/10.1007/978-3-031-40942-4_9

that influence the absorption and scattering of solar radiation. Their performance depends on the quality with which these variables are known, which are operationally estimated by satellite through inverse problems or by atmospheric models. An-other type of model, called statistical or empirical, does not attempt to model the physical attenuation phenomena through the atmosphere but adjusts the estimates to ground measurements using a set of coefficients or parameters. These models are therefore simpler to calculate but may have extrapolation problems to other sites where local conditions can be different. An intermediate category is that of hybrid models (semi-empirical), where a physical basis is assumed and parameters with physical meaning are adjusted to ground data.

Among the satellite models available for the Pampa Humeda region with a physical basis, some that are particularly relevant for this work are the CIM-ESRA [9] and the Heliosat-4 [19]. The first is a semi-empirical model based on information from the visible channel of the GOES-16 satellite (located at latitude 75° W), operated by NOAA, while the second is a physical model based on information from the European Meteosat Second Generation (MSG) satellite, located at the Greenwich meridian.

The CIM-ESRA model replicates the strategy used by other satellite models such as SUNY [16, 18] or Heliosat-2 [21]. In these models, global horizontal irradiance (GHI) is estimated as the irradiation that would occur under clear sky conditions modulated by an empirical factor based on a cloudiness index (CIM is due to Cloud Index Model) obtained from satellite images. That is,

$$I = I_{cs}F(C) \tag{1}$$

where I is the estimated solar irradiance, Ics is the irradiance that would occur under clear sky conditions (estimated by a clear sky model), and F is a cloud attenuation factor adjusted locally (or regionally) that depends on a cloudiness index (C). CIM-ESRA uses the ESRA clear sky model [21], whose only input variable is the Linke turbidity for an air mass equal to two, TL [12]. This variable represents the state of the cloud-free atmosphere using a single parameter, which models the aerosols and water vapor effects. The CIM-ESRA model uses seasonal average cycles of TL for its operation [10].

The operational model of the Copernicus Atmosphere Monitoring Service (CAMS) is Heliosat-4 [19]. This model consists of two combined physical sub-models: McClear [11], which estimates irradiance under clear sky conditions, and McCloud, which adds the effect of cloudiness. Both McClear and McCloud are based on outputs from the radiative transfer model LibRadTran [4], which is computationally expensive. McClear uses inputs such as aerosols properties, the precipitable water column, and ozone obtained from the CAMS reanalysis database (atmospheric modeling), as well as daily estimates of land surface albedo obtained from the MODIS satellite instrument (a low-earth orbit meteorological satellite). McCloud estimates the attenuation of solar radiation in the presence of clouds with MSG images, and the use of an adapted APOLLO/SEV methodology [7]. The Heliosat-4 estimates are available as a free internet service for the geographic coverage of the MSG satellite and are widely used (on the other hand, the McClear model is available with global coverage).

Currently, machine learning techniques such as artificial neural networks (ANN), k-nearest neighbors (kNN), support vector regression (SVR), extreme learning machines (ELM), and tree-based ensembles are also used to estimate solar radiation [5]. The input variables used in some works include the month, latitude, longitude, and altitude, as well as meteorological variables such as vapor pressure, land surface temperature, day length, temperature, humidity, precipitation, cloudiness, wind speed, evaporation, and the global solar radiation is the output of the models [20]. The data is divided into training and validation sets, the models are trained with the training set and validated with the remaining data.

Other works use an empirical clear sky model combined with variables such as temperature, humidity, and pressure obtained from available meteorological databases on land as input to a neural network [6]. A second work in this same line uses values from meteorological stations similar to those mentioned above [22], proposing different models (different combinations of input variables) all based on neural networks. A third work [15] compares the use of neural networks for different sky conditions where, according to the authors, they find poor performance. All these works make use of ground measurements. Works using satellite information under the ML framework are scarce for solar radiation [5, 23]. It is interesting to note that the use of ground-based measurements limits the estimation tools significantly, both in terms of data availability and extrapolation capacity to sites where there are no ground measurements. Satellite information does not have these limitations, as it is accessible and available, even operationally, and is capable of observing all points in large continental regions with spatial resolution suitable for solar energy projects (the pixel width is typical of 1 km, enough to model a large-scale solar photovoltaic plant). Therefore, satellite-based methods have a much higher potential.

## 2   Materials and Methods

### 2.1   Ground-Based Measurements

The GERSolar R&D group manages a ground-based solar radiation measurement network that covers the Buenos Aires Province. The global horizontal irradiance (GHI) measurements are recorded in all stations with a 1-min resolution, being the most common solar radiation data. In this work, a 10-min time scale is used, which is the same as the GOES-16 satellite image rate. Therefore, the minute resolution ground data are averaged to obtain their 10-min value, following the criterion that each average should have at least 2/3 of the corresponding minute data. The quality of measurements is a prerequisite for any meaningful use. The 10-min GHI data series were subjected to a quality control algorithm consisting of four successive filters (Table 1) and a visual inspection of the series to eliminate shading periods or other anomalous data. The selected filters are standard in the field [14]. The objective of the quality procedure is to select a typical data set, where missing, anomalous, or error-affected data, and measurements affected by isolated or short-lived phenomena (such as over-irradiance) are excluded [2].

The first filter sets a minimum solar altitude of 7° and excludes samples taken during sunrise and sunset. This filter aims to eliminate ground data with higher relative error due to the measuring equipment, which presents known directional errors at high incidence angles. The second filter uses a widely used criterion that establishes a range of values for extremely rare cases. This criterion is based on the solar zenith angle [13] and is recommended by the worldwide Baseline Solar Radiation Network (BSRN). The third

**Table 1.** Filters applied to ground-based measurements

| Filter | Criterion | Description |
|--------|-----------|-------------|
| 1 | $\alpha_s > 7^\circ$ | Minimun solar height |
| 2 | $-2W/m^2 < I_h < I_0 . 1.2 . cos\theta_z^{1.2} + 50W/m^2$ | BSRN levels (Long y Shi, 2008) |
| 3 | $0W/m^2 < I_h < I_h^{ESRA}(TL = 1.8)$ | Elevations of a clear sky model |
| 4 | $ktp < 0.89$ | Bound Perez clarity index |

filter imposes an upper limitation on the measured values, which correspond to clear sky conditions. This filter uses the ESRA model with very low atmospheric turbidity (TL = 1.8), which ensures an upper limit for GHI [1]. Finally, the fourth filter imposes a maximum value on the modified clearness index by Perez et al. [17]. The modified clearness index is defined as a regular clearness index (the GHI normalized by its corresponding top-of-the-atmosphere value) but without its dependence on solar altitude. In summary, each filter has its own criteria and is used to exclude inaccurate or unreliable data. In this section, the results for the Luján station operated by GERSolar along with INTA for the years 2019–2021 are shown, and its precise location is indicated in Table 2.

**Table 2.** Location of the measurement station and its measurement equipment. The total number N (filtered) corresponds to the reliable 10-min measurements in the 2019–2021 period.

| Estation | Latitude (Degrees) | Longitude (Degrees) | Equipment | N Totals (leaked data) |
|----------|--------------------|--------------------|-----------|------------------------|
| **Luján, ARG** | −34.558 | −59.062 | CMP11 & CMP21 | 62,592 |

The solarimetric station in Luján has data loggers from Campbell Scientific and uses two Kipp & Zonen CMP11 and CMP21 pyranometers as measurement equipment. These devices are Class A according to the equipment classification standard for solar radiation measurement (ISO 9060:2018). The data series was assembled by selecting the higher quality equipment during any concurrent measurement period, and one of the data series was chosen when the other device failed or the measurement had errors. Figure 1 shows the distribution of the data points for the period considered in this article, after the series underwent the quality control. The white gaps correspond to missing data.

## 2.2  Satellite Images

The visible channel images (C02 channel, centered at 0.64 μm) of the GOES-16 meteorological geostationary satellite were used. This satellite is part of the geostationary satellite network for Earth observation that covers the entire globe. This particular satellite is operated by the National Oceanic and Atmospheric Administration (NOAA) of the United States and has been generating images for the entire American continent since 2018 with a time interval between 10 and 15 min. The satellite is located over the

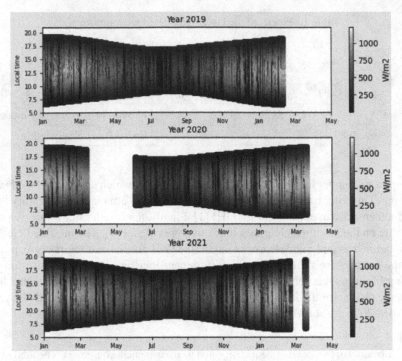

**Fig. 1.** Plot of ground data after subjecting it to quality control algorithms.

Earth's equator at −75°W longitude in geostationary orbit. Its spatial resolution varies along the image, being 500 m at its nadir. Over the Pampa Húmeda region, the pixel size varies between 1 and 3 km. The visible channel is suitable for estimating solar radiation because diurnal cloudiness is recognizable and quantifiable. Clouds are typically more reflective than the background (the Earth's surface), and therefore distinguishable.

The two classical variables calculated from visible channel satellite images are the reflectance factor (FR) and the planetary reflectance (RP). The latter is also known as Earth albedo and is denoted as ρ. The FR is a normalization of the radiance measured by the satellite from each pixel with respect to the maximum it is capable of measuring (i.e., the solar radiation incident on the top of the atmosphere normalized by the spectral response of the satellite radiometer). It is therefore in the interval [0, 1] and contains, in addition to daylight cloudiness information, spatial information about the variable illumination of the Sun over the Earth's surface. The quantity RP contains the additional normalization to remove this spatial dependence and is effectively the reflectivity of the Earth, in its strict physical sense.

## 2.3 Data Set Configuration

The following input variables were used for the machine learning algorithms:

- Cos(z) - Cosine of the solar zenith angle. It is the angle between the local zenith (the local vertical) and the Sun's direction. This quantity varies instantaneously according to the relative movement between Earth and the Sun and also depends on the position on Earth's surface (latitude and longitude of the site).
- McClear estimates - The McClear clear sky model is widely used in solar radiation simulation. Its main advantages include that the estimates are freely available to download, and that it is one of the most accurate models [24]. The model was developed by Lefèvre et al. [11] and uses atmospheric information such as pressure, temperature, humidity, and aerosol optical thickness. The model employs a physics simulation algorithm based on radiative transfer calculations and atmospheric modeling to estimate direct, diffuse, and global solar radiation under clear sky conditions for a specific location. These estimates were downloaded here from the CAMS web portal.
- Multiscale satellite information (F01-F18 and R01-R18) - These are spatial averages of the Reflectance Factor and Earth Albedo, respectively, in square latitude-longitude cells of incremental size. The numbers from 01 to 18 indicate the increasing cell size in which the satellite information is averaged, meaning cell sides from $0.01°$ to $0.90°$ respectively. The relationship between the cell side and numbering is not linear. For smaller cell sizes, the spacing between sides has a higher resolution, and vice versa for larger cell sizes.

## 2.4 Definition of Training and Validation Sets

The aim of the ML algorithms is to learn how to estimate GHI from satellite data by adjusting their parameters to ground measurements. The annual seasonality of GHI is characteristic. Hence, it is an adequate choice to select the training and testing data sets on an annual basis. A data set corresponding to two of the three available years was used for training and the remaining year for validation. This was done for all possible year permutations. Taking the validation set in this way avoids three possible biases. The first one is related to the random distribution of data in the training and validation sets as consecutive time samples can be very similar to each other. The second one is related to the particularities of each year as one year could be sufficiently different from another. The third one is related to incomplete data as there is a two-month gap in 2020 that was unrecoverable, and for the years 2019 and 2021, the month of December is missing.

## 2.5 Supervised Learning Models

Three ML models were considered: a linear multiple regression, which allows for a quick white box estimation; a Feed Forward Neural Network that uses a 100 neurons hidden layer, ReLU activation function, and Adam optimizer; and a Random Forest with 30 estimators. The latter two are non-linear models.

## 3   Results and Discussion

### 3.1   Performance Reference

GHI estimations from the CIM-ESRA and Heliosat-4 satellite models were downloaded for the Luján station and the period 2019–2021 from the websites http://les.edu.uy/online/stack-loc/ (CIM-ESRA, LES web portal) and https://www.soda-pro.com/web-services (Heliosat-4, CAMS web portal). The CIM-ESRA estimations are available on a 10-min scale for different Latin American stations, including Luján, Argentina. The CAMS estimations are not available at the 10-min temporal resolution used in this article, so one-minute data were downloaded and then integrated into the 10-min time scale. The data from these models were used as a performance reference for the developed statistical ML models against available databases for the region.

The performance metrics used in this work are the MBE, RMSE, MAE, and $R^2$ (Mean Bias Error, Root Mean Square Error, Mean Absolute Error, and R-squared) respectively. For the first three, their corresponding relative values are also reported, which are named as MBEn, RMSEn, and MAEn, respectively. These metrics are expressed as a percentage of the measurement average value, which is 420 W/m$^2$ for this station. MBE is the systematic bias of the models, and RMSE and MAE measure the error dispersion with different weighting laws, being the former more sensitive to outliers. The evaluation results of these models can be seen in Table 3.

**Table 3.**   Performance metrics of the Heliosat-4 (CAMS) and CIM-ESRA models. MBE, RMSE, and MAE are measured in W/m$^2$, their relative versions in %, and $R^2$ is dimensionless.

|          | MBEn   | RMSE  | RMSEn | MAE   | MAEn  | $R^2$ |
|----------|--------|-------|-------|-------|-------|-------|
| **CAMS** | −0.99  | 93.38 | 22.22 | 54.94 | 13.07 | 0.894 |
| **CIM-ESRA** | 1.63 | 74.79 | 17.07 | 49.34 | 11.26 | 0.928 |

It is possible to notice that the estimates from the CIM-ESRA model fit more accurately to the region compared to those obtained by the Heliosat-4 model. The superior performance of CIM-ESRA is due to two reasons: (a) it uses GOES-16 information instead of MSG, which has better-viewing angles for the Pampa Húmeda region, and (b) it is a semi-empirical model whose adjustable parameters were determined for the region (previously) by using information from 10 sites in the 2010–2017 period [8]. The performance reference is therefore given by the CIM-ESRA model, which also uses information from the same satellite as the input data used for the machine learning algorithms in this work.

### 3.2   Implementation of Machine Learning Models

The variables detailed in Sect. 2.3 were used as input for the implemented models. Different combinations of input variables were tested for the implemented models, and it was found that for the black box algorithms, it was sufficient to have information from the satellite image variables. Tables 4 and 5 show the results. The metrics are presented for each validation year, with the fit to the other two remaining years of the 2019–2021 period. The last column shows the average performance over the 3 validation years, which is used here as a comparison value with the CIM-ESRA reference in Table 3.

**Table 4.** Results of ML models using all input variables.

| Metric | Linear Regression | | | | Neural Networks 100 Hidden ReLU- Adam | | | | Random Forest n = 30 | | | |
|---|---|---|---|---|---|---|---|---|---|---|---|---|
| | 2019 | 2020 | 2021 | Mean | 2019 | 2020 | 2021 | Mean | 2019 | 2020 | 2021 | Mean |
| MBE | 0.08 | −1.32 | 1.10 | **−0.05** | −0.59 | −1.45 | −2.52 | **−1.52** | 1.26 | −1.99 | 1.73 | **0.33** |
| MBEn | 0.02 | −0.28 | 0.25 | **0.00** | −0.14 | −0.31 | −0.58 | **−0.34** | 0.30 | −0.43 | 0.40 | **0.09** |
| RMSE | 70.49 | 69.05 | 70.79 | **70.11** | 68.84 | 67.19 | 68.61 | **68.21** | 71.88 | 69.14 | 70.44 | **70.49** |
| RMSEn | 16.86 | 14.79 | 16.37 | **16.01** | 16.47 | 14.40 | 15.87 | **15.58** | 17.19 | 14.81 | 16.29 | **16.10** |
| MAE | 45.08 | 40.88 | 44.98 | **43.65** | 40.74 | 37.59 | 39.81 | **39.38** | 42.29 | 39.16 | 42.21 | **41.22** |
| MAEn | 10.78 | 8.76 | 10.40 | **9.98** | 9.74 | 8.05 | 9.21 | **9.00** | 10.12 | 8.39 | 9.76 | **9.42** |
| $R^2$ | 0.94 | 0.95 | 0.94 | **0.94** | 0.94 | 0.95 | 0.95 | **0.95** | 0.94 | 0.95 | 0.94 | **0.94** |

**Table 5.** Results of the ML models using only satellite variables (excluding the clear sky model and the geometric variable Cos(z)).

| Metric | Linear Regression | | | | Neural Networks 100 Hidden ReLU- Adam | | | | Random Forest n = 30 | | | |
|---|---|---|---|---|---|---|---|---|---|---|---|---|
| | 2019 | 2020 | 2021 | Mean | 2019 | 2020 | 2021 | Mean | 2019 | 2020 | 2021 | Mean |
| MBE | −0.95 | 18.50 | −9.97 | **2.53** | −5.33 | −0.26 | 0.40 | **−1.73** | 0.45 | 0.82 | 2.35 | **1.21** |
| MBEn | −0.23 | 3.96 | −2.31 | **0.48** | −1.28 | −0.06 | 0.09 | **−0.41** | 0.11 | 0.18 | 0.54 | **0.28** |
| RMSE | 176.82 | 211.23 | 179.33 | **189.13** | 70.13 | 67.73 | 69.64 | **69.16** | 72.08 | 69.16 | 71.28 | **70.84** |
| RMSEn | 42.29 | 45.26 | 41.48 | **43.01** | 16.77 | 14.51 | 16.11 | **15.80** | 17.24 | 14.82 | 16.49 | **16.18** |
| MAE | 135.59 | 150.77 | 141.22 | **142.53** | 44.20 | 41.07 | 42.67 | **42.65** | 44.21 | 41.40 | 44.51 | **43.37** |
| MAEn | 32.43 | 32.31 | 32.66 | **32.47** | 10.57 | 8.80 | 9.87 | **9.75** | 10.58 | 8.87 | 10.29 | **9.91** |
| $R^2$ | 0.62 | 0.54 | 0.63 | **0.60** | 0.94 | 0.95 | 0.94 | **0.95** | 0.94 | 0.95 | 0.94 | **0.94** |

When using all variables, the statistical techniques exhibit similar performance, although it is possible to notice that the neural network's performance is slightly better. If we look at, for example, RMSEn, the neural network's performance is 0.4% higher than the others on average. It also shows a 1.5% RMSEn gain compared to the CIM-ESRA reference. When comparing the linear regression with and without the clear sky estimates and the Cos(z) variable, a marked downgrade in performance is noticed, unlike what happens in the case of nonlinear models (only a loss of 0.2% in RMSEn is observed). This suggests that for these types of techniques, the satellite variables would suffice to estimate solar radiation (F01-F18 and R01-R18), but this is not the case for the simple linear regression algorithm. In that case, linear regression loses the necessary temporal reference to estimate a magnitude with a marked geometric daily and annual component like the GHI. However, machine learning algorithms do not lose it. The geometric information is implicit in the relationship between FR and RP, and ML algorithms are capable of learning from it. Figure 2 shows the predictions of the neural network that only uses satellite information for two days with cloudy sky conditions corresponding to January (top) and July (bottom). Figure 3 shows the estimation of the same model but for two clear days during the year.

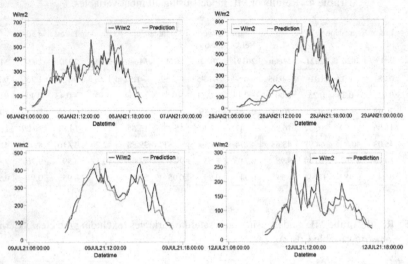

**Fig. 2.** Comparative plots between ground measurements and the neural network that uses only satellite variables for two days in January 2021 (top) and two days in July (bottom) under cloudy sky conditions.

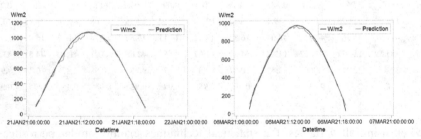

**Fig. 3.** Comparative plots between ground measurements and the neural network that uses only satellite variables for two days with clear sky conditions.

It can be appreciated in the previous plots that the model is capable of capturing, in general, the presence of clouds and their effect on GHI with a good level of success. This is reflected in the metrics of Table 5. In the case of clear sky days, it can be observed that the predicted curve is not completely smooth. This could be due to the non-use of the clear sky model or the calculated geometric information of Cos(z), and could be indicating the approximate temporal positioning of the algorithm derived from the joint use of FR and RP.

# 4 Conclusions and Future Work

In this study, it was observed that the neural network algorithm had the best performance, followed by the random forest method, even after eliminating input variables such as the clear sky model and cosine of the solar zenith angle. In contrast, a simple linear regression showed poor performance when these input variables were removed, as it could not reconstruct the necessary temporal reference to estimate GHI. In terms of comparison with the CIM-ESRA reference model, better performance was observed for the empirical ML models. The comparative metrics between CIM-ESRA and the neural network are all favorable to the latter, with MAEn of 11.3% vs 9.7%, RMSEn of 17.1% vs 15.8%, and MBEn of + 1.6% vs −0.4%. However, it will be important in future work to analyze the behavior of the empirical model in other locations in the Pampa Húmeda region, i.e., to analyze its spatial extrapolation using a testing set in different measuring sites. For future work, it would also be appropriate to consider other relevant satellite variables, such as the satellite cloud index [3] and information from the satellite's infrared channels. These parameters can provide additional information about the cloud cover or atmospheric transmissivity, which could improve the accuracy of ML solar radiation estimates. Therefore, it would be valuable to evaluate the inclusion of these variables in the model and measure their impact on its performance.

# References

1. Abal, G., Aicardi, D., Alonso-Suárez, R., Laguarda, A.: Performance of empirical models for diffuse fraction in Uruguay. Sol. Energy **141**, 166–181 (2017)
2. Aristegui, R., Iturbide, P., Stern, V., Lell, J., Righini, R.: Variabilidad de corto plazo y valores extremos de la irradiancia solar en la Pampa Húmeda Argentina. Avances en Energías Renovables y Medio Ambiente (AVERMA) **23**, 19–30 (2019)
3. Cano, D., Monget, J., Albuisson, M., Guillard, H., Regas, N., Wald, L.: A method for the determination of global solar radiation from meteorological satellite data. Sol. Energy **37**, 31–39 (1986)
4. Emde, C., et al.: The Libradtran software package for radiative transfer calculations (version 2.0.1). Geosci. Model Dev. **9**, 1647–1672 (2016)
5. Huang, G., et al.: Estimating surface solar irradiance from satellites: past, present, and future perspectives. Remote Sens. Environ. **233**, 111371 (2019). https://doi.org/10.1016/j.rse.2019.111371
6. Jiménez, V.A., Will, A., Rodríguez, S.: Estimación de radiación solar horaria utilizando modelos empíricos y redes neuronales artificiales. Cienc. Tecn. **17**, 29–45 (2017)
7. Kriebel, K., Gesell, G., Kastner, M., Mannstein, H.: The cloud analysis tool APOLLO: Improvements and validations. Int. J. Remote Sens. **24**(12), 2389–2408 (2003)
8. Laguarda, A., et al.: Validación de modelos satelitales Heliosat-4 y CIM-ESRA para la estimación de irradiancia solar en la Pampa Húmeda. Energías Renovables y Medio Ambiente **48**, 1–9 (2021)
9. Laguarda, A., Giacosa, G., Alonso-Suárez, R., Abal, G.: Performance of the site-adapted CAMS database and locally adjusted cloud index models for estimating global solar horizontal irradiation over the Pampa Húmeda region. Sol. Energy **199**, 295–307 (2020)
10. Laguarda, A., Abal, G.: Clear-sky broadband irradiance: first model assessment in Uruguay. In: Proceedings of the ISES Solar World Congress, pp. 1360–1371, ISBN:978-39-81465-97-6. https://doi.org/10.18086/swc.2017.21.05

11. Lefevre, M., et al.: McClear: a new model estimating downwelling solar radiation at ground level in clear-sky conditions. Atmos. Meas. Techn. **6**(9), 2403–2418 (2013)
12. Linke, F.: Transmissions-koeffizient und trübungsfaktor. Meteorol. Mag. Beiträge Zur Physik der Atmosphäre Beitr **10**, 91–103 (1922)
13. Long, C.N., Shi, Y.: An automated quality assessment and control algorithm for surface radiation measurements. Open Atmos. Sci. J. **2**(1) (2008)
14. McArthur, L.: Baseline Surface Radiation Network (BSRN) Operations Manual. Td-no. 1274, wrcp/wmo, World Meteorological Organization (WMO, www.wmo.org)
15. Olivera, L., Atia, J., Amet, L., Osio, J., Morales, M., Cappelletti, M.: Uso de redes neuronales artificiales para la estimación de la radiación solar horaria bajo diferentes condiciones de cielo. Avances en Energías Renovables y Medio Ambiente-AVERMA **24**, 232–243 (2020)
16. Perez, R., et al.: A new operational model for satellite-derived irradiances: description and validation. Sol. Energy **73**, 307–317 (2002)
17. Perez, R., Ineichen, P., Seals, R., Zelenka, A.: Making full use of the clearness index for parameterizing hourly insolation conditions. Sol. Energy **45**(2), 111–114 (1990)
18. Perez, R., Schlemmer, J., Hemker, K., Kivalov, S., Kankiewicz, A., Gueymard, C.: Satellite-to-irradiance modeling - a new version of the SUNY model. In: 42nd Photovoltaic Specialist Conference (PVSC), pp. 1–7 (2015)
19. Qu, Z., et al.: Fast radiative transfer parameterisation for assessing the surface solar irradiance: The Heliosat-4 method. Meteorol. Z. **26**(1), 33–57 (2017)
20. Raichijk, C.: Estimación de la irradiación solar global en Argentina mediante el uso de redes neuronales. Energías Renovables y Medio Ambiente **22**, 1–6 (2008). (ISSN:0328-932X)
21. Rigollier, C., Lefevre, M., Wald, L.: The method Heliosat-2 for deriving shortwave solar radiation from satellite images. Sol. Energy **77**(2), 159–169 (2004)
22. Sayago, S., Bocco, M., Ovando, G., Willington, E. A.: Radiación solar horaria: modelos de estimación a partir de variables meteorológicas básicas. Avances en Energías Renovables y Medio Ambiente **15** (2011)
23. Verbois, H., Saint-Drenan, Y.-M., Becquet, V., Gschwind, B., Blanc, P.: Retrieval of surface solar irradiance from satellite using machine learning: pitfalls and perspectives, EGUsphere [preprint], https://doi.org/10.5194/egusphere-2023-243
24. Yang, D.: Choice of clear-sky model in solar forecasting. J. Renew. Sustain. Energy **12**, 026101 (2020). https://doi.org/10.1063/5.0003495

# An Architecture and a New Deep Learning Method for Head and Neck Cancer Prognosis by Analyzing Serial Positron Emission Tomography Images

Remigio Hurtado[1]([✉])(iD), Stefanía Guzmán[2](iD), and Arantxa Muñoz[3](iD)

[1] Universidad Politécnica Salesiana, Calle Vieja 12-30 y Elia Liut, Cuenca, Ecuador
rhurtadoo@ups.edu.ec
[2] Servicio de medicina nuclear, Hospital Central de la Defensa Gómez Ulla, Madrid, Spain
[3] Universidad Internacional de La Rioja, Avenida de la Paz 137, La Rioja, Spain

**Abstract.** In the U.S. it is estimated that there are more than 20,000 cases of head and neck cancers per year. Radiomics is a much discussed topic in nuclear medicine. The radiomic characteristics of metabolic imaging modalities such as Positron Emission Tomography (PET) have been postulated as surrogates for underlying tumor biology and thus prognosis. Radiomic data can be extracted to discover characteristics and patterns of evolution (in serial images, their changes over time) and to provide a response to treatment. In oncology it has been shown that the degree of tumor heterogeneity is a prognostic factor for survival and an obstacle to cancer control. One of the main obstacles to radiomics research is the lack of understanding among clinicians and data scientists. For this reason, in this paper, we propose a case study, an architecture and a Deep Learning method for the processing and analysis of PET tomographic images for the detection of head and neck cancers. Our architecture consists of three phases: 1) Image preparation, 2) Deep learning method using convolutional neural networks for dimensionality reduction and image feature extraction, and recurrent neural networks for serial image learning of PET, and 3) Optimization. A public dataset is used and the quality of the method is demonstrated using standard quality measures such as Accuracy, Precision, Recall and F1-Score.

**Keywords:** Deep Learning · Data Science · Medical Imaging · Optimization · Molecular Imaging · Disease Modeling and Analysis

## 1 Introduction

Cancer is a disease in which abnormal cells divide uncontrollably and destroy body tissues. The prevention, detection and treatment of cancer is a great challenge for mankind. A person's cancer may or may not be curable depending on the type and stage of the cancer, as well as the type of treatment, among other

M. Naiouf et al. (Eds.): JCC-BD&ET 2023, CCIS 1828, pp. 129–140, 2023.
https://doi.org/10.1007/978-3-031-40942-4_10

factors. Head and neck cancers have been increasingly studied in recent years, especially oropharyngeal cancers, with more than 20,000 cases annually expected in the U.S. Radiomics is a hotly debated topic in nuclear medicine. Several groups have shown that radiomic signatures developed in cancers of the head and neck among other tumor sites can correlate with survival outcomes. The radiomic features of metabolic imaging modalities, such as 18F-fluorodeoxyglucose Positron Emission Tomography (18F-Fluorodeoxyglucose PET o 18F-FDG PET), have been postulated as surrogates for underlying tumor biology and thus prognosis [1].

PET is based on tomographic imaging of the three-dimensional distribution of ultra-short half-life radiopharmaceuticals, which after administration to patients are incorporated into tumor cells, enabling their external detection. Malignant cells suffer alterations in the mechanisms of cell growth regulation, show neovascularization and need a greater incorporation of fundamental substrates to maintain high energy consumption (glucose), all these biological and metabolic changes differentiate the tumor cell from the normal cell. PET allows imaging and quantification of the metabolic and pathophysiological parameters of neoplastic tissue. The correlation of PET findings with those obtained by other radiological imaging techniques (CT, MRI) is very important because it allows greater precision in the localization of tumor lesions. The most widely used radiopharmaceutical in PET for oncological applications is a glucose analog, in which the hydroxyl group of Carbon 2 has been replaced by an 18F atom, called 2-[18F] fluoro-2-deoxy-D-glucose (18FDG). 18FDG allows imaging and quantification of one of the most interesting physiological parameters in the tumor cell, namely glycolytic metabolism. The uptake of 18FDG varies greatly according to the histology of each tumor; however, high uptake is generally associated with increased expression of the GLUcose Transporter (GLUT), hexokinase activity and the existence of a large number of viable cells, factors characteristic of a high histological grade [1].

Radiomics is a much discussed topic in nuclear medicine, and there are several scenarios in which radiomic features extracted from metabolic imaging techniques such as PET can be useful. Radiomics aims to obtain quantitative and ideally reproducible information from diagnostic images. It can be used to capture the properties of tissues and lesions, such as shape and heterogeneity and, in serial imaging, their changes over time, such as during treatment or follow-up. In oncology, the degree of tumor heterogeneity has been shown to be a prognostic factor for survival and an obstacle to cancer control. Radiomic data can be mined, which means that, in sufficiently large data sets, it can be used to discover previously unknown markers and patterns of disease progression, progression and response to treatment [2].

However, one of the main obstacles to radiomics research is the lack of communication between clinicians and data analysts, in particular, the lack of a common language [2]. Therefore, in this paper we propose a case study, an architecture and a Deep Learning method for the processing and analysis of PET tomographic images for the detection of head and neck cancers. Our architecture consists of three phases: 1) Image preparation for deep learning, 2) Deep learning method using convolutional neural networks for dimensionality reduction and image feature extraction, and recurrent neural networks for serial image learning of PET, 3) Hyperparameter optimization and evaluation of the proposed method. A public dataset is used and the quality of the method is demonstrated using standard quality measures such as Accuracy, Precision, Recall and F1-Score. The method is limited to the preparation and analysis of images previously obtained from a public dataset. Image collection and visualization techniques have not been developed.

The highlights and most important contributions of this work are:

1. A phased data science architecture and a novel deep learning method for the preparation and analysis of tomographic images obtained using Positron Emission Tomography.
2. A set of experiments using a public dataset, standard quality measures and the comparison and discussion of machine learning methods.
3. A set of notebooks for reproducibility of experiments and for the development of new methods from this case study.
   Code: https://www.kaggle.com/code/remigohurtado/notebookee6a3293bf

The rest of this paper is structured as follows: Sect. 2 mentions the most relevant related work, Sect. 3 presents the architecture and the deep learning method used, Sect. 4 presents the design of experiments. Subsequently, in Sect. 5, the results and discussion are presented. Finally, Sect. 6 presents the conclusions and future work from this research.

## 2   Related Work

This section presents some relevant papers related to this research.

A deep learning-based time-to-event analysis with PET, CT and PET/CT imaging for head and neck cancer prognosis is performed in [3]. High predictive ability is demonstrated. In [4], automated lung cancer segmentation is performed using a PET and CT dual-modality deep learning neural network. This generates clinically useful lung cancer contours that are highly acceptable at physician review. In [5] a deep learning model in non-small cell lung cancer that improves the predictive value of TNM staging with PET/CT imaging features is performed. The results suggest that textural and PET imaging features are significant predictors of outcome in lung cancer. In [6], automated lung cancer segmentation is performed using a dual-modality deep learning network with PET and CT images. It is able to generate clinically useful lung cancer contours that are quantitatively similar to the truth and highly acceptable in physician review. In [7] using deep learning, breast cancer (BC) detection is performed.

As a result, it is obtained that early detection of breast cancer can improve the survival rate of patients. The rapid development of Artificial Intelligence-based techniques in Medical Image Analysis (MIA) has made it possible to fully utilize large datasets to improve BC diagnosis and the accuracy of medicine by automatically extracting relevant features.

In [8], a deep learning-based multimodality image analysis for cervical cancer detection is performed. It is concluded that PET/CT fusion is more beneficial for cervical cancer detection than using either alone. In [9], multiscale and multitask learning is performed for outcome prediction in 3D PET images. This enables higher performance of radiomic analysis by extracting enriched information from intratumoral and peritumoral regions. A systematic review of recent advances in deep learning-based lung cancer detection is performed in [10]. The study includes an in-depth analysis of deep learning algorithms for identifying and classifying lung cancer nodules. Researchers are provided with an overview and comparison of various techniques used to diagnose lung cancer. In [11], automated lung cancer detection is performed on ultra-low-dose PET/CT using deep neural networks. These results suggest that machine learning algorithms can aid fully automated lung cancer detection even at very low effective radiation doses. Further refinement of this technology could improve the specificity of lung cancer detection and lead to new applications of FDG-PET. In [12], a fully automated method for segmentation and detection of metabolically active lesions in wholebody F-FDG PET/CT is developed. The system achieves competitive results in terms of detection and segmentation metrics, and outperforms a direct segmentation approach trained on the same dataset. A validation of the low-dose PET-CT protocol for lung cancer and PET image enhancement by machine learning is performed in [13]. The LD PET-CT protocol is validated for lesion detection using ALD PET scans. Substantial image quality improvement or further dose reduction can be achieved while preserving clinical values using machine learning methods. Extensible and explainable deep learning for pan-cancer radiogenomic research is performed in [14]. This review summarizes the current status of deep learning in cancer radiogenomic research, discusses its limitations, and indicates possible future directions. A radiogenomic model based on deep learning for prediction of genetic mutations in lung cancer is performed in [15]. They take three different types of data and use all of them together to make predictions. They find that the EfficientNets network performs well for gene mutation prediction in lung cancer.

All these papers present deep learning methods, however, our proposed method provides a data science based process in order to establish a case study for better understanding between expert clinicians and data scientists. In addition, we present a composite deep learning method using a convolutional neural networks for dimensionality reduction and image feature extraction, and recurrent neural networks for serial image learning of PET images.

# 3   Data Science Architecture and Deep Learning Method

This section first presents the architecture designed and the proposed method to perform the predictive analysis. Figure 1 shows the architecture of the proposed method, which consists of three phases: 1) Image preparation, 2) Image analysis with deep learning, and 3) Hyperparameter optimization and evaluation. Each phase is described below:

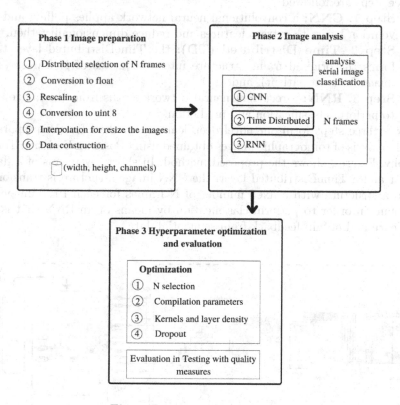

**Fig. 1.** Data science architecture

- **Phase 1 - Image preparation:** in this phase, six image preparation steps are developed.
    - **Step 1. Distributed selection of N frames:** in this step the distributed selection of N frames for each serie of images of a patient is performed.
    - **Step 2. Conversion to float:** each frame is converted to float to avoid overflow or underflow.
    - **Step 3. Rescaling:** at each frame the grayscale is rescaled between 0-255.

- **Step 4. Convesion to uint8:** each frame is converted to unsigned integer (uint8).
  - **Step 5. Interpolation for resize the images:** all frames are transformed to the same dimensions.
  - **Step 6. Data construction:** the image dataset is built to be analyzed by machine learning and deep learning techniques.
- **Phase 2 - Image analysis with deep learning:** in this phase, basically three steps are followed:
  - **Step 1. CNN:** a convolutional neural network applies polling and convolution layers to extract features and reduce dimensionality, then,
  - **Step 2. Time Distributed (TD):** the TimeDistributed layer transforms the original frame structure into a sequence of N frames (serial image for each patient), and
  - **Step 3. RNN:** a recurrent neural network learns from the image series to perform classification and prediction.

These three steps form our novel deep learning method for the preparation and analysis of tomographic images obtained using Positron Emission Tomography. Figure 2 shows the proposed method. In short, by means of a flatten layer and a TimeDistributed layer, the CNN image structure is transformed into a structure with a fixed number of N frames for each PET image of a patient, in order to perform classification by means of an RNN that is able to learn and obtain feedback from sequential data.

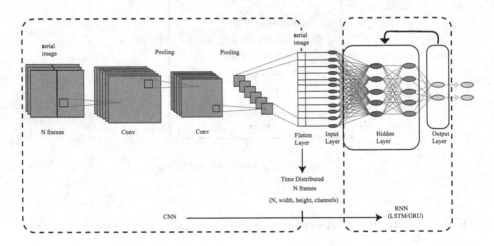

**Fig. 2.** Deep learning method

- **Phase 3 - Hyperparameter optimization and evaluation:** in this phase, four steps are followed for the optimization and evaluation of our deep learning method:
  - **Step 1. N selection:** N is the number of frames of each PET image for each patient. In the design of experiments section we present the values to be tested in our method for each parameter. For each value of N the method is evaluated in Testing. The N that generates the best prediction results will be the optimal value, i.e. the optimal number of frames for each PET scan of a patient.
  - **Step 2. Compilation parameters:** the performance of the method to find the best combination of neural network compilation parameters, such as: number of epochs, batch size, optimizer, etc., is evaluated.
  - **Step 3. Kernels and layer density:** the performance of the method is evaluated to find the best combination of layers and neurons in the method.
  - **Step 4. Dropout:** the performance of the method is evaluated to find the appropriate dropout rate to provide adequate generalization of the method.

## 4   Design of Experiments

This section presents the characteristics of the dataset, the parameters for optimization of the methods in the learning phase, and the quality measure.

**1) Characteristics of dataset:** Table 1 presents the general description of dataset and their most relevant characteristics.

**2) Optimization parameters of predictive methods:** Table 2 presents the parameters to be experimented to train and optimize the methods.

**3) Quality measures:**   For the evaluation of the methods, the Cross-Validation K-Folds technique (with K=5) has been used in order to obtain an adequate generalization of the results. The quality measures used are: Precision, Recall, F1-Score and Accuracy. The average of K experiments with the best parameters of each method is presented in the results section.

**Table 1.** General description of the dataset

| Dataset | Number of samples PET images (serial image) | Dimensions of each frame | Classes |
| --- | --- | --- | --- |
| 18F-FDG     PET Radiomics Head and Neck Cancer [16] | 124 | $(128 \times 128)$ | presence or absence of malignant tumor |

**Table 2.** Optimization parameters of predictive methods

| Method | Parameters |
| --- | --- |
| Proposed method (CNN-TD-RNN) | **Compilation:**<br>epochs:10,20,30,40,50<br>batch size:10,20,30,40<br><br>optimizers:<br>Adaptive Gradient Algorithm (AdaGrad),<br>Adadelta (AdaGrad variant),<br>Root Mean Square Propagation (RMSprop),<br>Adaptive moment estimation (Adam).<br>Adam combines the best of the other optimizers<br><br>activation functions:<br>Linear, Sigmoid, Hyperbolic Tangent,<br>Rectified Lineal Unit (ReLU)<br><br>**Kernels, layer density and dropout:**<br>**CNN**<br>One to four levels of the following layers:<br>layer (Conv): 16,32,64,128,256,512. For each one: (2,2), (3,3)<br>layer (Conv): 16,32,64,128,256,512. For each one: (2,2), (3,3)<br>layer (MaxPooling): (2,2), (3,3)<br>Dropout: 0, 0.1, 0.25, 0.5<br><br>**Flatten Layer and TimeDistributed (TD)**<br>GlobalMaxPooling<br>TimeDistributed with shape (N frames, 128, 128, 3)<br>**RNN**<br>GRU and LSTM with: 16,32,64,128,256,512<br>**Dense**<br>Dense layer: 16,32,64,128,256,512,1024<br>Dropout: 0,0.1,0.2,0.3,0.4,0.5<br>Output layer: 2 classes, activation='softmax' |
| Transfer Learning | Pre-trained CNN networks: MobileNet, VGG16, ResNet50, Xception and InceptionResNetV2 |
| Random Forest (RF) | number of estimators: 5,10,15,20,30,40,50,100,200<br>maximum depth: 5,10,15,20,40 |
| Support Vector Machine (SVM) | penalty (C): 0.001, 0.01, 0.1, 1, 10, 100<br>kernel: linear, polynomial, sigmoid, radial basis function (rbf)<br>epsilon: 0.0,0.1,0.2,0.3,0.5,1 |
| K-Nearest Neighbors (KNN) | number of neighbors: 5,10,20,30,40,50<br>metrics: euclidea, manhattan |

$$\text{Precision} = \frac{TP}{TP + FP} \tag{1}$$

$$\text{Recall} = \frac{TP}{TP + FN} \tag{2}$$

$$\text{F1-Score} = 2 \cdot \frac{Precision \cdot Recall}{Precision + Recall} \tag{3}$$

$$\text{Accuracy} = \frac{TP + TN}{TP + TN + FP + FN} \tag{4}$$

where $TP$, $TN$, $FP$ and $FN$ are the number of True Positives, True Negatives, False Positives and False Negatives, respectively.

## 5   Results

This section presents the results of the selection of the optimum number of frames and of the methods of prediction. Figure 3 shows the selection of the optimum number of frames. It is observed that the best results in all quality measures is $N = 10$ and $N = 20$, however, the process with $N = 10$ is more efficient than $N = 20$, since fewer frames are required for each PET image. The final parameters of the learning methods are presented in Table 3. Table 4 shows the comparison of the results of methods of prediction. It can be seen that the optimized method of deep neural outperforms the other machine learning and deep learning methods. Figure 4 shows the confusion matrix of the proposed method.

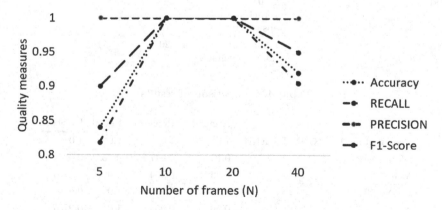

**Fig. 3.** Selection of number of frames (N)

**Table 3.** Final parameter values

| Method | Parameters |
|---|---|
| Proposed method (CNN-TD-RNN) | **Compilation:**<br>epochs: 20<br>batch size: 10<br>optimizer: Adam<br>activation function: ReLU in all layers except for the output layer<br><br>**Kernels, layer density and dropout:**<br>**CNN**<br>first level: 64 neurons with kernel (3,3)<br>second level: 128 neurons with kernel (3,3)<br>third level: 256 neurons with kernel (3,3)<br>fourth level: 512 neurons with kernel (3,3)<br>Dropout at the four levels: 0.25<br><br>**Flatten Layer and TimeDistributed**<br>GlobalMaxPooling<br>TimeDistributed with shape (10 frames, 128, 128, 3)<br><br>**RNN**<br>GRU with: 64 neurons<br><br>**Dense**<br>Dense layer: 512 neurons<br>Dropout: 0.2<br>Output layer: 2 (two classes), activation='softmax' |
| Transfer Learning | Pre-trained networks: MobileNet (9 layers to train), VGG16,<br>ResNet50 (pooling='average'), Xception and InceptionResNetV2 |
| RF | number of estimators: 30<br>depth: 20 |
| SVM | C: 0.01<br>kernel: linear<br>epsilon: 0.2 |
| KNN | number of neighbors: 20<br>metric: euclidea |

**Table 4.** Comparison of results

| Method | Accuracy | Precision | Recall | F1-Score |
|---|---|---|---|---|
| Proposed method (CNN-TD-RNN) | 1.0 | 1.0 | 1.0 | 1.0 |
| MobileNet | 0.72 | 0.9474 | 0.75 | 0.8372 |
| VGG16 | 0.96 | 0.9545 | 1.0 | 0.9767 |
| ResNet50 | 0.96 | 0.9545 | 1.0 | 0.9767 |
| Xception | 0.96 | 0.9545 | 1.0 | 0.9767 |
| InceptionResNetV2 | 0.84 | 0.84 | 1.0 | 0.913 |
| RF | 0.84 | 0.84 | 1.0 | 0.913 |
| SVM | 0.96 | 0.9545 | 1.0 | 0.9767 |
| KNN | 0.72 | 0.9474 | 0.75 | 0.8372 |

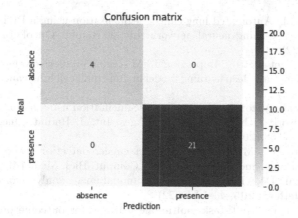

**Fig. 4.** Proposed method: confusion matrix with N=10. 25 patients in the Testing set.

## 6    Conclusions

Detecting cancer in a person is a great challenge, it may or may not be curable depending on the type and stage of the cancer, type of treatment, among other factors. One of the main obstacles to radiomics research is the lack of understanding among clinicians and data scientists. For this reason, we have provided a case study, an architecture and a Deep Learning method for the processing and analysis of PET tomographic images for the detection of head and neck cancers. We have provided a set of experiments using a public dataset, standard quality measures and the comparison and discussion of machine learning methods. We have provided a set of notebooks for reproducibility of experiments and for the development of new methods from this case study. As future work, we consider, in addition to an inductive approach, to explore a hybrid approach that adds deductive artificial intelligence supported by expert knowledge modeling, in order to significantly improve the results. We intend to develop methods and experiment with modern learning techniques, such as reinforcement learning, ensemble methods, and techniques from other artificial intelligence approaches, such as rule-based, case-based, evolutionary, logic-based, and probability theory approaches. We also consider articulation, future image collection, processing and modeling, working together with medical institutions.

## References

1. Cenzano, C., et al.: La tomografía por emisión de positrones (PET) en oncología (Parte I). Revista Española de Medicina Nuclear. **21**(1), 41–60 (2002)
2. Mayerhoefer, M.E., et al.: Introduction to radiomics. J. Nucl. Med. **61**(4), 488–495 (2020)
3. Wang, Y., et al.: Deep learning based time-to-event analysis with PET, CT and joint PET/CT for head and neck cancer prognosis. Comput. Methods Progr. Biomed. **222**, 106948 (2022)

4. Wang, S., et al.: Automated lung cancer segmentation using a PET and CT dual-modality deep learning neural network. Int. J. Radiat. Oncol. Biol. Phys. **115**, 529–539 (2022)

5. Giovannini, E., et al.: 918P Improving TNM staging predictive value with PET/CT imaging features and deep learning model in non-small cell lung cancer. Ann. Oncol. **33**, S966 (2022)

6. Wang, S., et al.: Automated lung cancer segmentation using a dual-modality deep learning network with PET and CT images. Int. J. Radiat. Oncol. Biol. Phys. **114**(3), e557–e558 (2022)

7. Dar, R.A., Rasool, M., Assad, A.: Breast cancer detection using deep learning: datasets, methods, and challenges ahead. Comput. Biol. Med. **149**, 106073 (2022)

8. Ming, Y., et al.: Deep learning-based multimodal image analysis for cervical cancer detection. Methods **205**, 46–52 (2022)

9. Amyar, A., et al.: Multi-task multi-scale learning for outcome prediction in 3D PET images. arXiv preprint arXiv:2203.00641 (2022)

10. Dodia, S., Annappa, B., Mahesh, P.A.: Recent advancements in deep learning based lung cancer detection: a systematic review. Eng. Appl. Artif. Intell. **116**, 105490 (2022)

11. Schwyzer, M., et al.: Automated detection of lung cancer at ultralow dose PET/CT by deep neural networks-initial results. Lung Cancer **126**, 170–173 (2018)

12. Dirks, I., et al.: Computer-aided detection and segmentation of malignant melanoma lesions on whole-body 18F-FDG PET/CT using an interpretable deep learning approach. Comput. Methods Progr. Biomed. **221**, 106902 (2022)

13. Nai, Y.-H., et al.: Validation of low-dose lung cancer PET-CT protocol and PET image improvement using machine learning. Phys. Med. **81**, 285–294 (2021)

14. Liu, Q., Pingzhao, H.: Extendable and explainable deep learning for pan-cancer radiogenomics research. Curr. Opin. Chem. Biol. **66**, 102111 (2022)

15. Tripathi, S., et al.: Radgennets: deep learning-based radiogenomics model for gene mutation prediction in lung cancer. Inform. Med. Unlocked **33**, 101062 (2022)

16. Fuller, C., Elhalawani, H., Mohamed, A.: MICCAI 2018 - Computational Precision Medicine Challenge: 18F-FDG PET Radiomics Risk Stratifiers in Head and Neck Cancer, 29 July 2021 (2022). https://doi.org/10.6084/m9.figshare.15075195.v2

# Smart Cities and E-Government

# Designing a Data Strategy for Organizations

Fabiola del Toro Osorio[1](✉) (iD), Victoria Eugenia Ospina Becerra[1] (iD),
and Elsa Estévez[2] (iD)

[1] Escuela Colombiana de Ingeniería, Bogotá, Colombia
{fabiola.deltoro,victoria.ospina}@escuelaing.edu.co
[2] Department of Computer Science and Engineering, Universidad Nacional del Sur (UNS),
Institute of Computer Science and Engineering, UNS-CONICET, Buenos Aires, Argentina
ece@cs.uns.edu.ar

**Abstract.** Data are an invaluable asset for the private sector as well as for government and non-government organizations, the academy and, in general, for all communities. During the last few years, different frameworks have appeared proposing practices to obtain the greatest value from data organizationally. The use of data has been mainly understood in data governance as the central axis of the design and implementation of strategies that expect data to be really captured, transformed, and used in an accurate way within the organization. A data strategy is the instrument that allows aligning the data with strategic objectives, so data governance as the central axis without an efficient data strategy will not generate the expected results. Therefore, this article presents a model for the design of data strategy. The main contributions of the proposed model are the focus on strategic objectives, the use of best practices from previous research combined with the incorporation of data knowledge and its behavior in early stages, and the design of a work plan that encourages the appropriation and incorporation of the data strategy in an organization. In addition to presenting the model, we discuss the results of its implementation, we analyze and outline the issues identified for its adaptation in the context of a smart city, and we also explain the first version of such adaptation.

**Keywords:** Data Strategy · Smart Cities · Smart Territories

## 1 Introduction

Currently, the use of data in different industries is unquestionable. This is the case of healthcare systems that have been transformed using medical technology, information systems, electronic medical records, portable and intelligent devices [13]. Similarly, private sector companies use data to better understand their customers' preferences and generate marketing campaigns that are closer to their needs. In this context, the development of data strategies is the first step for organizations to focus on data by identifying it as a strategic asset in the organization [5]. The foundation for getting the most value from data is aligning data with organizational strategies. For this purpose, to be fulfilled, it is also necessary to ensure that the required data is in the necessary conditions to be used by the organization, supported by the required processes and technology, and

M. Naiouf et al. (Eds.): JCC-BD&ET 2023, CCIS 1828, pp. 143–156, 2023.
https://doi.org/10.1007/978-3-031-40942-4_11

the people, aware of their roles and responsibilities, are adequately trained and have the willingness to actively participate in data management and data governance initiatives. To do this, this research is based on the strategic use of data to achieve organizational business goals, through the definition of a data strategy.

In addition to the use of data by the private sector, local governments, in their efforts pursuing the development of smart cities, they are looking for solutions that allow them to solve social, economic, and political problems [6], through a more efficient use of data. Due to the digital transformation of smart cities (SCs), there is the possibility to collect and use data that can be used as key resources for services to improve the citizens' quality of life [11] as well as to improve economic competitiveness.

This article presents a model for the design of an organizational data strategy, the results of its application, and the identified considerations for its adaptation to a smart city context. The structure of the paper is as follows. After this introduction, in Sect. 2 we explain the methodology used for conducting the research work. Next, in Sect. 3, we include a discussion with related work. In Sect. 4, we introduce the model and summarize the result of its application, a kind of model validation. Following, we present our first approach to adapting the model to the smart city context. Finally, in Sect. 5, we summarize our conclusions and outline our future work.

## 2   Research Methodology

Figure 1 presents the research methodology used for conducting our research work.

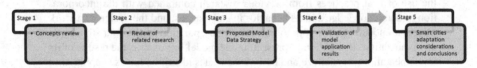

**Fig. 1.** Research method. Source: own elaboration.

Stage 1 begins with the review of concepts. It starts with the documentation of the concepts associated with a Data Strategy to set up the scope of the research. In Stage 2, we identify and analyze related work using the Scopus database and complement its results with the bibliography of interest referenced in the identified articles (snowflake technique). Subsequently, in Stage 3, we synthesize and present the proposed model for the design of a data strategy. In Stage 4, we summarize the results of its application. Finally, in Sect. 5, we present the first considerations for the adaptation of the proposed model to the smart city context, and we elaborate conclusions and future work.

## 3   Related Research

To identify related work, we conducted ten searches in the Scopus database: eight searches in December 2022 and two in January 2023, identifying in total 1715 articles. The ones in December were limited to articles published between 2020 and 2022, containing in the title the words "Data and Strategy" or "Data and Management" or "Data and Governance" or "Information Management" or "Decision Making" or "Big Data" or "Data Handling"; and belonging to the subject areas "Computer Science" and "Engineering". The type of documents selected were "article" at the "final" stage. The search produced 674 results. The searches in January 2023 used the keyword Strategy, and the subject area "Business, Management and Accounting" and were limited to articles published between 2018, 2020, and 2022.

Of the 1715 articles, 82 were pre-selected, using pre-defined criteria on publication date, number of citations and abstract revision to ensure that the selected papers were closed to the objective of this research. Many of the non-selected papers were oriented to uses of data such as data science, business intelligence and artificial intelligence; another large number were concerned with frameworks oriented to a specific use, such as health applications, among others. Below, we summarize the related work most relevant to the focus of this research work.

To understand the business model, the research conducted by Giourka et al., the book Data Strategy and the Business Data Executive, and the book Data Strategy by Bernard Marr were mainly considered. First, the study by Giourka revises the developed business models and proposes a tool to adapt the components of the canvas business models and to add others to adapt them to smart cities [4].

In the case of detailed knowledge of organizational needs, the research developed by professors of the Universität Hamburg and Universität Duisburg-Essen, presents the Data-driven Citizen Journey Map (DCJM), [11]. One of the main particularities of this work is the orientation to the citizen as the center of the designed services. The exercises of understanding what organizationally is called business needs is oriented by Muschkiet to identify the needs of the citizen as the central axis of the services to be offered. In the case of Bernard Marr's book, how to benefit from a world of Big Data, Analytics and the internet of things, the author discusses a business view on the use of data. This book also states as possible uses the improvement of decision-making, the improvement of activity and, the conversion of data into money [10].

We consider the knowledge of data management capabilities as part of the data strategy design. In the research of Corinna Cichy and Stefan Rass, the authors present 12 data quality models and compares them [2]. Regarding the capabilities associated with data security and privacy, the diversity of the research is wide. For example, Xabier a's research, which considers legal aspects such as the General Data Protection Regulation from the European Union and extends the healthcare industry architecture reference model with tools for consent management and data hiding [9].

As for other capabilities, such as the use of best practices in the use of data, the literature review yields numerous studies mainly oriented to data science, artificial intelligence, and internet of things, among others. Obtaining the greatest value from data is one of the main concerns and ensuring its efficient use is one of the main variables of this exercise. However, confusion about the scope of new disciplines and technological tools is becoming increasingly evident. There is no clarity about the scope of data science [12]. Provost and Fawcett's research presents what they call good reasons why the precision of data science's definition is not straightforward.

To ensure that the different data management strategies are the right ones, the model proposes to involve in the planning the design and implementation of the data governance strategy. In this area, the research on data governance for reliable artificial intelligence stands out [7], they propose a framework for data governance for Big Data Algorithmic Systems (BDAS) supported by 13 principles ranging from data quality assessment to data usability. In addition, the book Data Strategy and the Enterprise Data Executive presents the main concepts for designing an organizational data strategy, highlighting three key components to ensure good use of data, namely, data literacy, data supply chain, and standard data assets [5].

After revising major related work, we argue that the model proposed in this article integrates the different practices with the purpose of ensuring the design of a consolidated plan to obtain the greatest value from data in an organization. By establishing the boundaries between the different disciplines with a focus on ensuring that data truly guides and drives organizational goals, we start from a deep knowledge of the business model, business initiatives, necessary and missing data, as well as the current and necessary capabilities to obtain such value, involving the assurance of the expected and current participation of people to achieve this purpose. The main contribution of this model lies in the integration of best practices identified by previous researchers together with a holistic knowledge of the data, its behavior, and main risks; as well as in the incorporation of an ownership stage that promotes the participation of the different actors in the exercise.

## 4  Model for the Design of the Data Strategy

In phase 3 of our methodology, we propose a model for designing a data strategy for an organization. Below, we present the model details.

### 4.1  Model Description

The proposed model is based on the fact that the data strategy will be clearly oriented to ensure compliance with organizational requirements. Usually, such requirements are outlined in a business strategy, which is a document defining the goals that the organization aims to achieve in the next three to five years. Based on such strategy, a data strategy aims at ensuring that the organization possess and can properly manage all the data needed to achieve the business goals. Figure 2 illustrates the vision of a data strategy, management and data governance that supports the proposed model. Subsequently, we explain the main elements.

*Knowledge of the Data.* The activities conducted here are used to understand the data needs of businesses, the data that the organization has, new data needed to achieve each management goal, and the flow of data.

*Data Organization.* Is based on data architecture management and is designed on following the definition of enterprise architecture.

*Data Trust.* Ensures that the data meets the specific quality characteristics for its purpose. We use risk management and the quality attributes proposed by ISO to achieve this goal.

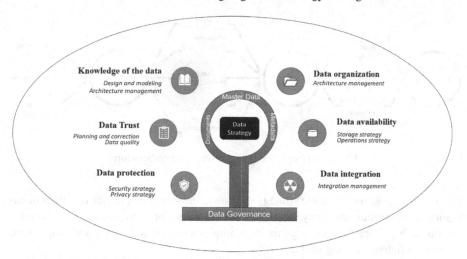

**Fig. 2.** Strategy, management, and data governance. Source: Own elaboration.

*Data Availability.* Comprises the standards and procedures to ensure the availability of data to satisfy business requirements.

*Data Protection.* Is oriented towards the design and implementation of best practices to achieve a secure and private data environment.

*Data Integration.* Is one of the most important activities in data management and is oriented to define the most reliable sources and the business rules to consolidate all data possessed by an organization in repositories, like data warehouse, data lakes or lake houses.

*Data Governance.* Oversees the articulation and decision-making processes of all the other elements to ensure the successful implementation of a data strategy.

*Data Strategy.* Is the instrument that allows aligning the data with strategic objectives.

### 4.2   Design Stages of a Data Strategy

Figure 3 shows the stages of the proposed model for designing a data strategy. Below, we explain the details of each stage.

*Knowledge.* In this first stage of the model, the goal is to know the organizational strategies, the data needed for implementing such strategies with their associations and life cycle, and the current state of organizational capabilities and culture to ensure the reliability, availability, security, and privacy of such data.

The model begins with the knowledge and analysis of the business strategy. For the development of this analysis, the existing documents of the organization are studied. In addition, data can be collected through interviews, surveys, and brainstorming sessions. Such data collection activities should be planned, designed, and conducted, and the results are consolidated using different methodological tools such as Canvas, Pestel,

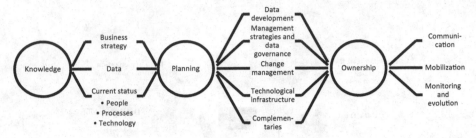

**Fig. 3.** Strategy design – Source: Own elaboration

SWOT, among others. Once the strategy is known, the associated initiatives, their prioritization and indicators are analyzed; the model proposes a prioritization scheme based on criteria such as impact on the organization, implementation feasibility and dependence on other initiatives, among others.

The model highlights the identification and conceptual modeling of the data necessary to meet the identified needs and the analysis of the availability of such data in the organization, as well as the identification of its macro life cycle. For this purpose, we propose to integrate the enterprise architectural vision, presented by DAMA International, which involves the design of an Enterprise Data Model (EDM) and the Data Flow Design [3]. We particularly propose to currently use a conceptual model. The conceptual model could be considered as a visual dictionary of relevant abstractions, domain vocabulary and domain information [8]. The data flow design defines the requirements and the steps for storage and processing across databases, applications, platforms, and networks [3]. In our proposed model for the design of a data strategy, we enrich this vision by considering that the data life cycle will also consider the areas, business processes, and business managers associated with each stage to have a comprehensive view of the data and its passage through the organization. This documentation of both the conceptual model and the life cycle is developed with a strategic vision, highlighting the data that are prioritized during the knowledge, due to their relevance for business initiatives and risk management related to them. In addition, we also include in this knowledge phase the necessary instruments to know the state of methodological and technical capacities in data management and governance. To guide this knowledge, we follow the knowledge areas presented in Fig. 2. For each of them, we propose instruments, such as interviews and pre-designed surveys, to determine the status and expectations of those involved, which have been developed using reference frameworks such as ISO (8000, 38500, 2500, 33000), TOGAF, and maturity models such as the one proposed by Carnie Mellon University and DAMA.

Finally, to generate, transform and use the needed data, it is necessary to have technological tools to support them. Thus, the model proposes to identify both the technological requirements and the type of initiatives that are currently being worked on in the organization. For example, business intelligence projects, data science, artificial intelligence, among others, and the technological infrastructure that supports them.

*Planning.* Based on the knowledge developed in the previous stage, we propose the development of a specific plan to obtain the greatest value from data in an organization. The model proposes the inclusion of data development, management, and governance activities aligned with the strategic objectives. The prioritization of the projects is defined with a balanced vision between the priorities in the business initiatives, allowing the achievement of the strategic objectives, and the feasibility analysis of their implementation, as well as the valuation of the results for the organization.

The model we present in this article suggests that data development does not correspond exclusively to software development projects per se, the scope of data development is much broader, and its objective is to have the data that have been identified as missing at the time of performing knowledge activities. Likewise, data development involves other strategies, such as adaptation of business processes which have the technological tools but are not generating the data identified as necessary but is missing. Planning, in turn, involves the design and implementation of data management strategies to ensure the correction and/or expansion of those processes, procedures, indicators, and practices which do not comply with best practices and are causing problems in obtaining the greatest value from the data. In addition, planning involves culture strategies to ensure the participation of all the people of the organization and the management support.

Throughout the planning process, the model proposes the generation of indicators to periodically measure the implementation results of the designed plan. This measurement is recommended within the plan, involving both the indicators associated with business initiatives, documented during the knowledge stage, and the indicators associated with the design and implementation of data development, management, and governance strategies, as well as data related to cultural change management strategies.

*Ownership.* Ensuring the development of the proposed plan involves the design and implementation of communication and mobilization mechanisms that permeate the organization's designed data strategy. In the planning context, these strategies are established. Therefore, the appropriation phase will be oriented toward implementing the designed strategies. However, given the importance of this phase in the success of the data strategy, the model highlights its development as the last activity in the design of the data strategy. Similarly, the definition of monitoring and evolution plans are incorporated in the planning phase.

### 4.3  Model Validation

The proposed model has been validated in developed consulting projects and training workshops in Colombia and other Latin American countries (Research method stage 4 - Validation of model application results). One of the greatest challenges identified in applying the model was that people considered that the primary need was to govern data, based on the erroneous concept of governing for the sake of governing. One of the main achievements, at the end of the application of the model or the training workshops conducted, is that the participants acquire a strategic vision of data and its real importance for each case, ensuring that data initiatives are oriented towards the needs of each organization.

To validate the results of the model implementation, interviews were conducted with people from the companies in which, through consulting, the use of the data based on the proposed model was oriented, as well as with people who participated in the training workshops. We interviewed a leader from each company or course involved in the validation. In total, 7 interviews were conducted, covering the same 6 different organizations. In one of the organizations, 2 leaders were interviewed: one from data governance area and a manager from the business area. The interviews were carried out on average between 6 and 12 months after the execution of the project and/or training. Below, we summarize the most important findings.

Most of the interviewees said that the design of the data strategy has changed their conception of how to approach business initiatives. For example, one of the organizations that received the proposed model, in its data governance team for Latin America, stated that it had been developing data governance and master data management initiatives and that the proposed model had changed its work plan, allowing it to participate more effectively in the organization, manage data strategically, encourage the participation of other business areas and expand its coverage.

In the case of an energy operator in Colombia, the participants in the training workshop stated that the knowledge of the model allowed them to establish a plan oriented toward business initiatives. In this organization, one of the managers of the business areas was also interviewed, who stated that there is now an inventory of data completeness that has allowed them to focus sales actions and customer relations in an assertive way, achieving growth in the generation of opportunities. He also stated that the governance teams of the different units began to define their initiatives in terms of business strategies, changing the way they relate to the business areas. It is important to note that the workshop was only oriented toward officers of this organization.

In the case of a Colombian construction company, a positive result is identified around the data management of the data domain called project. In this case, the business area has identified a reduction in costs since the data flows have been organized based on the application of the model.

Students were also interviewed in workshops involving staff from different organizations, obtaining varying results. For example, one of the interviewees stated that he was unable to apply the knowledge of the model due to lack of managerial support and lack of knowledge of both the data strategy and the value of the data. In another case, the student was able to partially use the model, so he was able to guide the business team, which he supported, to orient data towards business initiatives, but he was not able to apply it holistically in the organization and what he did apply did not involve the whole model. Particularly, its best results were in the orientation of the initiatives to the business and the application of ADKAR to change the culture of the business team involved.

## 4.4  Adapting the Model to Smart Cities

In this section, we explain our first approach to adapting the model to the smart cities' context (Fig. 4).

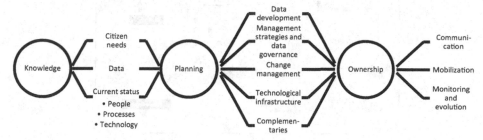

**Fig. 4.** Data strategy in smart cities. Source: own elaboration.

Specific considerations for each stage of the model are presented below.

## 4.5  Knowledge

The proposed model for the design of the data strategy is based on knowledge of the organizational strategy. When adapting the model to smart cities, it is necessary to consider knowledge related to the citizens' needs. The central axis of smart city solutions is focused on meeting the citizens' needs; in this way, smart cities are increasingly oriented to listen to the citizen, to understand their needs and create solutions together with the government and users with the goal of increasing the quality of life and well-being [1].

The research developed on the value of data in smart cities at the University of Duisburg-Essen proposed a roadmap that starts with the citizens' vision. Likewise, to continue with the adaptation of the model, it is necessary to point out that a complete knowledge about the design of the business model for smart cities is essential to motivate investment proposals, promoting communication and participation of those who will be able to ensure such solutions in the long term [4]. We propose the integration between the understanding of the needs raised in Muschkiet's research, which has been adapted by the authors as presented in the figure "Roadmap smart cities solutions evolution" and the use of the canvas model proposed by Giourka et al. Muschkiet's research, presented a roadmap to support smart city actor's collaboration, in the creation of ideas and the design of data-driven services (Fig. 5).

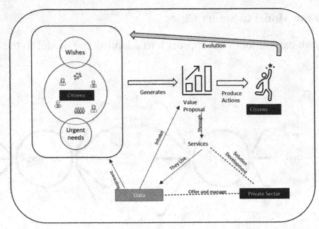

**Fig. 5.** Roadmap smart city solutions evolution. Source: Own elaboration based on Ontology for the roadmap [11].

Giourka et al.'s proposed canvas model highlights data as a key resource, as shown in the figure highlighting data as a key resource in the canvas for smart cities. Giourka et al. highlight that data is becoming increasingly essential in the development and improvement of smart cities, pointing out that data generated by sensors and connected in real time, as well as data generated by end users enable innovation and the creation of business and innovation while improving the quality of life in the city [4] (Fig. 6).

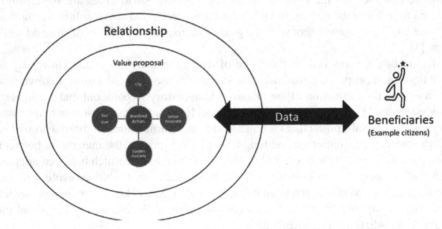

**Fig. 6.** Data as a key resource in Canvas for smart cities. Source: Own elaboration based on Canvas model for smart cities [4].

The model also proposes the identification of the data needed to meet these needs and whether they exist in the organization; as well as the establishment of the processes that capture, transform and/or deliver such data, and the risks associated with this process. In the case of smart cities, knowing both the necessary and existing data generates important challenges, understanding that each required solution may involve different organizations.

The model also proposes knowing the status of the implemented processes for data management and the culture associated with them. To adapt the model to smart cities, it is necessary to expand the design of the data life cycle to specify each of the processes associated with the use, transformation, and use of data in return for the organizations involved in them. The life cycle designed in the organizational environment, during the data strategy, has a broader vision than in a smart city given the challenges of having so many entities involved. This extension is rewarded with automatic data generation using, for example, the internet of things, which should reduce the quality risks caused by human error. In addition, a more detailed exploration of the security and privacy risks of personal data will be necessary, precisely because of the participation of so many involved actors and the use of personal data in an environment that could be less controlled than in an organization and supported by technologies such as the internet of things.

## 4.6 Planning

The model proposes to develop a specific plan to achieve the greatest value from the data in the organization. In the case of smart cities, the prioritization of the projects to be developed will have an added criterion that is associated with the analysis of the most pressing citizen needs and the prioritization of the Sustainable Development Goals (SDGs) that are currently driving and establishing the order of the initiatives around the world.

The design, development, and implementation of solutions to the challenges posed and the transformation of cities into smart cities cannot be a task of the government alone, it requires collaborative work. This article considers collaboration as a basic structure for the development of smart cities. Thus, in the planning stage, it is necessary to adapt the change management dynamics of organizations to ensure the effective participation of these involved actors. For example, ensuring that involved actors have the necessary skills is an additional challenge in the adaptation. Referring to this, Wolf states that "society has been increasing its trust in data, making it necessary to ensure that all citizens have the necessary skills to be data literate" [15].

The model involves planning the generation and use of data that represent the indicators needed to assess the evolution of smart cities. It is proposed to take as a basis the indicators proposed in the research conducted by John Smiciklas (BOMA Canada) and others. The indicators will allow cities to measure their progress over time, compare their performance with other cities and through analysis and sharing allow for the dissemination of best practices and for setting standards for progressing in achieving the SDGs at the city level [14].

This adaptation will also end up benefiting the model for organizations, since companies must also prioritize SDGs. In future projects, feedback from the adaptation to smart cities towards the model oriented to organizations is considered.

### 4.7 Ownership

In the case of the appropriation of the data strategy in smart cities, it will be crucial to involve the beneficiaries. These beneficiaries may include citizens, private companies, research organizations, government, and non-governmental enterprises [4]. To ensure that the greatest value is obtained from the data, it is essential to ensure government transformation. The plans developed during the design of the data strategy imply added challenges, the adaptation of the model has opportunities for improvement in the appropriation stage, as well as it is necessary to distinguish these appropriation activities in an organizational environment vs. an environment with a diversity of involved actors, as is the case of smart cities.

## 5 Discussion and Conclusions

The data strategy design model presented in this article has fulfilled its purpose. Both in the results originally evaluated and, in the interviews, the model gives good results in ensuring that those who know it, understand the importance of aligning data initiatives to the business and in doing so in a concrete way that can be implemented. Likewise, the model allows establishing the boundaries between data strategy, management, and governance, ensuring its implementation according to the needs of each organization. It is also evident that the incorporation of knowledge of data and its associations, which is one of the main contributions of the model, is a successful approach. The three proposed stages- knowledge, planning and appropriation are evidenced as adequate.

As some of the limitations of this work, is necessary to expand the support tools that guide the customization of the instruments prepared in the model to the specific needs of each organization. There is also a need to enrich the documentation of the model for its use independent of the author's participation. Another fundamental point to be improved is the use of methodological and technological tools that allow the valuation of the data. Likewise, it is necessary to strengthen the specific follow-up activities of the organization's results when applying the model, particularly considering evidence that it is being effectively adopted culturally.

As for our future work, we plan to enrich the model with the development of guidelines for the customization and enrichment, in each organization, of the instruments designed for the knowledge stage.

In the case of smart cities, an effective data strategy will allow the government, the private sector, and citizens to make better decisions in each of the smart city dimensions, improve the operation of offered services, and comply with the regulations associated with each of them. It will also allow academia to focus on the research, training, and support necessary to achieve the purpose of smart cities and allow citizens to participate in the definition, implementation and monitoring of services.

In this research we provide the first version of the proposed model for the design of an effective data strategy for smart cities. For the adaptation of the model, some considerations must be made. The first consideration is associated with the need to provide methods that sufficiently address the problems of smart cities. There is a lack of research to provide methods that sufficiently address the problems of smart cities to make the data valuable for the services offered [11]. As presented in the introduction, it reflects that due to the digital transformation of smart cities, improved access to digital technologies can enable the collection and use of data that can serve as key resources for services to improve the quality of citizens' lives. The adaptation of the model responds to this need to provide such methods, best practices, and strategies.

In terms of the benefits of adapting the model, we highlighted those smart cities face challenges in making data valuable for the design of data-driven services [11]. The concern about obtaining the greatest value from data in smart cities is being outlined in different academic and business environments and the adaptation of this model drives to achieve such value by the integration of different research and the use of the proposed validated model. The third consideration is oriented toward the risks that may be involved in applying the model. The first risk we identified is associated with the diversity of those involved in the exercise, the support of the government and the community itself, and the appropriation and effective application of the model by those involved. In addition, there are risks mitigating in the application of the different instruments, both in terms of knowledge and planning, with an orientation of the services to improve the quality of life of the community. Another risk is ensuring that the services proposed are aligned with one of the main focuses of smart cities, sustainability. The fourth consideration is the need to customize the model, considering the mitigation of identified risks and the enhancement of benefits.

# References

1. Blasi, S., Gobbo, E., Sedita, S.R.: Smart cities and citizen engagement: evidence from twitter data analysis on Italian municipalities. J. Urban Manag. **11**(2), 153–165 (2022). https://doi.org/10.1016/j.jum.2022.04.001
2. Cichy, C., Rass, S.: An overview of data quality frameworks. IEEE Access **7**, 24634–24648 (2019). https://doi.org/10.1109/ACCESS.2019.2899751
3. Deborah Henderson, C., Susan Earley, C., Laura Sebastian-Coleman, C.I. (eds.) 2nd ed. DAMA International. Data Management Body of Knowledge, Technics Publications (2017)
4. Giourka, P., et al.: The smart city business model canvas—a smart city business modeling framework and practical tool. Energies **12**(24) (2019). https://doi.org/10.3390/en12244798
5. Harbour T, Aiken P.:Data strategy and the enterprise data executive: ensuring that business and IT are in synch in the post-big data era (Data Literacy Book 1) (2017)
6. Janowski, T.: Digital government evolution: from transformation to contextualization. In: Government Information Quarterly, vol. 32, no. 3, pp. 221–236. Elsevier Ltd (2015). https://doi.org/10.1016/j.giq.2015.07.001
7. Janssen, M., Brous, P., Estevez, E., Barbosa, L. S., Janowski, T.: Data governance: organizing data for trustworthy artificial intelligence. Government Inf. Q. **37**(3) (2020). https://doi.org/10.1016/j.giq.2020.101493
8. Larman, C.: UML y Patrones. Introducción al análisis y diseño orientado a objetos. Pearson Educación S.A., ed.; 2nd ed (2003)
9. Larrucea, X., Moffie, M., Asaf, S., Santamaria, I.: Towards a GDPR compliant way to secure European cross border Healthcare Industry 4.0. Comput. Stand. Interfaces **69** (2020). https://doi.org/10.1016/j.csi.2019.103408
10. Marr, B.: Data strategy: how to profit from a world of big data, analytics, and the internet of things (1st edn, ed.) (2017)

11. Muschkiet, M., Kühne, B., Jagals, M., Bergan, P.: Making data valuable for smart city service systems-a citizen journey map for data-driven service design augmented reality-enabled enterprise architecture management view project Projekt portfolio management view project (2022). https://www.researchgate.net/publication/358644525

12. Provost, F., Fawcett, T.: Data science and its relationship to big data and data-driven decision making. Big Data 1(1), 51–59 (2013). https://doi.org/10.1089/big.2013.1508

13. Nazir, S., et al.: A comprehensive analysis of healthcare big data management, analytics, and scientific programming. Elsevier (2020)

14. Sustainable Cities, S. (n.d.). Collection methodology for key performance indicators for smart sustainable cities united smart sustainable cities 4 Montevideo office collection methodology for key performance indicators for smart sustainable cities ii foreword

15. Wolff, A., Gooch, D., Montaner, J.J.C., Rashid, U., Kortuem, G.: Creating and understanding of data literacy for a data driven society.J. Commun. Inf. 12(3), 9 (2016)

# A Maturity Model for Data Governance, Data Quality Management, and Data Management

Ismael Caballero[1,4][(✉)] ⓘ, Fernando Gualo[1,4] ⓘ, Moisés Rodríguez[2,3,4] ⓘ, and Mario Piattini[4] ⓘ

[1] DQTeam SL, 13005 Ciudad Real, Spain
`{Ismael.Caballero,Fernando.Gualo}@uclm.es`
[2] AQCLab, 13005 Ciudad Real, Spain
`Moises.Rodriguez@uclm.es`
[3] University of Castilla-La Mancha, 13001 Ciudad Real, Spain
[4] Alarcos Research Group, University of Castilla-La Mancha, 13001 Ciudad Real, Spain
`Mario.Piattini@uclm.es`

**Abstract.** Data governance is an important activity for data-centric digital transformation. One of the main elements of data governance is a data maturity model. In this paper, we summarize the main existing data maturity models. We also describe the Alarcos' Model for Data Maturity (MAMD in Spanish). MAMD is an ISO/IEC 33000-based framework for data governance, data management, and data quality management. MAMD consists of a Process Reference Model (PRM) and a Process Assessment Model (PAM), including a Maturity Model. One of the most important components of the PAM is a maturity model. Some practical experiences using this model are also presented.

**Keywords:** Data maturity model · Data Governance · Data management · Data Quality Management

## 1 Introduction

In recent years, the importance of data has been emphasized, and expressions such as *"data is the new currency,"* *"data is the new oil,"* *"data is the hidden mine"* ... have become popular. Digital transformation is affecting all sectors, from agriculture to industry, tourism, healthcare, etc., and data has become any organization's most powerful potent enabler. This is because, as [1] points out, data enables organizations to implement different strategies: data centricity, industry convergence, hybrid services, and customer-centricity.

All countries are driving the data economy; for example, the European Data Strategy foresees a 530% increase in the overall volume of data being generated and moved within the European Union. For this reason, there is a demand for the creation of adequate data governance mechanisms in organizations so that they can be competitive players in the data market and improve the well-being of citizens.

M. Naiouf et al. (Eds.): JCC-BD&ET 2023, CCIS 1828, pp. 157–170, 2023.
https://doi.org/10.1007/978-3-031-40942-4_12

The expected benefits of data governance are (1) Optimization of the organizational value of data through alignment with organizational strategy; (2) Optimization of risks related to the acquisition, use, and exploitation of data, ensuring compliance with regulatory standards; and (3) Optimization of the human and technological resources needed and used to provide more efficient support to the various operations involving data.

These data governance mechanisms must address vertical aspects related to the acquisition, holding, sharing, use, and exploitation of data in business processes while addressing cross-cutting aspects of their management: quality, ethical and privacy aspects, interoperability, knowledge management, and control over data assets through the related policies, and deployment of organizational structures with appropriate separation of data governance roles from data management roles. One of the main elements of data governance is the maturity model.

At Grupo Alarcos, we have been working for twenty years on data maturity models [2], which we have been applying in several organizations and refining and completing with various standards and frameworks. This work has given rise to the MAMD model (Alarcos Model for Data Maturity), which has recently been updated following the development by the Spanish Government's Data Office and UNE (Spanish Standardization Organization) of three technical specifications for governance (UNE 0077 [3]), quality management (UNE 0078[4]) and data management (UNE 0079 [5]), based on MAMD and other standards such as DAMA [6] and ISO/IEC 38505 [7].

Section 2 summarizes the main existing data maturity models, Sect. 3 presents the latest version of the MAMD model, Sect. 4 summarizes some practical applications of the model, and Sect. 5 presents conclusions and future work.

## 2  Maturity Models

As in software, a field in which dozens of maturity models have been created for different processes, among which the best known is the CMM/CMMI driven by the SEI and the ISO/IEC 15504/33000 family of standards, several maturity models have also been created for data. In this section, we summarize the most relevant ones.

### 2.1  Dama

Regarding the assessment of data management maturity, DAMA proposes a six-level model [6]:

- **Level 0 - No capabilities**. There are no organized data management practices or formal organizational processes to manage data. Only some organizations are typically at this level 0.
- **Level 1 - Initial.** General purpose data is managed using a limited set of tools with little or no governance. Data management is mainly dependent on a few experts. Roles and responsibilities are defined in "silos."
- **Level 2 - Repeatable**. At this level, the implementation of consistent tools and role definition for process execution support arises. The organization begins to use centralized tools and provide more oversight for data management.

- **Level 3 - Defined**. This level considers the introduction and institutionalization of scalable data management processes, which acts as organizational enabler. Characteristics include replication of data across an organization with some controls in place and a general increase in overall data quality, along with coordinated policy definition and management. A more formal process definition leads to a significant reduction in manual intervention.
- **Level 4 - Managed**. Institutional knowledge gained from growth in Levels 1 through 3 allows the organization to predict outcomes when tackling new projects and tasks and begin to manage data-related risks. Data management includes performance metrics.
- **Level 5 - Optimized**. When data management practices are optimized, they are highly predictable due to process automation and technology change management. Organizations at this maturity level focus on continuous improvement. At this level, tools allow data to be seen across all processes.

### 2.2 Aiken's Model

In [8], a model is proposed whose main objective is to increase data management maturity levels to positively impact the coordination of data flow between organizations, human resources, and systems. To improve the organization's data management practices, this model proposes to start with a self-assessment against the maturity level and develop a roadmap to achieve improvement. The model states that data management consists of six interrelated and coordinated processes:

1. **Data Coordination Program**, the purpose of which is to provide an appropriate data management process and technology infrastructure.
2. **Organizational Data Integration**, which is intended to achieve appropriate organizational data exchange.
3. **Data Management**, which consists of achieving the integration of data from the thematic area of the business.
4. **Data Development**, to achieve the exchange of data within a business area.
5. **Data Operations Support** to provide reliable access to the data.
6. **Active Use of Data**, the purpose of which is to leverage data in business activities.

All organizations implement their data management practices in a way that can be classified into one of the five maturity model levels.

### 2.3 Data Management Maturity Model (DMM)

The SEI (Software Engineering Institute) published the DMM (Data Management Maturity Model) [9], which is analogous to the maturity model for software processes, CMMI (Capability Maturity Model Integration) but focused on data governance, management, and quality processes.

This model was withdrawn at the end of 2021. Its content is supposed to be subsumed by the CMMI V2 model.

## 2.4 IBM Model

The IBM Data Governance Maturity Model has been developed by the IBM Data Governance Council and is focused on helping to make the strategy more effective. The maturity model defines the scope and who should be involved in governing and measuring how organizations govern their data. This model measures data governance competencies based on eleven maturity categories [10] arranged in four interrelated groups:

- **Outcomes**. These are the intended outcomes of the data governance program, which tend to focus on reducing risk and increasing value; these outcomes are driven by reduced costs and increased revenue.
- **Enablers**. Includes areas of organizational structures and knowledge, policies, and data stewardship.
- **Core disciplines**. Includes data quality management, data lifecycle management, and data security and privacy.
- **Supporting disciplines**. It includes data architecture, classification and metadata, and logging and audit reporting.

In each of these groups, it is possible to find the following eleven categories:

- **Data compliance and risk management**. A methodology in which risks are identified, rated, quantified, accepted, avoided, mitigated, or transferred.
- **Value creation**. A process by which data assets are qualified and quantified to maximize the value created by the data assets.
- **Organizational structures and knowledge**. Refers to the level of mutual accountability between business and IT and the recognition of fiduciary responsibility for governing data at different levels of management.
- **Stewardship**. A quality control discipline designed to ensure data stewardship for asset enhancement, risk mitigation, and organizational control.
- **Policy**. The written articulation of organizational performance.
- **Data quality management**. Refers to methods for measuring, improving, and certifying the quality and integrity of production, testing, and archive data.
- **Information lifecycle management**. A systematic approach to the policy-based collection, use, retention, and disposal of information.
- **Information security and privacy**. Refers to the policies, practices, and controls an organization uses to mitigate risks and protect data assets.
- **Data architecture**. The architecture design of structured and unstructured data systems and applications that enable availability and distribution to appropriate users.
- **Classification and metadata**. Refers to the methods and tools for creating standard semantic definitions for business and IT data models and repositories.
- **Audit logging and reporting**. Refers to the organizational processes for monitoring and measuring the value and risks of data and the effectiveness of data governance.

## 2.5 Gartner's Enterprise Information Management Model

Gartner states that enterprise information management cannot be implemented as a single project but that organizations must implement it as a coordinated program that evolves over time. Therefore, it proposes an information management maturity model called

EIM (Enterprise Information Management), which can be adapted to support a small business unit or the entire organization.

The EIM makes it possible to identify what stage of maturity organizations have reached and what actions they need to take to reach the next level. The maturity model has five levels that look at seven dimensions or building blocks that Gartner has identified as essential for information management maturity: vision, strategy, metrics, governance, people, process, and infrastructure [11].

The maturity levels and indicators themselves are aligned with the organizations' current and near-term capabilities:

- **Level 1:** Organizations are aware of critical issues and changes, but they need more resources, budgets, and/or leadership to address or make significant changes in EIM.
- **Level 2:** Organizations work reactively application-centric until information-related problems manifest themselves significantly in business losses or lack of competitiveness.
- **Level 3:** Organizations have become more proactive in identifying specific areas of information management and have begun to identify the "organization" in information systems. Some programs are operational and practical, but there needs to be more leverage or alignment between programs and investments.
- **Level 4:** They take a managed approach to information management, committing to coordination across the organization with influential people and effective processes and technologies.
- **Level 5:** Typically, model organizations in which many (if not most) aspects of information acquisition, management, and application have been optimized as tangible organizational assets with high-performance organizational structures and advanced technologies and architectures.

## 2.6  DCAM

The Data Management Capability Assessment Model (DCAM) [12] was created by members of the Enterprise Data Management (EDM) Council as a set of assessment standards to measure the level of data management capability. DCAM documents 38 capabilities and 136 sub-capabilities associated with developing a sustainable data management program.

These capabilities are specific to components, which are the artifacts to be considered in creating a data management program, according to DCAM. The components are data management strategy, data control environment, data quality, technology architecture, data architecture, data management business case, data governance, and data management program. Coordination of the components into a cohesive operational model ensures that controls are consistently placed throughout the lifecycle in alignment with organizational privacy and security policies.

DCAM proposes a maturity model with six levels, from Not Initiated, the first level, to Improved, the last level.

# 3 MAMD (Alarcos' Model for Data Maturity)

Based on our experience, we believe that the development of a maturity model should be based on international standards, especially on the ISO/IEC 33000 family of standards [13–15]. This brings the following benefits: Facilitates self-assessment, provides a basis for use in process improvement and process capability determination, supports the evaluation of other process characteristics in addition to process capability, produces a process rating, addresses the capability of the process to achieve its purpose, is appropriate for different application domains and organization sizes, and can provide an objective benchmark across organizational processes.

These benefits were already proven in developing maturity models for software processes such as COMPETISOFT [16, 17] and MMIS [18, 19].

The MAMD model is two-dimensional (see Fig. 1), whose first dimension defines the different processes to be evaluated and the expected results for each of them in case they are correctly implemented. In the case of this technical specification, the processes to be used are those defined in the technical requirements for data governance, management, and quality management. In the second dimension, the model deals with the "capability" of the process, which consists of a series of process attributes grouped into capability levels and which identify whether the process, in addition to being implemented (level 1), is managed, established, etc.

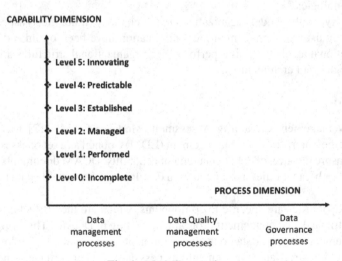

**CAPABILITY DIMENSION**

Level 5: Innovating

Level 4: Predictable

Level 3: Established

Level 2: Managed

Level 1: Performed

Level 0: Incomplete

**PROCESS DIMENSION**

Data management processes

Data Quality management processes

Data Governance processes

**Fig. 1.** MAMD overview

## 3.1 Capability Dimension

For the measurement of the capability of a process, ISO/IEC 33020 defines a set of process capability levels and their corresponding process attributes (PA). It is important to note that, to achieve a capability level, a process must meet the process attributes of

| Capability level | ID | Process attribute |
|---|---|---|
| Level 0. Incomplete Process | | |
| Level 1. Performed Process | AP 1.1 | Process realization |
| Level 2. Managed Process | AP 2.1 | Realization management |
| | AP 2.2 | Work product management |
| Level 3. Established Process | AP 3.1 | Process definition |
| | AP 3.2 | Process deployment |
| Level 4. Predictable Process | AP 4.1 | Quantitative analysis |
| | AP 4.2 | Quantitative control |
| Level 5. Innovating Process | AP 5.1 | Process innovation |
| | AP 5.2 | Innovation implementation |

**Fig. 2.** Capability levels and process attributes.

that level and the process attributes of the levels above it. The list of process attributes and capability levels is shown in Fig. 2.

Within the process measurement framework proposed by the ISO/IEC 33000 family of standards, a process attribute is a measurable property of the process capability, which is measured using the following ordinal scale:

- **(N) Not Implemented**: there is little or no evidence of achievement of the defined process attribute in the assessed process. As an indication, a process attribute is "*not implemented*" when its achievement degree is between 0 and $< = 15\%$.
- **(P) Partially implemented**: There is some evidence of a focus and some achievement of the process attribute defined in the assessed process. If the achievement degree of the process attribute is $> 15\%$ and $< = 50\%$, its rating is "*partially implemented.*"
- **(L) Largely Implemented**: There is evidence of a systematic approach and significant achievement of the defined process attribute in the assessed process. A process attribute is rated as "*largely implemented*" if its achievement degree is $> 50\%$ and $< = 85\%$.
- **(F) Fully implemented**: There is evidence of a complete and systematic approach and full achievement of the defined process attribute in the assessed process. If the degree of achievement of the attribute is $> 85\%$ and $< = 100\%$, its rating is "*fully implemented.*"

The data governance, data quality management, and data management process outcomes specified in the process definition are considered to evaluate capability level 1: it must be inspected if the mentioned processes achieve their defined process outcomes. For capability levels 2 to 5, the process attributes in Fig. 2, which are cross-cutting to all processes, are used.

The process results and process attribute results can be characterized as an intermediate step to provide a process attribute rating. Based on the results obtained in the assessment of each of the process attributes of a specific process under evaluation, a rating of the capability level of that process can be issued. This rating is achieved by an aggregation method based on the assumption that a process has a given capability level if all process attributes of the previous levels have a rating of *"fully achieved"* (F) and the process attributes of that capability level have a rating of at least "largely achieved" (L).

## 3.2 Process Dimension

The process dimension is constituted by the processes of the three technical specifications mentioned above [1–3]. Each process is described in terms of its name, purpose, and process results. In addition, the description is completed with base practices, work products, and their relationship to the process results. For example, the *"Establishment of organizational structures process"* is presented in Table 1.

## 3.3 Organizational Maturity Model

The MAMD model is aligned to ISO 8000-6x [20–23] and consists of five maturity levels, as shown in Fig. 3.

The maturity levels proposed in MAMD [24], along with their meaning and the processes included, are detailed below:

- **Maturity Level 1 – Accomplished:** At this level, the organization can demonstrate that it uses a set of best practices to provide the minimum necessary support for managing the data required in its business processes. An organization at this level pays no attention to data governance or data quality. The processes that make up maturity level 1 are Data processing and Data technology infrastructure management.
- **Maturity Level 2 – Managed:** The organization can demonstrate that it uses a set of best practices to control the data quality used in its business processes. Therefore, there is some assurance that the organization has the minimum necessary data management processes in place to provide an acceptable outcome for its business processes. The processes that make up maturity level 2 are Data requirements management, Data configuration management, Historical data management, Data security management, Metadata management, Data quality monitoring and control, and Establishment of data policies, best practices, and procedures related to data governance.
- **Maturity Level 3 – Established:** The organization can demonstrate that it uses the complete set of data management best practices to ensure that the data used in its business processes are of appropriate levels of quality and that the data used in its business processes are aligned with organizational strategy. The processes that are included in the maturity level 3 are Data architecture and design management; Data sharing, brokerage, and integration; Master data management; Human resources management; Data lifecycle management; Data analytics; Data quality planning; Establishment of data strategy; Establishment of organizational structures for data governance, management, and use of data, and Data risk optimization.
- **Maturity Level 4 – Predictable:** The organization can demonstrate that it uses a set of best practices to monitor that the organizational data strategies are really effective, enabling it to ensure data quality and optimize data value. The processes that conform the maturity level 4 are Data quality assurance and Data Value Optimization.

**Table 1.** Process for the *"Establishment of organizational structures"*

| Process ID | EstOrg |
|---|---|
| Name | Establishment of organizational structures for data governance, management, and use |
| Purpose | The purpose of this process is to create and maintain the organizational structures necessary to assume the responsibilities related to the governance, management, and use of data; these structures must be provided with sufficiently skilled human resources to address these responsibilities successfully |
| Process outcomes | PO1. The most appropriate working model for data governance, management, and use is chosen<br>PO2. The organizational structures necessary to perform data governance, data management, and data quality management are created and maintained<br>PO3. Chains of authority, responsibility, and accountability are established to enable decision-making and conflict-resolution in data governance, management, and use<br>PO4. Escalation mechanisms are established for decision-making and problem-solving<br>PO5. The skills, knowledge, and competencies required for the roles that perform the established responsibilities are identified<br>PO6. It is ensured that the people who perform the specific roles related to the data have the identified knowledge and skills<br>PO7. The performance of organizational structures is monitored |
| Base practices | • Define an organizational structure for data governance, management, and use [PO1, 2, 3, 4]<br>• Establish the necessary skills and knowledge [PO5, 6]<br>• Monitor the performance of organizational structures [PO7] |

Work products
• Organizational structures for data governance, management, and use [PO 1, 2]
• Authority levels of the components of organizational structures [PO 3]
• Chains of responsibility and accountability of organizational structures [PO 3, 4]
• Stakeholder communication and control mechanisms [PO 4]
• Knowledge, skills, and competencies needed to perform the responsibilities assigned to each role [PO 5, 6]
• Reports on the degree of performance of organizational structures [PO 6, 7]

– **Maturity Level 5 - In Innovation:** The organization can demonstrate that it uses a set of best practices to ensure that data governance, management, and quality management processes are continuously improved to optimize data value and reduce risks, contributing to the organizational strategy. The process that makes up maturity level 5 is Data quality improvement.

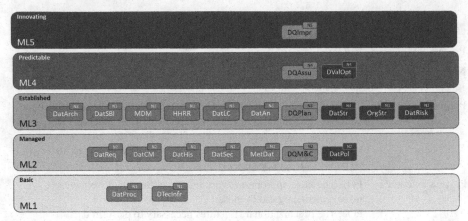

**Fig. 3.** MAMD Maturity Model for Data Governance, Data Management, and Data Quality Management.

### 3.4 Difference Between MAMD and Other Models

Some notable differences between MAMD and the remainder of the model shown in Sect. 2 are:

- **MAMD** is based and aligned to international open standards like ISO 8000–61 or ISO 38505–1
- **MAMD** is not proprietary, it is open and free (it can be downloaded for free).
- **MAMD** can be used with any type and size of organization, ranging from multinationals to small and medium companies.
- **MAMD** brings together unified the most relevant concept on data governance, data quality, and data quality management around international standards.
- **MAMD** addresses the process approach.
- **MAMD** incorporates a maturity model aligned to ISO 33000, with common requirements for process capability-driven assessment and a systematic and rigorous process assessment methodology.
- **MAMD** can be used to certify the level of data maturity of organizations.

## 4    Practical Applications

MAMD has been successfully applied to different organizations, public and private, with mainly three purposes:

1) Define projects to select and implement or improve the data governance, data management, and data quality processes.
2) Assess the level of organizational data maturity to improve the less capable processes.
3) Combine MAMD as a body of knowledge with some other domain-specific frameworks to tailor new maturity models for given domains considering the specific concerns of data governance, data management, and data quality management in the domain.

Due to length paper restrictions, we introduce examples of the two first purposes in Subsects. 4.1 and 4.2.

## 4.1 Insurance Company: Building a "Source of Truth" Repository

This experience is related to a large insurance company. Due to regulatory compliance, the insurance company must build specific reports to be submitted to the national agency to meet Solvency II's requirements. These reports were built upon data from different transactional databases related to the insurance operations (e.g., new contracts of insurance policies and customers' claims). These reports are vital to determine the company's capability to keep on the market, as Solvencia II requires. Consequently, the data used to produce this report must be of the highest quality possible. The insurance company invested lots of resources in assuring the quality of the data coming from every transactional data source, and consequently, they were at high risk of making any mistakes.

To prevent these mistakes, the insurance company decided to build a master data repository that could be used as the only source of truth from which data required to build the report was extracted. After introducing MAMD to the people in charge of the project, the initiative was no longer understood as a technological project but also a managerial project in which data had to be conveniently governed. The project was structured in three stages:

1) Development of the "source of truth" repository. This repository was a master data repository. Several data management processes from MAMD ("data requirements management," "data architecture and modeling," "data technology infrastructure management," "master data management," "data sharing, brokerage, and integration," "data security management" and "data configuration management") were considered the essential reference for this subprojects stage.
2) Improvement of the quality of the data in the "source of truth" repository. Once the repository was populated with data from various sources, people in charge of the initiative considered some MAMD processes ("data quality management" processes of "data quality planning," "data quality monitoring and controlling," and "data quality assurance") to improve the current state of quality of the data. They also use these processes to revisit the ETL processes feeding the master data repository to ensure that the collected data quality requirements were correctly implemented. Interestingly, they consider this stage as iterative and incremental, assuming some risk in every iteration of the stage and leading efforts to reduce the existing risks continuously.
3) Governance of the data in the "source of truth" repository. People in charge of the project understood over time that the repository became an essential asset for the company. Consequently, they became convinced of the need to maintain the data contained in the master data repository aligned with the organizational strategy. To achieve this goal, they complemented the data life cycle information with some policies (not only to meet Solvency II requirements and to better performance in other data operations). Some other MAMD processes, like "data life cycle management" and "establishment of data policies, best practices, and procedures related to data governance," were followed to support these last stages.

## 4.2  University Library: Assessing the Organizational Maturity

This experience was conducted in a Spanish University Library [8]. This project's main aim was to assess the organizational maturity level of the library to determine how well they were governing and managing the data. This requirement was essential for them because they needed to internally share data with other university organizations and externally with other university libraries and other institutions of Public Administration.

Similar to the previously described experience, several business processes were chosen as the source of evidence of the adequate implementation of the data governance, data quality management, and data management processes included in MAMD. On this occasion, the selected processes were:

– As Main Process (MP): cataloging procedure.
– As Auxiliary Process 1 (AP1): funds movement procedure and
– As Auxiliary Process 2 (AP2): user load procedure / external users

**Fig. 4.** Certification of having achieved the organizational data maturity level of 2 granted to University Library

The assessment scope was selected to maturity level 2. It was relatively easy to determine that the University Library has achieved Maturity Level 1. As the Head of the Library considered that achieving maturity level 2 would bring significant benefits to the institution, they launched a process improvement project to amend the various problems found during the internal audit. In this sense, several corrective actions affecting the working methods and the data repositories were successfully executed. As a consequence, almost all problems were fixed. The University Library decided to go ahead with an external certification audit to be granted a certificate. AENOR International oversaw conducting the external audit for certification, and they found that the University Library has achieved the required rating for the process attributes for the Maturity Level 2. Consequently, AENOR International granted the University Library a certificate of Maturity Level 2 (See Fig. 4.)

## 5  Conclusions and Future Work

In addition to further refining the model through its use in real organizational settings, especially in the public sector, we also want to investigate the extent to which a model such as MAMD can be useful for the implementation of data spaces.

On the other hand, a maturity model is a piece of a much more complex system such as a data governance system, so we are investigating the development of a process for the creation and optimization of the data governance system and the creation of a technological infrastructure to support the creation of a governance system.

**Acknowledgements.** This work has been partially funded by the ADAGIO project (Alarcos' DAta Governance framework and systems generatIOn), JCCM Consejería de Educación, Cultura y Deportes, and FEDER funds (SBPLY/21/180501/000061).

## References

1. Aiken, P.: Experience: succeeding at data management – BigCo attempts to leverage data. ACM J. Data Inf. Q. **7**(1–2), 1–35 (2016). art. 8
2. Caballero, I., Piattini, M.: CALDEA: a data quality model based on maturity levels. In: QSIC, pp. 380–387 (2003)
3. UNE-0077. Especificación técnica para el gobierno del dato. Asociación Española de Normalización (2023)
4. UNE-0078 Especificación técnica para la gestión del dato. Asociación Española de Normalización (2023)
5. UNE-0079. Especificación técnica para la gestión de la calidad del dato. Asociación Española de Normalización (2023)
6. DAMA. DAMA-DMBOK: data management body of knowledge (2ª ed.). Bradley Beach, Technics Publications, Nueva Jersey (2017)
7. ISO/IEC 38505-1:2017 information technology — governance of IT — governance of data — Part 1: Application of ISO/IEC 38500 to the governance of data
8. Aiken, P., Allen, M.D., Parker, B., Mattia, A.: Measuring data management practice maturity: a community's self-assessment. Computer **40**(4), 42–50 (2007)
9. SEI. DMM: data management maturity model. Software Engineering Institute Pittsburgh (2014)
10. Soares, S.: The IBM data governance unified process: driving business value with IBM software and best practices, MC Press, LLC (2010)
11. Laney, D.B. Infonomics. How to monetize, manage, and measure information as an asset for competitive advantage. Nueva York, EE.UU. Bibliomotion (2018)
12. DCAM framework. EDMCouncil. https://edmcouncil.org/frameworks/dcam/
13. ISO/IEC 33001 - Information technology - process assessment - concepts and terminology (2015)

14. ISO/IEC 33003 - Information technology - process assessment - requirements for process measurement frameworks (2015)
15. ISO/IEC 33004:2015: information technology — process assessment — requirements for process reference, process assessment, and maturity model, ISO, (2015)
16. Oktaba, H., García, F., Piattini, M., Ruiz, F., Pino, F.J., Alquicira, C.: Software process improvement: the Competisoft project. Computer **40**(10), 21–28 (2007)
17. Pino, F.J., García, F., Piattini, M., Oktaba, H.: A research framework for building SPI proposals in small organizations: the competisoft experience. Softw. Qual. J. **24**(3), 489–518 (2015). https://doi.org/10.1007/s11219-015-9278-2
18. Pino, F., Rodríguez, M., Piattini, M., Fernández, C.M.: Delgado modelo de madurez de ingeniería del software V2.0 (MMIS V.2), AENOR, Madrid (2018)
19. Rodríguez, M., Verdugo, J., Pino, F.J., Delgado, B., Piattini, M.: Software development process assessment with MMIS vol 2, an ISO/IEC 33000-based model. IT Prof. **23**(6), 17–23 (2021)
20. ISO/TS 8000-60:2017. Data quality — Part 60: Data quality management: overview
21. ISO 8000-61:2016 Data quality — Part 61: Data quality management: process reference model, ISO (2016)
22. ISO 8000-62:2018 Data quality — Part 62: data quality management: organizational process maturity assessment: application of standards relating to process assessment, ISO (2018)
23. ISO 8000-63:2019 data quality — Part 63: data quality management: process measurement, ISO (2019)
24. MAMD. Modelo Alarcos de Madurez de Datos v4, DQTeam (2023)

# Examining Factors of Acceptance and Use of Technology in Digital Services in the Context of Ecuador

Pablo Pintado[1,2]($\boxtimes$) (iD), Sebastián Wiesner[1] (iD), Daniela Prado[3] (iD),
and Elsa Estevez[4]($\boxtimes$) (iD)

[1] Universidad del Azuay, Cuenca, Ecuador
ppintado@uazuay.edu.ec
[2] Facultad de Informática, Universidad Nacional de la Plata (UNLP), La Plata, Argentina
[3] Universidad de Cuenca, Cuenca, Ecuador
[4] Departamento de Ciencias e Ingeniería de la Computación, Universidad Nacional del Sur
(UNS), Instituto de Ciencias e Ingeniería de la Computación (UNS-CONICET), La Plata,
Argentina
ecestevez@gmail.com

**Abstract.** Today, users of digital services demand sophisticated quality attributes
to decide for their adoption. Thus, knowing which factors influence the acceptance and use of technologies for the adoption of digital services is most relevant
for planning and designing such services. Despite the existence of a variety of
research on techniques and models of acceptance and use, little research exists
for understanding the behavior of these factors by economic activity, and users'
demographic attributes, like gender, age, educational level, and location, in the
context of digital services in Ecuador. Aiming at filling this research gap, this
article presents; 1) a selective state-of-the-art review on the proposed topic: 2)
based on case study methodology complemented with survey research method, an
analysis of the results obtained from the behavior of the factors of acceptance and
use of digital services by the units of analysis in Ecuador; and 3) a characterization
of the variable behavior of the factors of acceptance and use of digital services in
general and by unit of analysis. The main contribution of our research is that the
obtained results provide insights and knowledge about factors required for users
to accept, use and adopt digital services in Ecuador.

**Keywords:** case study · survey · acceptance and usage factors · digital
transformation · scrum · design thinking · bot · characterization · digital services

## 1 Introduction

The industrial revolution 4.0 facilitated by the adoption of new technologies, motivates
innovation, transformation of business processes and the design of innovative digital
services, available to society at large. As a result, users are becoming more informed,
more practical and more demanding of high-quality digital services. However, to adopt

M. Naiouf et al. (Eds.): JCC-BD&ET 2023, CCIS 1828, pp. 171–185, 2023.
https://doi.org/10.1007/978-3-031-40942-4_13

new services and based on the increasing demands, there are some factors of acceptance and use of technologies that must be carefully consider. In [1], the authors present a systematic literature review of such factors and indicate that there is variation in the behavior of acceptance and use factors by economic activity, and they recommend future studies applying other research techniques to determine the behavior of acceptance and use factors in specific regions. Based on our study, we found previous works in the literature on technology acceptance and usage factors of digital service in Ecuador that focus on certain digital services and only with certain acceptance and usage models. For instance, [2] evaluated the quality of educational game applications for children in Ecuador by applying Technology Acceptance Model (TAM), ISO 9241–210 and ISO 25010. In [3], the authors analyze the use of scrum to actuate agile software development that allows early user testing, promoting early use and acceptance of the application. The work presented in [4] analyzes the use of chatbots in complex virtual environments, communicating with human characteristics. One of the results is that the chatbot response speed increases user satisfaction. Based on our knowledge, we understand that there is a gap in the state of the art that motivates to obtain the characterization of the priority factors of acceptance and use of digital services in Ecuador considering in particular the units of analysis of economic activity, and users' demographic data, like gender, age, educational level, and location.

To address the identified research gap, we use the case study research methodology [5], following an exploratory approach applied to the Ecuadorian context, complemented with a survey with a descriptive approach to collect standardized information from a specific population. The collected data enable us to perform a quantitative data analysis [6], whose result is the input to characterize the factors of acceptance and use of digital services in Ecuador.

The rest of this document is structured as follows. Section 2 provides the state of the art conducted to analyze previous works existing in the literature. Section 3 explains the case study methodology used for this research. Section 4 presents the analysis and characterization of the results obtained from about the factors of acceptance and use of digital services in general and by units of analysis. Finally, Sect. 5 discusses conclusions, recommendations and future work.

## 2 Background

A selective literature review was conducted in ACM, IEEE Xplore and Springer aiming at identifying previous research works on the perception of the factors of acceptance and use of digital services and technology in Ecuador. For thus, we conducted searches, on December 2022, looking for papers published in the last five years and with the following keywords.

In the title:

"(((Acceptance model) OR (Acceptance and Use of Technology) OR (ISO 9241-210) OR (ISO-9421-210) OR (ISO-IEC-25010) OR (ISO/IEC-25010) OR (ISO/IEC 25010) OR (ISO IEC 25010) OR (Digital Services) OR (Robotic Process Automation) OR (Straight-through processing) OR (Design Thinking) OR (SCRUM)) AND (Ecuador))"

Or in the abstracts:

"((((Acceptance model) OR (Acceptance and Use of Technology) OR (ISO 9241-210) OR (ISO-9241-210) OR (ISO-IEC-25010) OR (ISO/IEC-25010) OR (ISO/IEC 25010) OR (ISO IEC 25010) OR (Digital Services) OR (Robotic Process Automation) OR (Straight-through processing) OR (Design Thinking) OR (SCRUM)) AND (Ecuador)))".

As a result, 42 records were found in ACM, seven in IEEE Xplore, and 15 in Springer. The abstracts of the papers were analyzed by the researchers for considering their relevance for this research. In conclusion, we selected three of the ACM papers, three of IEEE Xplore and none from Springer. In the following sections, we summarize the previous works considered as a reference for this research.

### 2.1 Models and Theories of Acceptance and Use of Technologies

There are research works on TAM, the Unified Theory of Acceptance and Use of Technology (UTAUT), the ISO 9241–210 (Ergonomics of human-system interaction) and the ISO 25010 (System and software quality models). As example, the case of the research in [7] explains the existence of TAM2 and TAM3 as extensions of TAM. The revised models consider more factors than TAM, including social influence, cognitive process of experience, perceived enjoyment, objective usability related to anxiety and taste of technology use. The research in [8], explains UTAUT2 model related to the adoption and use of technology, and shows that UTAUT2 with its new factors is a high-quality acceptance model, with its predictive ability much higher than UTAUT.

Regarding research work considering specific features of the context in Ecuador, the research in [2] evaluated the quality of educational game applications for children in Ecuador by applying TAM, ISO 9241–210 and ISO 25010. In [9], the authors apply the experimental research methodology using a quantitative approach and a structured questionnaire, employing the TAM model to verify the acceptance or rejection of the new technology in gamification resources for virtual teaching. Additionally, the research in [10] validates the efficiency of the application of virtual reality in teaching processes at the university level; however, although it validates the efficiency factor, it does not apply acceptance models and use of technologies for its validation.

In [1], the systematic literature review conducted by the authors indicate that there is variation in the behavior of acceptance and use factors by economic activity, so they recommend that future studies apply other research techniques such as surveys in specific regions to determine the behavior of acceptance and use factors.

### 2.2 Agile Methods for Software Development

In [3], the research conducted in Ecuador shows the use of techniques, such as Scrum, to drive agile software development with early deliverables that allow obtaining early user-tested tests, promoting early use and acceptance of the application.

### 2.3 Problem Identification and Problem Resolution Methods

In the scientific review in [11], the authors compare Human-Computer Interaction (HCI) and design thinking, concluding that they have similar procedures, and can the approaches can complement each other in various ways in applications for research and industry. For instance, design thinking manages empathy to understand the users, to generate ideas/solutions, that translate into facilities in the user's life.

### 2.4 Process Simplification and Automation Methods

Methods or best practices for process simplification and automation, such as Business Process Management (BPM) and Straight Through Processing (STP), are analyzed in [12]. As well as today with robotics, it is possible to automate processes using bots, which are software robots that execute repetitive tasks automatically through autonomous functions. The research in [13] describes robotic automation of processes, emphasizing the use of artificial intelligence tools allowing improving the operational processes of institutions. Another research conducted in Ecuador [4] analyzes the use of chatbots in complex virtual environments, automatically executing tasks and communicate with human characteristics. They deduce that the speed of response of chatbots increases user satisfaction, generating a feeling of constant attention, with a positive user experience.

Based on the revised studies related to models and theories of acceptance and use of technologies in certain practices of digital transformation in Ecuador, we observe that they focus on digital services on specific areas, like education, gaming and conversational services, and only with certain models of acceptance and use. Therefore, we understand that there is a gap in the state of the art and, through the research presented in this paper, we propose to obtain the characterization of the priority factors of acceptance and use of digital services in Ecuador as explained before.

## 3 Methodology

As research methodology, we apply the case study method of [5] with an exploratory approach, as shown in Fig. 1. We complement the activities following a survey research method with a descriptive approach to collect standardized information from a specific population or sample, and we perform a quantitative data analysis with descriptive statistics [6].

**Fig. 1.** Case study methodology. Source: [5]

The inputs we consider for this research, part of the context, include: the factors of acceptance and technological use of the UTAUT, TAM and the ISO models, as well as certain specific practices used for digital transformation. In addition, we consider the economic activities, as classified by the International Standard Industrial Classification (CIIU); and the following demographic attributes: gender (female, male), age (in the ranges of 0–14, 14–65, 65 and older), educational level (basic, high school, technical, university, master's, doctorate), and location (urban, rural). Finally, we also took into account the digital channels used for delivering digital services, including websites, social networks and mobile applications.

### 3.1 Case Design

We apply an embedded type of case study, which preserves the context and the case to be analyzed, having more than one unit of analysis [5] (see Fig. 2).

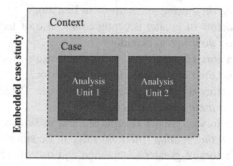

**Fig. 2.** Type of case study - Embedded. Source: [5]

To describe users' behavior and perception of the highest priority factors of acceptance and use of digital services technology by the users' economic activity and demographic characteristics, the embedded case study covers users of digital services in Ecuador with different characteristics that form instances of units of analysis by economic activity, age, education level, gender, location where they live, and digital channels used for consuming the service (see Fig. 3).

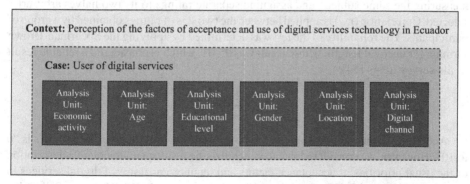

**Fig. 3.** Embedded case study - Factors of acceptance and use of digital services in Ecuador

As part of the case study design, we define the following objectives, research questions and other design elements.

**Objectives:** 1) To identify the factors of greater acceptance and use of digital services in Ecuador; and 2) to determine the relationships between the factors of greater acceptance and use of digital services with economic activities, age, educational level, gender, location, and digital channels used for receiving services, in Ecuador.

**Research questions:** We formulated one generic question (RQ1) and one specific for each unit of analysis (RQ2 to RQ7), seven in total:

RQ1 - What are the factors of greater acceptance and use of technology for users of digital services in Ecuador?

RQ2 - What are the factors of greater acceptance and use of technology for users of digital services *based on their economic activity* in Ecuador?

RQ3 - What are the factors of greater acceptance and use of technology for users of digital services *based on their age* in Ecuador?

RQ4 - What are the factors of greater acceptance and use of technology for users of digital services *based on their educational level* in Ecuador?

RQ5 - What are the factors of greater acceptance and use of technology for users of digital services *based on their gender* in Ecuador?

RQ6 - What are the factors of greater acceptance and use of technology for users of digital services *based on the location where they live* in Ecuador?

RQ7 - What are the factors of greater acceptance and use of technology for users of digital services *based on the digital channels they use* in Ecuador?

## 3.2 Preparation for Data Collection

For data collection, we conducted a survey, its questions were duly validated, data was collected and a quantitative analysis of the collected data was performed.

This 19-item survey was validated with a pilot test to 32 heterogeneous participants; this validation of reliability consists of the relative absence of measurement errors in the survey scores. This reliability with the approach of "internal consistency" and specifically of "division by halves" of Spearman-Brown, took the test composed of two parts measuring the same subject, and assigning separate ratings to its two halves arbitrarily selected. Correlation ($r_{oe}$) is applied between the two sets of ratings obtained by a group of participants. The reliability of the test was determined by applying the Spearman-Brown formula for unequal length, whose result was 0.701, which is considered a reliable result of the survey items [14]:

$$r_{11} \frac{2r_{oe}}{1 + r_{oe}}$$

According to the methodology in [6], the minimum sample size for case studies is "6 to 10". However, we considered that to generalize the results, and to obtain a description of the usual priorities of acceptance factors and technological use of digital services in Ecuador, we invited 7,200 users from the main provinces in Ecuador -i.e., Pichincha, Guayas, Azuay-, aged over 18 years, with different social demographic characteristics of gender, educational level, location and economic activity. Finally, we obtained 420 valid surveyed records, which are the sample of this case study.

## 3.3  Data Collection

Duly tested the 19-item survey for reliability and invited 7,200 users from the main provinces of Ecuador to complete it online. The complete survey form is available online (https://tripetto.app/run/C1HCO0M0DK). The survey was conducted from March 25 to April 5, 2022. Four hundred and twenty-two users completed the survey. The results were tabulated, validated, and we obtained 420 good records. We note that a user was able to inform more than one criterion in the same unit of analysis, e.g. perform more than one economic activity or use several channels, Thus, there may be overlaps in quantities (adding more than 420 responses) and percentages (see Table 1).

**Table 1.** Valid surveys per unit of analysis

| Analysis Unit | | Quantity | Percentage |
| --- | --- | --- | --- |
| Gender | Male | 274 | 65% |
| | Female | 146 | 35% |
| Age | 14–65 | 400 | 95% |
| | > 65 | 20 | 5% |
| Location | Urban | 380 | 90% |
| | Rural | 40 | 10% |
| Educational level | Basic | 5 | 1% |
| | High school | 28 | 7% |
| | Technical | 15 | 4% |
| | University | 152 | 36% |
| | Master | 204 | 49% |
| | Doctorate | 16 | 4% |
| Digital channel | Web | 219 | 52% |
| | Mobile application | 317 | 75% |
| | Social network | 98 | 23% |
| Economic activity | Financial | 370 | 88% |
| | Commercial | 306 | 73% |
| | Public services | 346 | 82% |
| | Education | 278 | 66% |
| | Health | 190 | 45% |
| | Tourism | 250 | 60% |
| | Transportation | 199 | 47% |
| | Others | 46 | 11% |

## 3.4  Analysis of Collected Data

To determine which are the most relevant factors of acceptance and use of digital services in Ecuador based on the results of the valid structured survey, we apply a quantitative data analysis, with descriptive statistics, using measures of central tendency to obtain the mean values of the distribution of the measurement scale of the percentages of the factors considered of interest by users. Although the "mean" is the most used measure of central tendency [6, 15] there are other options such as the median. I study [15], they analyzed the usability factor to find the best solution for most users by applying Fitts' law in web applications, using the Likert-type classification through Schulze's method and Borda's count, and concluded that they had more consistent results with the "mean" than with the "median". Likewise, in [16], they propose an improved decision tree algorithm, and they use the arithmetic mean in order to select the highest attribute from the average value and thus configure the decision tree branches. Based on such previous research works, observing that for cases where there are values that are distributed and classified within a measurement scale, the measure of central tendency "mean" is the best option, we were able to determine which are the most relevant factors that have higher values than the arithmetic mean, for each unit of analysis. In addition, the frequency distribution was used to present graphically the behavior of the factors, as well as the most relevant factors for each unit of analysis.

The 420 records were classified according to the factors of acceptance and use, their demographic and social segmentation. Table 2 shows the descriptive statistics with a "general approach" to the factors of acceptance and use of digital services in Ecuador.

**Table 2.**  Descriptive statistics - Factors of acceptance and use of digital services in Ecuador with a general approach.

| Descriptive Statistics | Value | Percentage |
|---|---|---|
| Mean | 0,879194118 | **87,92%** |
| Median | 0,9524 | 95,24% |
| Mode | 0,9571 | 95,71% |
| Standard error | 0,032642859 | 3,26% |
| Standard deviation | 0,134589954 | 13,46% |
| Sample variance | 0,018114456 | 1,81% |
| Range | 0,4619 | 46,19% |
| Minimum | 0,5286 | 52,86% |
| Maximum | 0,9905 | 99,05% |

Following a general approach, we call "priority factors" the most relevant factors of acceptance and use of digital services in Ecuador and consider those whose percentages of interest of users are above average (87.92%). The factors having a lower value than the mean, and with a general approach, were called "non-prioritizing factors". Table 3 shows the factors.

Table 3 shows that the priority factors include "Perceived Security" with 99.05%, and is the highest one. This result differs from the obtained in [1], in which the authors conducted a systematic review of the factors of technological acceptance, and the security factor did not score. This means that, although in the articles published worldwide at the time of this research the security factor was not relevant, however, when applying the survey to users of digital services in a specific context, i.e., in Ecuador, this factor is considered relevant.

In the following section, we discuss the results of the factors of acceptance and use of digital services in Ecuador for each unit of analysis, based on the case study described in Fig. 3.

**Table 3.** Priority and non-priority factors of acceptance and use of digital services in Ecuador

| Priority Factors | | Non-Priority Factors | |
|---|---|---|---|
| Factor | Percentage | Factor | Percentage |
| Perceived Security | 99,05% | Price/Value | 81,67% |
| Accessibility | 99,05% | Trust | 77,86% |
| Perceived Usefulness | 96,96% | Pandemic | 77,38% |
| Performance Expectation | 96,96% | Design thinking | 61,90% |
| Digital Culture | 96,19% | Automation/Robotization | 52,86% |
| Habit | 95,71% | | |
| Behavior Intention | 95,71% | | |
| Usage Behavior / Adoption | 95,71% | | |
| Hedonic Motivation | 95,24% | | |
| Facilitating Conditions | 91,43% | | |
| Ease of Use / Expectation of Effort | 90,71% | | |
| Social Influence | 90,24% | | |

## 3.5 Report

Based on the research methodology shown in Fig. 1, the last activity, namely Report, synthesizes all the relevant information to this research work. In the next section, we present and discuss the results obtained.

## 4 Data Analysis and Results

In the first instance of the analysis of the survey results with a general approach, we identified 12 most relevant factors of acceptance and use, called "priority factors" of digital services in Ecuador. Such factors were those that exceed the average (87.92%).

They include: 1) Perceived Security, 2) Accessibility, 3) Perceived Usefulness, 4) Performance Expectation, 5) Digital Culture, 6) Habit, 7) Behavior Intention, 8) Behavior Use/Adoption, 9) Hedonic Motivation, 10) Facilitating Conditions, 11) Ease of Use / Expectation Effort, and 12) Social Influence. The remaining five factors: 1) Price/Value, 2) Trust, 3) Pandemic, 4) Design Thinking, and 5) Automation/Robotization were considered "non-priority factors".

### 4.1   Results by Unit of Analysis of the Case Study

In the second instance of the analysis, a specific approach was applied for each unit of analysis of the case study, to obtain the priority acceptance and use factors per unit. Considering the "economic activity" unit of analysis, Fig. 4 describes the identified factors of acceptance and use of digital services. We can observe that despite the average of the factors of acceptance and use of users who have used digital services in Ecuador varies by 0.42% in relation to the general approach (Table 3), the general priority and non-priority factors remain the same.

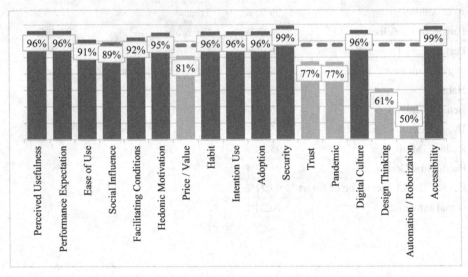

**Fig. 4.** Factors of acceptance and use of digital services in Ecuador by "commercial activity"

Similarly, we can conclude that there is a small variation in the percentages of the mean of the factors between the units of analysis of "economic activity", "gender" and "age". Such units of analysis maintain the same priority and non-priority factors, as in the general case. However, the unit of analysis related to location (urban and rural) shows a different behavior. In the rural sector, it is evident that of the 12 general priority factors, two factors, i.e., Social Influence and Facilitating Conditions become non-priority since they do not exceed the mean (see Fig. 5).

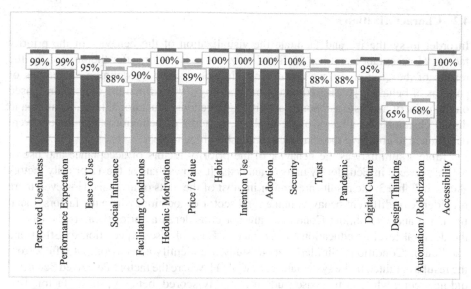

**Fig. 5.** Factors of acceptance and use of digital services in Ecuador by "rural sector"

Another particularity was found in the unit of analysis related to "educational level", specifically in people who have a doctorate academic level. Figure 6 shows such results, in which out of the 12 general priority factors, two factor, i.e., Ease of Use/Expectation of Efforts and Facilitating Conditions, become non-priority factors.

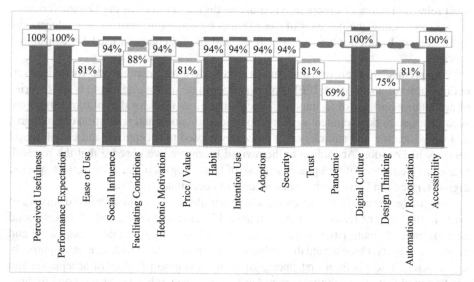

**Fig. 6.** Factors of acceptance and use of digital services in Ecuador by PhD educational level

## 4.2  Characterization

In order to synthesize and facilitate the visualization of the behavior of the priority factors of acceptance and use of digital services in Ecuador, after the analysis of the results of the case study, we opted for a characterization by defining archetypes or patterns of behavior [6]. Based on the methodology, we defined the dimensions based on the units of analysis: economic activity, age, gender, educational level, location and digital channels. As a result of the analysis, patterns of behavior of the factors were determined to conceive the characterization shown in Table 4.

Table 4 summarizes the behavior of the priority factors of acceptance and use of digital services in Ecuador by units of analysis. It shows that for the 12 priority factors shown in Table 3, the results are similar in most of the units of analysis. However, there is evidence of different behavior in the rural sector of location, where the factors Social Influence and Facilitating Conditions are not considered as priority, as is the case at the doctoral level of education for the factors Ease of Use/Expectation of Effort and Facilitating Conditions. Similarly, in our study, we identify a behavior that differs from the results obtained in the systematic review of [1], where the factor "Perceived Security" did not score, while in this case study it is highly scored, being a priority factor. This confirms the importance of contextualization and that it cannot be generalized that all the priority factors of acceptance and use are the same for all digital services, since their behavior may vary by the different units of analysis and even by region.

## 5  Discussion

The objective of this research was to conceive through a case study, the knowledge of the most relevant factors of acceptance and use of digital services in the Ecuador context. As well as to know the behavior of these factors by economic activity, age, educational level, gender, location where the user lives, and digital channels used for consuming services.

As a premise there are previous studies relevant to this research work. We revised scientific publications in ACM, IEEE Xplore and Springer discussing methods and theories of acceptance and use of technology, specific practices used for digital transformation, such as software development agile methods, identification and resolution of problems, and simplification and automation of processes related to acceptance and use of digital services in Ecuador. According to the revised literature, we observe that the research related to the factors of acceptance and use of technologies in focus on certain specific digital services and only with certain models of acceptance and use.

We conducted case study research, with a sample of 420 valid completed surveys of users in the main provinces of Ecuador, aged 18 years and older, with different social demographic characteristics of gender, location where they live, educational level and economic activity. Once we did the analysis of the survey results with a general approach, it was possible to obtain a first finding of 12 most relevant factors of acceptance and use "priority factors" of digital services in Ecuador (see Table 3). As a second finding, within the 12 identified priority factors is the factor "Perceived Security" with 99.05%, which is one of the highest values. A third finding, applying a specific approach for each unit of analysis, we found in the unit of analysis of "economic activity" that the behavior

**Table 4.** Characterization of priority factors for acceptance and use of digital services in Ecuador

| | | Patterns – dimensions | | | | | | | | |
|---|---|---|---|---|---|---|---|---|---|---|
| | | General | Economic activity | Age | Educational level | PhD Educational level | Gender | Location | Rural location | Digital Channel |
| Factors | Perceived security | * | * | * | * | * | * | * | * | * |
| | Accessibility | * | * | * | * | * | * | * | * | * |
| | Perceived Usefulness | * | * | * | * | * | * | * | * | * |
| | Performance Expectation | * | * | * | * | * | * | * | * | * |
| | Digital Culture | * | * | * | * | * | * | * | * | * |
| | Habit | * | * | * | * | * | * | * | * | * |
| | Behavior Intention | * | * | * | * | * | * | * | * | * |
| | Usage behavior / Adoption | * | * | * | * | * | * | * | * | * |
| | Hedonic Motivation | * | * | * | * | * | * | * | * | * |
| | Facilitating Conditions | * | * | * | * | | * | * | | * |
| | Ease of use / Expectation of effort | * | * | * | * | | * | * | * | * |
| | Social Influence | * | * | * | * | * | * | * | | * |

of the commercial economic activity is similar to the rest of the economic activities, and that although the average of the factors varies by 0.42% in relation to the general approach, the priority factors are maintained. A fourth finding is that the unit of analysis "location" has a different behavior for people living in the rural sector, since for them, the two factors - Social Influence and Facilitating Conditions - become non-priority. Similarly, in the unit of analysis of "educational level", specifically in people who have an academic level of doctorate, the two factors Ease of Use/Expectation of Effort and Facilitating Conditions were not prioritized.

We consider that the contribution of this research refers to valuable knowledge synthesized for software developers, researchers and others interested in the relevant factors of acceptance and use of digital services in the Ecuador context. However, we highlight that the findings of this research cannot be generalized, i.e., that all the priority factors of acceptance and use are the same for all digital services in Ecuador, since their behavior may vary by the different units of analysis and even by region. Our results should be taken into account by implementers of digital services and researchers to have greater certainty that the implemented digital services will be adopted by users.

Finally, our future work will apply other qualitative research methods such as focus groups with experts in the field to validate the contributions of this research but applied in different contexts, like specific government areas, such as educational, health and security services.

# References

1. Pintado, P., Jaramillo, I., Prado, D., Estevez, E.: Taxonomy of factors of acceptance and use of technologies for HCI in digital services (2023)
2. Solorzano Alcivar, N.I., Gallego, D.C., Quijije, L.S., Quelal, M.M.: Developing a dashboard for monitoring usability of educational games apps for children. In: ACM International Conference Proceeding Series, pp. 70–75, March 2019. https://doi.org/10.1145/3328886.332 8892
3. Rocha, Associação Ibérica de Sistemas e Tecnologias de Informação, and institute of electrical and electronics engineers. In: 2019 14th Iberian Conference on Information Systems and Technologies (CISTI) : proceedings of CISTI'2019 - 14th Iberian Conference on Information Systems and Technologies : 19 to 22 of June 2019, Coimbra, Portugal (2019)
4. Chilcanan, D., Cuzco, C., Uyaguari, A.: Monitoring of residential drinking water service consumption using human machine interaction (HCI) techniques. In: ACM International Conference Proceeding Series, pp. 152–156, October 2019. https://doi.org/10.1145/3369114. 3369137
5. Runeson, P., Host, M., Rainer, A., Regnell, B.: Case Study Research in Software Engineering: Guidelines and Examples. Wiley, Hoboken (2012)
6. Hernández Sampieri, R., Fernández Collado, C., Baptista Lucio, P.: Metodologia de la Investigación (Sexta edición), Mc Graw Hill, New York (2014)
7. Lai, P.: The literature review of technology adoption models and theories for the novelty technology. J. Inf. Syst. Technol. Manage. **14**(1) (2017). https://doi.org/10.4301/S1807-177 52017000100002
8. Tamilmani, K., Rana, N.P., Wamba, S.F., Dwivedi, R.: The extended unified theory of acceptance and use of technology (UTAUT2): a systematic literature review and theory evaluation. Int. J. Inf. Manage. **57** (2021). https://doi.org/10.1016/j.ijinfomgt.2020.102269
9. Elizabeth Freire Espin, S., Marcelo Rodriguez Cortez, D.: Nearpod as a gamification resource for teaching in virtual education: a mathematical case study. In: 2022 Inter-national Conference on Inventive Computation Technologies (ICICT), pp. 177–183, July 2022. https://doi.org/10.1109/ICICT54344.2022.9850488
10. Cabrera Duffaut, A.M., Llorente, P., Iglesias Rodríguez, A.: Efficiency in the application of virtual reality in the teaching processes to generate competences in the university environment. In: ACM International Conference Proceeding Series, pp. 1008–1013, October 2020. https://doi.org/10.1145/3434780.3436608
11. Park, H., McKilligan, S.: A systematic literature review for human-computer interaction and design thinking process integration. In: Marcus, A., Wang, W. (eds.) DUXU 2018. LNCS, vol. 10918, pp. 725–740. Springer, Cham (2018). https://doi.org/10.1007/978-3-319-91797-9_50
12. Hong, V., Kiet, T., Wojciechowski, R.: Straight through processing for corporate foreign exchange trading lessons learned from a web service based implementation (2005)
13. Ribeiro, J., Lima, R., Eckhardt, T., Paiva, S.: robotic process automation and artificial intelligence in industry 4.0 - a literature review. Procedia Comput. Sci. **181**, 51–58 (2021). https://doi.org/10.1016/j.procs.2021.01.104

14. Aiken, L.R., Elena, M., Salinas, O., Varela Domínguez, R.W.: Tests Psicológicos y Evaluación (2003)
15. Sageder, J., Demleitner, A., Irlbacher, O., Wimmer, R.: Applying voting methods in user research. In: ACM International Conference Proceeding Series, pp. 571–575., September 2019. https://doi.org/10.1145/3340764.3344461
16. Bin Nie, J.L.D.P., Zhuo Wang, A.C.: Improved algorithm of C4.5 decision tree on the arithmetic average optimal selection classification attribute. IEEE (2017)

# Visualization

# UVAM: The Unified Visual Analytics Model. The Unified Visualization Model Revisited

María Luján Ganuza[1,2,3(✉)] , Dana K. Urribarri[1,2,3] ,
Martín L. Larrea[1,2,3] , and Silvia M. Castro[1,2,3]

[1] VyGLab Research Laboratory, UNS-CICPBA, Bahía Blanca 8000, Argentina
{mlg,dku,mll,smc}@cs.uns.edu.ar
[2] Department of Computer Science and Engineering, UNS, Bahía Blanca 8000,
Argentina
[3] ICIC, CONICET-UNS, Bahía Blanca 8000, Argentina

**Abstract.** Nowadays, the explosive growth of data generated from numerous sources results in ever-increasing volumes of data that are, therefore, difficult to understand, explore and analyze in order to extract information from them. The contribution of visualization to the exploration and understanding of these large datasets is very significant. Various application domains often require different visual representations, although several share the same intermediate steps, transformations, and/or manipulations of such data. These shared aspects lead to the requirement for a consistent and extensible visual analytics model across all application domains. In this context, we introduce the Unified Visual Analytics Model (UVAM), which combines the Unified Visualization Model (UVM) with the specific features of visual analytics. The UVAM is a state model represented as a flow between the many states that the data passes through throughout the process. It includes the user interactions with the data and its intermediate representations and how the user controls the transformations and, subsequently, modifications of the visualizations. This paper illustrates how the model includes various visual analytics processes and describes in detail a UVAM case study.

**Keywords:** Visual Analytics Model · Visualization Model · Visual Analytics Pipeline · Visualization Pipelines · Visualization

## 1 Introduction

Visualization is the process of creating interactive visual representations from a dataset enabling its visual analysis. It involves a cognitive process in which the users explore the data space iteratively and interactively, allowing for the identification and inference of possible relationships between the data [21,22, 27,29]. Visualization and automatic data analysis led to the development of visual analytics. It integrates the two formerly separate areas and substantially promotes interaction between people during the analysis process. In order to

M. Naiouf et al. (Eds.): JCC-BD&ET 2023, CCIS 1828, pp. 189–203, 2023.
https://doi.org/10.1007/978-3-031-40942-4_14

extract knowledge from data, the visual analytics process combines automated and visual analysis techniques with a close coupling through human involvement.

Visual analytics is widely used in various areas of science, like engineering and medicine, among others, in which the vertiginous growth in the amount of information generates even larger volumes of data that are difficult to understand and analyze without adequate visual support [4]. Although each application domain requires different treatment of the data and also different visual representations, several domains share intermediate data states and transformations and require similar view-level manipulations. The analysis of these common denominators in the different visual analysis processes exposes the need for a consistent visual analytics model valid for different application domains.

On the other hand, given the potentially complex and enormous datasets we are dealing with today, it is hardly feasible to indiscriminately visualize and interact with the whole dataset. In that case, our visual representations would be too crowded, and interaction would be time-consuming and expensive. In this context, computational analysis is required to support visual exploration [12, 24]. Thus, the complexity of the visual representations decreases, easing the preliminary analysis of the data by displaying essential features rather than the original data values. Then, the combination of visual analysis, interactive querying, and more automated calculations results in a deeper understanding of the data. This visual analytics approach must also integrate into the visualization model.

In this paper, we revisit the Unified Visualization Model (UVM) [15], a consistent visualization pipeline model valid for all visualization areas and different application domains, and define the Unified Visual Analytics Model (UVAM), an extension of the UVM that includes automated computational algorithms to facilitate interactive visual data analysis. Moreover, we expose the soundness of the UVAM to support visual analytics techniques. Additionally, a Case Study that illustrates how the UVAM supports visual analytics tasks and techniques is presented.

## 2    Related Work

Creating interactive visual data analysis solutions is a difficult task. The main challenge is to provide a suitable combination of computational, interactive, and visual tools that genuinely assist users in solving application-specific analytical issues. In the framework of interactive visual data analytics, several players are involved: designers, developers, and the final users [24]. Several abstract models of interactive visual data analysis were conceived from the perspectives of the previous players: design (designers), data transformation (developers), and knowledge creation (final users). Using a pipeline architecture enables us to quickly categorize the fundamental contributions of extremely diverse procedures that act on completely unrelated objects while also revealing their connections. This has resulted in visualization models being mostly pipelines. For this reason, in this manuscript, we will use model and pipeline interchangeably when there is no risk of confusion.

A visual analytics pipeline must provide effective abstractions for designing, implementing, and using visual analytics systems [26]. Then, a relevant model of visual analytics must cover automated data processing, visualization, and human interactions. Since 35 years ago, several visualization models were developed that partially covered different areas and/or were dedicated to different players of visualization [2,10,13,14,19,20,25].

In 1997, Card and Mackinlay [23] presented a taxonomy of the information visualization literature oriented to the data flow. This flow data model was subsequently expanded in [22] and consists of a succession of transformations that are represented by nodes, and the direction of data flowing between transformations is indicated by edges between them. In this model, three types of basic transformations are distinguished: data transformations, visual mapping transformations, and view transformations. Interactions are introduced as control parameters of these transformations, and although it constitutes a very rich design space, its interaction model is incomplete. In 1999, Chi and Riedl [7] presented a state model distinguishing four states (data, analytic abstraction, visual abstraction, and view), three transformations (data, view, and visual mapping transformation), and operators defined at each stage. In 2001, Duke [6] raised the need to work with a general reference model that is not based on the pragmatic differences between the nature of the data corresponding to Scientific Visualization and Information Visualization. In that work, he describes a conceptual data model that provides some level of integration between scientific datasets and more abstract data sources.

The Unified Visualization Model (UVM) [15], presented in 2003, can be used by designers, developers, and end users to create visualizations, regardless of the specific application domain, focusing on data states, transformations, and interactions. This model clearly depicts the available operations, the operands to which they may be applied, as well as the order of transformations included in the process. In 2009, Munzner [16] introduced the design process called the Nested Model for Visualization Design and Validation oriented to designers of a visualization. It consists of four nested levels that describe the path from a domain problem to an actual implementation of a solution.

In the early 2000s, the concept of *visual analytics* emerged as a result of research in fields such as information visualization, human-computer interaction, and data mining [5]. Visual analytics' goal is to facilitate data analysis and decision-making by providing users with interactive and intuitive visualizations that enable them to gain insights into the underlying patterns and relationships in the data. The first publication that considers a visual analytics model is Keim et al. [11]. In 2016, Wang et al. [26] presented a review of the previous work on visual analytics pipelines and individual modules from multiple perspectives: data, visualization, model, and knowledge. They discussed various representations and descriptions of pipelines inside the module and compared the commonalities and differences among them. Besides that, they presented a general pipeline that mainly consists of three major steps: feature selection and generation, model building and selection, and model validation. The problem with

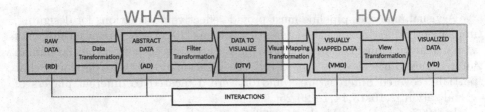

**Fig. 1.** Unified Visualization Model. A distinction is made between data-oriented states and transformations, i.e., those dedicated to manipulating the data to be displayed (rectangle WHAT, in green) and those dedicated to visually displaying the data (rectangle HOW, in orange). (Color figure online)

these last two models is that from the knowledge acquired by the user, the model only provides the interaction with the underlying data and not directly with the visualization or the data model. From the knowledge acquired by the user, no clear interaction with any other state is shown. However, a pipeline-based model offers the designers, developers, and final users a modular perspective of current developments, enabling new systems to be created or used.

## 3    Unified Visualization Model (UVM)

Intuitively, any visualization process can be thought of as a transformation of data into a visual representation. Although it is common for different application domains to require different visual representations, several of them may share intermediate states of the data, require similar manipulations at the level of views, or even require the same transformations of the data. In this context, The Unified Visualization Model [15] was defined, focusing on both the processes and the data states, and that applies to any type of visualization regardless of the data domain. Additionally, the UVM enables the explicit definition of user interactions through the definition of tasks, basic interactions, and low-level operators and operands.

This transformational process takes the user domain data (raw data) as input, goes through the processing to generate the visual representation, and is susceptible to user interactions. This processing is decomposed in a visualization pipeline (see Fig. 1) where the nodes represent the states of the data and the edges, the transformations required to go from one state to the next. As seen in Fig. 1, the user can interact in all stages, manipulating data in the different states and controlling the parameters of the transformations. Next, we briefly describe the stages and transformations of the UVM; for more details, see [15].

### 3.1    The States

The distinction between the states that data passes through throughout the process is not always due to structural differences but due to the different roles that data fulfill within the entire process.

**Raw Data (RD).** The RD corresponds to the initial state of the visualization process. This data comes from different application domains and constitutes the input to the visualization process. There is a wide variety of formats.

**Abstract Data (AD).** In this state, all the pre-selected data within the RD are stored in a suitable representation to facilitate the management of the datasets for the rest of the visualization process. In this state, in addition to the data of interest, the metadata generated in the data transformation is also available.

**Data to Visualize (DTV).** The DTV is the data that will be presented in the visualization that is generated in later stages. It is constituted by all the data in the AD or only a subset of them. The data representation in this state corresponds to the one in the preceding state (AD). This feature allows the exploration of different regions of the information space and their comparison.

**Visually Mapped Data (VMD).** This state constitutes the DTV enriched with the visual structure [22], which is the information necessary for supporting the visual representation of the data. The visual structure comprises the spatial substrate and the graphic substrate.

The *Spatial Substrate* refers to the underlying surface on which visual elements are displayed. The attributes of the spatial substrate reflect the organization of the space that the visualization technique will use. This includes the axes' layout and type and the dimensions of the space. The information in this state must be enough to determine the spatial organization of the view [22].

The *Graphical Substrate* includes the graphic elements used to represent the data in the view (visual marks) and their associated graphic properties (visual channels, which control the appearance of the marks) [17,22,28].

**Visualized Data (VD).** This is the last stage of the process, but not the end, since it constitutes the exploration space for the user. It is important to emphasize that for the same set of VMD, more than one VD can be generated by the application of different techniques that support the characteristics or the restrictions specified in the previous state.

### 3.2   The Transformations

The transformations are the processes that allow the data to pass from one state to the next one. The user can interact at the level of the transformations, as well as at the level of the data states.

**Data Transformation.** This transformation is in charge of transforming the RD from the application domain format to an internal format manageable through the rest of the process. The outcome is a set of AD coming from external data sources or other visualizations. This transformation can create a new AD set or incorporate new data into an existing one.

**Filter Transformation.** This transformation allows the selection of the data to be visualized and to perform tasks such as projection and filtering. New DTV sets are generated while maintaining the same AD set. Thus, the user can determine what he/she wants to visualize in a given instance, without worrying (yet) about how to do it.

**Visual Mapping Transformation.** This transformation is key in the visualization process and allows the user to define how he/she wants to visualize the data. It is in charge of visual mapping, i.e., in establishing which visual structures are appropriate, which attributes will be spatially mapped and how, and which marks and channels will be used.

**View Transformation.** This transformation is in charge of generating the visual representation on screen, according to what is expressed in the VMD. Once the visualization technique that supports the restrictions present in the previous state is selected, it is applied to generate the view. For a certain set of VMD, there may be several techniques that support it, then the user must choose one of them to obtain the VD.

## 4    The Unified Visual Analytics Model (UVAM)

To make visual analytics practical for applications is important to have an appropriate mental model of the visual analytics pipeline. Such a model provides effective abstractions for designing, developing, and using visual analytics systems. Figure 2 provides a summary of the various stages (represented by rectangles) and the data transformations (represented by arrows) in this UVAM pipeline.

To design this pipeline, we start with the definition of visual analytics and the UVM, considering that it is a visualization pipeline model regardless of the visualization area in focus. We take the definition of visual analytics that we consider the broadest. That is, the visual analytics process is a combination of automatic and visual analysis methods with a tight coupling through human interaction in order to gain knowledge from data [11]. Below, we describe the new features, i.e., the operations that were introduced to make the pipeline a Unified Visual Analytics Model.

### 4.1    Operations Within Data States

Most of the visualization pipelines have mainly two parts (see Fig. 1). One part is oriented to data, that is, WHAT data to visualize. The other part is dedicated to HOW to visualize that data. In order to extend the UVM pipeline to encompass computational analysis support, UVAM includes operations within the data-oriented states. These operations are symbolized by arrows starting from and arriving at the same state (see Fig. 2).

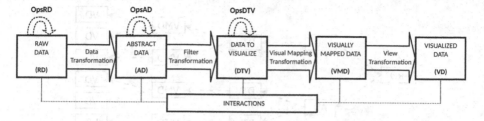

**Fig. 2.** Unified Visual Analytics Model. The UVAM modifies the UVM adding operations within the data-oriented states to support computational analysis.

**Operations on Raw Data (OpsRD).** RD constitutes the input to the visualization process, coming from different application domains in a given format. This RD can be inaccurate, unreliable, or noisy. Certain data pre-processing activities must be carried out in order to solve these issues and satisfy the requirements for the next stages. Data pre-processing is a flexible procedure that is determined by the RD. The OpsRD often relate to operations such as data conversions from one format to another, data cleaning (to identify and address data quality issues at this stage), data integration (to merge data from many sources based on a global schema), etc.

**Operations on Abstract Data (OpsAD).** The OpsAD correspond to operations carried out on AD in this state. The result of these operations could be, for example, derived or enhanced data. Data operations also correspond to the analysis-centric methods such as dimension reduction, regression, subspace clustering, feature extraction, and data sampling, besides data abstraction. In this state, in addition to having the data of interest, there is also the metadata generated as a result of the operations.

**Operations on Data to Visualize (OpsDTV).** The OpsDTV correspond to operations applied to the data that will be present in the visualization. They are the same operations as in the previous state. However, since DTV can be a subset of AD and the operations can be costly in time and/or space, applying them in this state can potentially improve the efficiency of the process.

## 5   Coordinated Views in the UVAM

The coordinated multiple-views technique has become a well-established technology for interactive visual analysis [18]. It is an exploratory visualization technique that allows users to explore their data through different representations. For the analysis of complex data, the user is usually required to consider different scenarios, arising the need to compare multiple visualizations generated from the same dataset.

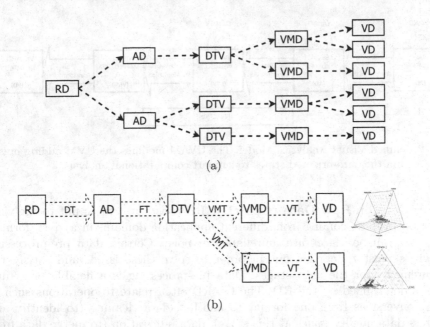

Fig. 3. Ramifications in the UVAM: Multiple views (a) and *Spinel Web* at the UVAM (b). Branches of the running model to represent two views, the 3D Prism and the triangular projection of the prism.

The Unified Visual Analytics Model supports multiple coordinated views. As mentioned above, multiple AD sets can be obtained from an RD set, either using a different representation for the same data or representing a different subset of the data present in the RD set. Similarly, multiple DTV sets can be obtained from a set of AD, the result of different filtering processes applied to the AD. Furthermore, as a result of applying different visual mappings from a single DTV set, multiple VMD sets can be obtained.

Finally, since for a given set of VMD there may be several techniques that support it, it is possible to generate multiple sets of VD. In all cases, the generation of multiple datasets from a single-source dataset results from applying multiple transformations to any state of the visualization process. Each new transformation will generate a branch in the visualization process. The visualization process will have the structure of a tree whose root will be the RD state and can branch in any of its transformations (see Fig. 3(a)).

In UVAM, all views will share (at least) the RD set. Therefore, the process can result in different visual representations from the same data set; this includes not only different representations of the same data set but also representations of different subsets or different data derived from the original data set.

Given that the Data Transformation transforms the data to an internal format manageable for the rest of the process, it is correct to assume that all the views generated by a visualization pipeline from the same AD state can correlate. Clearly, those views with shared DTV will show exactly the same data but not necessarily represented in the same way. This does not happen with those views that only share the AD state since it is possible that, due to the filtering or aggregation processes involved in the Filtering Transformation, the data displayed in one view differs from the one present in the others. The latter can bring with it consistency problems, since when linking two views that do not show exactly the same data, the effect on one view may not be reflected in the other if the data involved is not present in the second. However, keeping in mind that special treatment may be required in those coordinated views that do not share the DTV, it is possible to coordinate all the views generated from different branches of a pipeline in the UVAMs that share the AD state.

# 6 Case Study: Spinel Web

As a case study, we discuss a visualization application in the context of the UVAM, detailing how the underlying datasets are represented, what operations can be applied to them, and the data transformations through the model. For this matter, we select the *Spinel Web*, a web application for the visualization of the spinel group minerals [1]. The spinels serve as both outstanding tectonic environment indicators and priceless exploration instruments when looking for mineral resources of commercial relevance.

Geologists usually represent the composition of the spinel-group minerals in a prismatic space called spinel prism (see Fig. 4(a) (left)) [9]. The chemical composition of a spinel-sample is made up of its composition in terms of the *major chemical elements*, of the *oxides* of the *major chemical elements* and the 22 *end members*. Of all end-members, only eight are commonly used for representation on chemical diagrams. Magnetite and Ulvöspinel prisms, which are generally referred to as Spinel prisms, are examples of such diagrams. These are triangular prisms where each vertex represents one end member. Depending on the ratios of the elements in a mineral, the mineral is plotted at a specific position inside the prism (or on the border for minerals that do not have all end-members). Since these prismatic spaces are difficult to plot without dedicated software, geologists often use two-dimensional plots such as triangle plots and scatterplots to represent the projections of the prism faces. In 2001, Barnes and Roeder [3] defined a set of contours (standard contours) corresponding to compositional fields for spinel group minerals. These fields were defined using point-density contour plots (PDCPs) based on the spinel prism. These contours are used by geologists as empirical tectonic discriminators that empower them to estimate the tectonic environment where a spinel with a particular composition has been formed. In order to do this, they compare their data, consisting of several analyses, with the PDCPs from Barnes and Roeder.

*Spinel Web* integrates most of the diagrams commonly used for analyzing the chemical characteristics of the spinel group minerals and a 3D representation of the spinel prisms and their projections (see Fig. 4(a)). It also provides

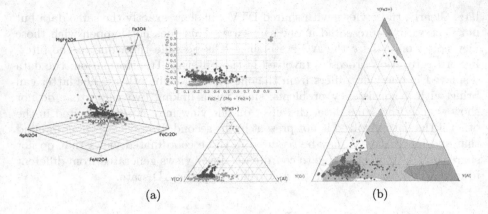

(a)    (b)

**Fig. 4.** (a) *Spinel Web*. Correlated views in the 3D Spinel Prism (left) and the corresponding projections in 2D (right). (b) *Contours in Spinel Web*. The 90% Barnes and Roeder's (green) overlapped with the 50% user's contours (purple).

coordinated views, appropriate interactions, it supports semi-automatic categorization of the geological environment of formation and overlapping of Barnes and Roeder's contours and density contours creation allowing visual clustering.

## 6.1   Spinel Web Across the UVAM

*Spinel Web* provides several linked views, a three-dimensional view representing the prismatic space, 3 two-dimensional views of the projections of the prism (see Fig. 4(a)), and a parallel coordinates view, among others. In this particular case study, we are considering only two views among all the views supported by *Spinel Web*: the prismatic view and the triangular projection of the prism. From a dynamic point of view, despite being a single RD, there will be several different VD as the result of a branch of the pipeline at some point in the process. Since the different visualizations show the same data but apply different visual mapping and visualization techniques, the underlying pipeline branches will share the states of RD, AD, and DTV, generating the branching in the *Visual Mapping Transformation* (see Fig. 3(b)).

**Raw Data.** The first step in the traditional workflow of spinel-mineral analysis consists of collecting the set of samples to be analyzed. At this stage, geologists take *in situ* samples that they consider representative of the problem they wish to solve. The samples, once collected, are chemically analyzed using a petrographic microscope in order to obtain the chemical composition of the minerals of interest. In addition to the chemical composition, each sample is assigned an identifier in order to be able to differentiate it during the exploration process. The result of this data collection process corresponds to the RD in *Spinel Web*. It is a file composed of as many rows as samples taken *in situ* and as many

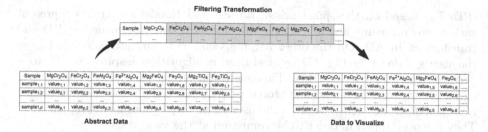

**Fig. 5.** *Abstract Data* in the *Spinel Web* (left) and *Data To Visualize* (right). The six final members necessary for the representation of the data in the Magnetite Prism were selected, together with the values of the oxides and the major elements for each sample.

columns as the sum of the number of major elements, oxides, and final members that make up its chemical composition.

**Operations on Raw Data.** The user's data can contain negative or missing values for some major elements and/or end members. The operations applied on the RD correspond to cleaning the dataset by eliminating the improper samples.

**Data Transformation.** In this transformation, the RD is transformed into an internal representation, the semantics and the type of the attributes are analyzed and those items and/or attributes that the user wants to keep are filtered. In this particular case, the expert geologist defines the semantics of the data, which is included in the RD and interpreted by the system. In *Spinel Web* the dataset is instantiated with a table, where each sample is a data item, and each column is an attribute of the data items. According to the Card et al. classification [22], the type of those attributes is quantitative ordinal. The identifiers of the samples, on the other hand, are categorical attributes. As detailed before, the position of a data item in the prismatic space is given by its chemical composition in terms of 6 of its 22 end members. In other words, to represent a data item within the two supported prismatic spaces, it is enough to keep, for each data item, the end members that make up the Magnetite Prism and the Ulvöspinel Prism. Since both prisms share their base, only 8 end members are needed to support both representations. This is why, this transformation performs attribute filtering to keep only these 8 end-members.

**Abstract Data.** The AD consists of the dataset of potentially viewable data stored in an internal format. The AD consists of a table of $m$ rows × $n$ columns, where $m$ corresponds to the number of samples and for each sample the $n$ attributes selected in the previous transformation are preserved (see Fig. 5(left)).

**Operations on Abstract Data.** The semi-automatic categorization of the geological environment requires the generation of point-density contour plots

(PDCPs) based on the spinel prism. Barnes and Roeder's contours represent various environments and all of them are standard contours loaded as RD and transformed in AD. On the other hand, specific contours are calculated from the user's dataset in the AD by a clustering algorithm inspired in [8], to a percentage selected by him/her. This operation on the AD allows the contour to be generated by demand and stored as AD. More than one contour can be represented. In Fig. 4(b), standard and user's generated contours are represented. They are overlapped in order to be compared at the view stage.

**Filtering Transformation.** In this transformation, the data that will be present in the visualization is selected. Depending on which prismatic space the user wants to represent, those six final members corresponding to its composition will be selected, discarding (perhaps momentarily) the remaining two. Attribute filtering is performed again.

**Data to Visualize.** The DTV is composed of the data that will be present in the display. In the *Spinel Web*, it has the same structure as the AD, keeping only six of the eight end members, the oxides, and the major chemical elements per data item (see Fig. 5 (right)).

**Operations on Data to Visualize.** In this case, the operations can be applied to the data the user has chosen to display. No operation at this stage has been implemented in *Spinel Web* yet.

**Visual Mapping Transformation.** In this transformation, the data to be displayed are associated with the information necessary for its representation on screen. The *Visual Mapping Transformation* generates a *visual mapping* representation of the DTV, their spatial substrate, and a collection of mappings between data and visual items.

As for this case study we are considering only two of the views supported by *Spinel Web*, we must construct two independent Transformations. The spatial substrate is similar for both views, but the visual marks differ. Then, two different sets of VMD will be generated, one for each view, and it is from this point that the visualization pipeline will branch (see Fig. 3(b)). The spatial substrate of both views, according to Card et al. [22], is unstructured axes. However, the 3D view uses spheres as visual marks and the 2D view uses points. The visual channels are also different. The 3D view uses size and color as visual channels for each visual element, while the 2D view uses only color.

**Visually Mapped Data.** The VMD constitutes the DTV enriched with the visual structure defined in the previous transformation.

**Visual Transformation.** This transformation applies the visualization technique. For the 3D view, an ad-hoc visualization technique is applied. This technique involves diagramming the prismatic space, the calculation of each sample position within the space, and finally, the representation of each data item in the previously calculated position with the color, size, and shape determined in the visual mapping transformation. The visualization technique applied to the triangular 2D view involves the diagramming of the triangular projection of the prism in 2 dimensions, the calculation of the position of each projected sample within the space, and finally the representation of each data item in the position previously calculated with the color determined in the visual mapping transformation.

**Visualized Data.** The VD is the output of the process. In this particular case, we have two VDs, one corresponding to the 3D view and the other corresponding to the triangular projection in the 2D view. Both datasets constitute the starting point for the exploration process that the user will carry out.

## 7    Conclusions

Creating interactive visual analytics solutions is a difficult task. The main challenge is to provide a suitable combination of computational, interactive, and visual tools that assist the players (designers, developers, and final users) involved in the framework of interactive visual analytics in solving application-specific issues. In this context, we recognize the need for a consistent visual analytics model valid for all different application domains, based on a single mental model, and that facilitates interactive visual data analysis of current big datasets. This necessity motivated the definition of the Unified Visual Analytics Model (UVAM), an extension of the UVM that includes automated computational algorithms to facilitate interactive visual data analysis. This new model constitutes a conceptual framework that allows the definition of any necessary interaction, including the specification of the operands it operates on, and output it produces, and how it affects the overall process. We also include a Case Study that illustrates how the UVAM supports visual analytics tasks and techniques.

**Acknowledgments.** This work was partially supported by PGI 24/N048, PGI 24/ZN39, PGI 24/N050, and PGI 24/ZN38 research grants from the Secretaría General de Ciencia y Tecnología, Universidad Nacional del Sur (Argentina), and by PIBAA 28720210100824CO granted by National Council for Scientific and Technical Research (CONICET).

**Competing interests.** The authors have declared that no competing interests exist.

## References

1. Antonini, A.S., et al.: Spinel web: an interactive web application for visualizing the chemical composition of spinel group minerals. Earth Sci. Inform. **14**(1), 521–528 (2021). https://doi.org/10.1007/s12145-020-00542-w

2. Ayachit, U.: The Paraview Guide: A Parallel Visualization Application. Kitware Inc., Clifton Park, NY, USA (2015)
3. Barnes, S.J., Roeder, P.L.: The range of spinel compositions in terrestrial mafic and ultramafic rocks. J. Petrol. **42**(12), 2279–2302 (2001). https://doi.org/10.1093/petrology/42.12.2279
4. Cleveland, W.S.: Visualizing data. Hobart press (1993)
5. Cook, K.A., Thomas, J.J.: Illuminating the path: the research and development agenda for visual analytics. Technical report, Pacific Northwest National Lab. (PNNL), Richland, WA (United States) (2005)
6. Duke, D.: Modular techniques in information visualization. In: Proceedings of the 2001 Asia-Pacific Symposium on Information Visualisation, pp. 11–18. APVis 2001, Australian Computer Society Inc., AUS (2001). https://doi.org/10.5555/564040.564042
7. Ed Huai-Hsin Chi, Riedl, J.T.: An operator interaction framework for visualization systems. In: Proceedings IEEE Symposium on Information Visualization, pp. 63–70 (1998). https://doi.org/10.1109/INFVIS.1998.729560
8. Ganuza, M.L., Ferracutti, G., Gargiulo, F., Castro, S.M., Bjerg, E.A., Gröller, E., Matković, K.: Interactive visual categorization of spinel-group minerals. In: Proceedings of the 33rd Spring Conference on Computer Graphics, pp. 1–11 (2017). https://doi.org/10.1145/3154353.3154359
9. Haggerty, S.E.: Oxide mineralogy of the upper mantle. In: Oxide Minerals, pp. 355–416. De Gruyter (1991)
10. Kitware Inc.: Volview (2009). https://www.kitware.com/volview/, May 2020
11. Keim, D., Kohlhammer, J., Ellis, G., Mansmann, F.: Mastering the Information Age: Solving Problems with Visual Analytics. Eurographics Assoc, Goslar (2010)
12. Keim, D.A., Robertson, G.G., Thomas, J.J., van Wijk, J.J.: Guest editorial: special section on visual analytics. IEEE Trans. Vis. Comput. Graph. **12**(06), 1361–1362 (2006)
13. Lee, J.P., Grinstein, G.G.: An architecture for retaining and analyzing visual explorations of databases. In: Proceedings Visualization 1995, pp. 101–108 (1995). https://doi.org/10.1109/VISUAL.1995.480801
14. Lucas, B., Abram, G.D., Collins, N.S., Epstein, D.A., Gresh, D.L., McAuliffe, K.P.: An architecture for a scientific visualization system. In: Proceedings of the 3rd Conference on Visualization '92. p. 107–114. VIS '92, IEEE Computer Society Press, Washington, DC, USA (1992)
15. Martig, S.R., Castro, S.M., Fillottrani, P.R., Estevez, E.C.: Un modelo unificado de visualización. In: IX Congreso Argentino de Ciencias de la Computación (2003)
16. Munzner, T.: A nested model for visualization design and validation. IEEE T VIS COMPUT GR **15**(6), 921–928 (2009). https://doi.org/10.1109/TVCG.2009.111
17. Munzner, T.: Visualization Analysis and Design. A.K. Peters visualization series, A K Peters (2014), http://www.crcpress.com/product/isbn/9781466508910
18. Roberts, J.C.: State of the art: Coordinated multiple views in exploratory visualization. In: Fifth International Conference on Coordinated and Multiple Views in Exploratory Visualization (CMV 2007). pp. 61–71 (2007). https://doi.org/10.1109/CMV.2007.20
19. Rosset, A., Spadola, L., Ratib, O.: Osirix: an open-source software for navigating in multidimensional dicom images. J. Digit. Imaging **17**(3), 205–216 (2004). https://doi.org/10.1007/s10278-004-1014-6
20. Schroeder, W.J., Lorensen, B., Martin, K.: The visualization toolkit: an object-oriented approach to 3D graphics. Kitware (2004)

21. Spence, R.: Information Visualization: Design for Interaction. Person Ed., (2007)
22. Stuart K Card, Jock D Mackinlay, Ben Shneiderman: Readings in information visualization: using vision to think. Morgan Kaufmann (1999)
23. Stuart K Card, Jock Mackinlay: The structure of the information visualization design space. In: Proceedings of VIZ'97: Visualization Conference, Information Visualization Symp. and Parallel Rendering Symp. pp. 92–99. IEEE (1997). https://doi.org/10.1109/INFVIS.1997.636792
24. Tominski, C., Schumann, H.: Interactive visual data analysis. CRC Press (2020)
25. Upson, C., Faulhaber, T.A., Kamins, D., Laidlaw, D., Schlegel, D., Vroom, J., Gurwitz, R., van Dam, A.: The application visualization system: a computational environment for scientific visualization. IEEE COMPUT GRAPH 9(4), 30–42 (1989). https://doi.org/10.1109/38.31462
26. Wang, X.M., Zhang, T.Y., Ma, Y.X., Xia, J., Chen, W.: A survey of visual analytic pipelines. J. Comput. Sci. Technol. 31, 787–804 (2016). https://doi.org/10.1007/s11390-016-1663-1
27. Ward, M.O., Grinstein, G., Keim, D.: Interactive data visualization: foundations, techniques, and applications. CRC Press (2010)
28. Ward, M.O., Yang, J.: Interaction spaces in data and information visualization. In: VisSym. pp. 137–145 (2004)
29. Ware, C.: Information Visualization: Perception for Design. Morgan Kaufmann (2004)

# Author Index

**A**
Alonso-Suarez, Rodrigo    118

**B**
Barraza, Fernando    75
Boixader, Francesc    45
Bruballa, Eva    45
Buccella, Agustina    57

**C**
Caballero, Ismael    157
Castro, Silvia M.    189
Cechich, Alejandra    57

**D**
De Giusti, Armando    31, 45
del Toro Osorio, Fabiola    143
Dufrechou, Ernesto    17

**E**
Epelde, Francisco    45
Estévez, Elsa    143
Estevez, Elsa    171
Ezzatti, Pablo    17

**F**
Faqir-Rhazoui, Youssef    3
Fernández, Alejandro    75
Freire, Manuel    17

**G**
Ganuza, María Luján    189
Garay, Francisco    31
García, Carlos    3
Gómez D'Orazio, Lucas    31
Gualo, Fernando    157
Guzmán, Stefanía    129

**H**
Hurtado, Remigio    129

**I**
Iturbide, Paula    118

**L**
Larrea, Martín L.    189
López Yse, Diego    105
Luque, Emilio    45

**M**
Marichal, Raul    17
Medina, Santiago    31
Montenegro, Ayelén    57
Montezanti, Diego    31
Muñoz, Angel    57
Muñoz, Arantxa    129

**N**
Naiouf, Marcelo    31

**O**
Ospina Becerra, Victoria Eugenia    143
Osycka, Líam    57

**P**
Piattini, Mario    157
Pintado, Pablo    171
Prado, Daniela    171

**Q**
Quiroga, Facundo    91

**R**
Ramirez, Carlos    75
Rexachs, Dolores    45
Rodriguez, Mariela    45
Rodríguez, Moisés    157
Ronchetti, Franco    91, 118

**S**
Stanchi, Oscar    91

M. Naiouf et al. (Eds.): JCC-BD&ET 2023, CCIS 1828, pp. 205–206, 2023.
https://doi.org/10.1007/978-3-031-40942-4

**T**
Torres, Diego   105

**U**
Urribarri, Dana K.   189

**W**
Wiesner, Sebastián   171
Wong, Alvaro   45

Printed in the United States
by Baker & Taylor Publisher Services